PROPERTY & SSAS SECRETS

Your step-by-step guide to creating powerful multi-generational wealth

Property & SSAS SECRETS

Your step-by-step guide to creating powerful multi-generational wealth

First published in Great Britain in 2021

© Copyright 2021 Sustainomics Limited

Email: mark.stokes@equassas.co.uk

Web: www.equaacademy.co.uk

The moral right of Mark Stokes to be identified as the author of this work has been asserted by him in accordance with the Copyright, Designs and Patents Act of 1988.

ISBN 978-1-5272-7557-7

A CIP catalogue record for this book is available from the British Library.

Cover design by Art by Avnie

Printed by Amazon.

DISCLAIMER

The information in this book does not constitute financial or other professional advice and is general in nature. It does not take into account your specific circumstances and should not be acted on without professional advice from fully qualified and independent advisors who should have a full understanding of your current situation, future goals and objectives.

Although the author has made every effort to ensure that the information in this book was correct at the time of printing, the author does not assume, and hereby disclaims any liability to any party for any loss, damage or disruption caused by errors or omissions, whether such errors or omissions result from negligence, accident or any other cause.

The author is <u>not</u> an Independent Financial Advisor, nor is he regulated in any way by the Financial Conduct Authority, and no inference should be taken in this book to suggest to the contrary.

DEDICATION

I would like to dedicate this book to my wife, Sharon, for her wonderful support, love, companionship and energy as well as to my four children: Ben, Jack, Katy and Emily who make me so proud.

They are my constant in life, my reason 'why' and who I firmly believe have the potential to make a positive change in the world and achieve great things.

I also dedicate this book to those that are prepared to create their 'North Star Vision', to believe in themselves, to step out of their comfort zone, to take action and to take control of their personal economy.

"It is not the critic who counts; not the man who points out how the strong man stumbles, or where the doer of deeds could have done them better. The credit belongs to the man who is actually in the arena, whose face is marred by dust and sweat and blood; who strives valiantly; who errs, who comes short again and again, because there is no effort without error and shortcoming; but who does actually strive to do the deeds; who knows great enthusiasms, the great devotions; who spends himself in a worthy cause; who at the best knows in the end the triumph of high achievement, and who at the worst, if he fails, at least fails while daring greatly, so that his place shall never be with those cold and timid souls who neither know victory nor defeat."

Theodore Roosevelt

TABLE OF CONTENTS

WHY I WROTE THIS BOOK

For over 25 years I worked tirelessly around the world for my employers, running businesses and global infrastructure projects. Each year a pension statement would land on my doormat with the same message of analysis and uninspiring news. Yes, my pension was a second thought for me, a brief ten minute each year interlude to my busy business and family life.

And yet it remained one of my largest bank accounts, left unattended apart from the monthly payroll contribution trickling in.

In 2014 at the age of 45, I decided that the life I was leading was upside down and something had to change. The more successful I was in my career, the more companies I was running for my employer (seven at the time). This meant more time away from the ones that I love – my family.

I decided to change that and leave corporate life to create a multi-generation legacy through assets and business of my own.

It was at this point that I became free. I had made that decision and commitment to exit my corporate career. The reality was that it took a further nine months to leave, but from that point on the roles were reversed - my employer was now funding my exit plan rather than me working for a salary.

This mindset shift was critical and lead to more opportunities than I could ever have imagined.

My commitment to my family was that by leaving my career, I would take full control of our personal economy – and I mean every aspect!

At aged 45, I realised quickly that the tough nut to crack was going to be my pensions, which had been relatively ignored, so I set about exploring what was in the art of the possible and after a brief search found out about SSAS (Small Self-Administered Scheme) pensions - it wasn't long before the power and accountability started to really resonate.

At this time no one had written a book on SSAS, SSAS Alliance didn't exist and Google searches came up fairly blank, so it was hard to find quality information. Not being one to procrastinate but being big on due diligence, my business partner, Nigel Greene, and I set out to research, plan and structure our SSAS and use it as a primary investment fund for our personal economy.

In only our second property acquisition we DOUBLED the value of my previous pension, which had taken 25 years to grow, in 12 months!

Now I should say that we are no strangers to property, construction and business having been involved in them for over 30 years now. However, these principles that we followed were not complicated and they enabled our wealth to grow exponentially as well as completely transforming our tax efficiency.

Becoming an author was a 35-year itch I wanted to scratch but it was only leaving corporate life that allowed me to have the bandwidth to connect with myself, to start to live a life of freedom of choice and to set about fully registering and achieving my goals.

My first book was 'Commercial to Residential Conversion: The essential manual for property developers'.

My second book was 'SSAS Pensions: Creating extraordinary levels of compounding wealth'. As more and more people started to relate to the power of SSAS in their lives, there became a constant stream of questions on all thing's property investing and how SSAS could play a crucial part.

I get asked so many questions almost on a daily basis now on the power of property and pensions and so I decided to write this book, to help guide others to create that route to certainty for their property investment plans.

Our experience has been gained with our own SSAS, as well as being large developers of major housing and apartment schemes, and holding a substantial amount of commercial property, buy to lets and HMO's.

What I will be sharing with you in this book is a step-by-step guide to help YOU become knowledgeable and confident in your true potential, revealing a roadmap you can create to unlock your powerful property asset base and to help you enable your personal vision and dreams.

We are all different. SSAS is part of the context of our overall wealth economy.

This book will make your think – it is designed that way. To enable you to turn over ideas in your head, to soul search and to enable you to understand that you can achieve great things. We all can.

You can be in control of your destiny ...... and should be!

This book is designed to help you come to the best solution for you and your loved ones.

It is your constant companion and reference manual to being 'eyes wide open' to the opportunity, and the risk, and to help you navigate the route to achieving your true potential in the powerful combination of property and SSAS.

Every SSAS trustee I have ever met has challenged tradition through direct action – that is what the game changing act of becoming a SSAS trustee is. It is the direct act of deciding to take control and accepting the responsibility for your actions, growing in stature, knowledge and confidence and embarking on a journey of self-ownership, discovery and accountability.

All trustees wear two hats. They are trustees, however they are also directors of their own business or businesses. They think on different levels constantly and one consistent point of reference comes up almost every single time – PROPERTY.

So, what can be achieved by combining SSAS and property along with business acumen and a strong personal drive? The possibilities as you are about to see in the chapters ahead, are bountiful and almost limitless for those prepared to put the effort in.

The rewards can be life changing and you will hear from many Trustees who have experienced exactly that.

This book should be the dog-eared book on your bookshelf, pages folded, post-it notes aplenty and highlighter pen and scribbles on every page. As your constant companion it should help you grow your strategy, hold you accountable, keep you compliant and be the fuel for your fire and enable your vision to become a reality.

We are only competing with what we are capable of.

What are you capable of? Let's find out!

I wish you every success as you embrace and master this game changing strategy of SSAS and property.

"Imagination is the source of all human achievement"

SIR KEN ROBINSON

FOREWORD

In the decades I have been helping business owners and employees create lasting wealth, it is the area of pensions that is consistently overlooked and undervalued.

Setting out to write a book of this magnitude was certainly an eye-opening prospect yet, in truth, it had been something that had been gnawing away at me for several years. To think that one person can collate all the vital lessons learnt to support and guide the next generation would probably be impractical, and most certainly arrogant!

Millions simply lose track of their pensions and become disconnected from what is often their largest single source of retirement wealth. The volatility of the stock market and the impenetrable language of pensions can leave people feeling cold, so they put pensions in a 'do not disturb' box until retirement and suffer a tragic reduction in income in their later life as a result.

Mark himself readily admits he was in the pension's wilderness during his corporate career.

He acknowledges that he would read the annual statements, wish they were better and file them away for another year of disconnection.

My wealth experience has also shown that the most popular asset used to build a future income is property. It is the easiest asset to replicate strategies and there is such a pent-up demand for homes that the Government themselves simply can't meet.

We have such a love affair with property in the UK with more than 2.5 million landlords renting out property to supplement or replace their pension disappointment. Many others have become property developers, creating value from commercial property or converting commercial property into residential units to help meet this demand.

The recent pandemic has changed the way so many businesses work, and we have seen the high street retail sector devastated by the lockdown and the changing nature of how we all shop.

The opportunity to convert these units into residential homes is a real growth area and so many other property strategies have gained huge traction.

Mark Stokes is a successful property investor, developer and business owner, always willing to challenge the norm and to look for solutions to problems as all outstanding entrepreneurs do. Having been touched by the tragic death of a business partner, he saw how traditional pensions didn't serve the family that was left behind. He made the decision to explore how he could solve his own pension situation by disconnecting the old employer pensions from the past and connecting these funds to his future in property.

He discovered the best kept secret for business owners called SSAS and dedicated himself to learning how the SSAS pension would serve his property business and his family. Once he discovered what was possible, he got off the stock market roller coaster and put his money to work, just like a business bank account, allowing him to create value in a number of property projects where his own expertise could shine. The remarkable result was a pension that took over 25 years to build in his corporate life, was doubled in as many months!

His passion for the extraordinary power of the SSAS pension was so strong that he decided to shine a light on it for others by writing his book 'SSAS Pensions: creating extraordinary levels of compounding wealth', to great acclaim. He also founded and spearheads a whole new movement called SSAS Alliance which is a growing community of enlightened business owners sharing knowledge and inspiration with each other. With Mark's help, thousands of trustees have been made aware of the art of what is possible and that pensions can be used in property.

In this book, Mark dives deeper into dozens of strategies and shows how SSAS pensions can help acquire or facilitate the ownership of property of all kinds. If you want to build wealth in property, this book is a must read and it will reveal sources of funding you didn't think were possible - it will challenge your thinking for sure and will be a valuable and inspirational guide for your own property journey.

Kevin Whelan
WealthBuilders

1. STRATEGY

Before we dive straight into exciting examples and scenarios, where property and SSAS can interact together, let us first pause for thought about our strategy.

So many times, this happens to many of us, I am sure. The urgency and enthusiasm to just get going is often at the expense of a first important step. To understand WHY we are about to do this.

How does your strategy fit your own personal economic equation, and to what end will it serve?

The Oxford Dictionary defines STRATEGY as 'a plan of action designed to achieve a long-term or overall aim'. Interestingly it also further describes as 'time to develop a coherent economic strategy'.

This is what we are looking to achieve for our personal circumstances – a coherent economic strategy that gets us to where we want to go. So often 'strategy' is only assumed to relate to business planning, but it absolutely relates to YOU and your family as well. It is a MUST!

You are the leader of your personal wealth creation. No-one is coming to save you. It is YOUR responsibility.

You simply must have a strategy otherwise you will have no point of reference, no guiding North Star and no roadmap.

Your strategy is not fixed either, it will evolve over time but as I often say to my mentees – "start with version one to get to version ten!"

Whether you are looking to create your strategy for the first time or refine and enhance it, this first section will frame the roadmap you intend to travel and set the context for which your relationship between SSAS pensions and property will flow.

1.1 YOUR WHY

A SSAS, or indeed a property portfolio, are generally not the end goal for most. I don't know anyone that came out of the womb wanting property!

It is what property as an asset class provides that is the end goal, not just property itself. Property is a vehicle to achieving wealth in all its forms.

Imagine a place where you are most at home, where you love the people you are around, the surroundings are idyllic, and you are doing what you love.

What would that look like to you? Freedom of choice springs to mind.

If you could find those one or two things in your life that you just get, they resonate with you, you feel authentic with, you are good at and they make you spring out of bed in the morning -now imagine doing that to achieve your goals!

How great would life be?

The late and great Sir Ken Robinson referred to this as 'finding your element'.

It is not what you DO in life, it is who you ARE – your very essence and being.

Sir Ken put it again very nicely when he encouraged us to 'see the world NOT as it is, but who I am'.

I want to be ENGAGED rather than DISENGAGED in everything I am.

Your Why is essential. It is your North Star, that omni-present drive that gives you inspiration, direction and drive to achieve it.

But you have to really want it – I mean truly desire it. Once you know what your Why is, your every effort goes towards achieving it.

Viktor Frankl said in his 1946 book, 'Man's Search for Meaning', "He who has a Why to live for can bear with almost any how". A truly remarkable book set in the heart of the suffering of a Nazi concentration camp.

Each of us have unique circumstances, backgrounds and visions for the future. We all see things differently through our own personal lens. Once you have your own Why, you will find distractions easy to identify and they will fade away rapidly.

Your Why can be boundaryless – make it huge, face your fears, live your dreams!

Once you understand the almost limitless potential of a SSAS combined particularly with property assets, you will find that achieving your dreams is not that far off after-all.

It is great fun exploring your true potential – a journey of self-discovery. It is incredible to understand what the power of the mind and the body can achieve if harnessed together.

Be bold, try new things, test yourself, expand your experience and continuously evolve. Share it with people so that they can relate to you and your aims. Those that become negative or non-supportive will become an unwelcome distraction and have a lesser part in your life.

So many of the great opportunities you have in your life are hidden away, out of sight, waiting to be discovered – like all precious minerals in nature. We have to explore and dig away the over-burden to reveal our own true potential. You simply can't plan your whole journey but what you can, and must do, is take those first steps. Then respond to what is in front of you and evolve forward, growing constantly.

I never want to live a life of any regrets, wondering what if.

'There is no heavier burden than an unfulfilled potential'
- Charles M. Schulz

1.2 YOUR ECONOMIC EQUATION

Each of us must have our own economic equation. FULL STOP.

Unless you understand what works for you, what the plan is and how each part dovetails together, it is difficult to see beyond a series of unplanned lurches forward, sideways or backwards!!

Each step we take should be a tactical advance to achieving our strategic vision and goals.

We all have different circumstances which define where we were, where we are and where we are going! I have always been acutely aware of the risk that some may fall into, of following the actions of others – almost a fear of missing out (FOMO) and SSAS can be no exception to that for some. That is why I have been very conservative in how I personally assess risk - yes, I can be inspired by others, and frequently am, however I am always grounded by our own circumstances and what is meaningful to myself, my family and my partners.

That is why our company, EquaAcademy, place such strong emphasis on having a clear vision and strategy for mentees and doing your own due diligence with the best resources available to you.

The extent of our personal circumstances are always going to be unique to each of us. These are some of the areas to consider when creating your own economic equation:

- Wealth in your SSAS
- Wealth outside of your SSAS
- Age
- Risk appetite
- Vision
- Family
- Tax status and efficiency
- Business interests

Make it one of your tasks to define what YOUR economic equation is, and your strategy, and where a SSAS may or may not fit in will become much clearer.

1.3 RISK V REWARD

We all have a very individual set of circumstances – we are unique. Yes, we can seek and take inspiration from others but seldom can we exactly copy others as our plan and path will be different.

The level of risk we are prepared to take, and the extent of the rewards we are targeting, is a careful balance. One of the most valuable things to have is the ability to lay your head on the pillow and sleep easy. Those that have lost it in the past will value it even more. Lack of sleep and constantly having an issue on your mind is so debilitating. Conversely, knowing your plan and being comfortable with what you are doing, serves to enhance the quality of life.

Finding your natural frequency to resonate at is crucial for you and your family.

Some of these factors that will be very specific to your risk and reward appetite, and profile, will include:

- Your personality and risk averse or risk-taking nature
- Your age
- Your current wealth
- Your dependents
- Employment
- Health
- Time availability
- Aspirations
- Goals
- Consideration for your life AND business partners – all of the above points relate to them too!

1.4 BUT I DON'T HAVE A SSAS

"What is the point of understanding pensions when I don't have one?"

If you do not have a SSAS that may be for many reasons. It maybe that, like myself during my corporate career, I just did not know they existed. You may have decided that a SSAS isn't for you – it certainly isn't for everyone.

This book is just as valuable and relevant to those who do not have a SSAS as it is for those that do, for a number of reasons:

- You are looking to raise investment funds from others that are SSAS trustees
- You may consider a SSAS due to future successes, such as proceeds from a business sale or conclusion of a property development
- You may wish to 'walk a mile in a SSAS Trustees shoes' to understand what can and can't be done, before making any considerations or approaches
- You may have zero pension to date
- You may be planning to start contributing to a pension
- You may want to have traditional pensions AND a SSAS

Irrespective of your position I hope this book will illuminate the huge array of options available to you.

In my experience in life, positive and successful people like to engage in positive and stimulating dialogue where opportunity abounds; Trust is built, and the creation of shared value sits at the heart of the outcome.

There is so much learning to be gained from the right qualified counsel AND from those that are actually doing it!

A Chinese proverb says:

'Those who say it cannot be done, should not interrupt those doing it'.

Whilst you may not currently have a pension or it may be small, it may be that establishing a SSAS for all future contributions could be particularly appealing for you. This would need your due diligence, of course, and will depend on your age, your income, background and financial circumstances etc. Nonetheless it could significantly enable the growth of your wealth.

A SSAS is one source of wealth and should you not have a SSAS it is certainly a very positive conversation that you could have on how best to collaborate with those that are SSAS Trustees.

In many respects the SSAS economy is an extension of a far greater and more meaningful life study of the evolutionary journey to mastering one's person economy.

I spent 25 years in corporate life not knowing that a SSAS pension even existed - sometimes we don't know what we don't know!

1.5 STATEMENT OF INVESTMENT PRINCIPLES

Given the vast array of SSAS investment options available to Trustees, and not just purely in property, it is important to dial in to a clear strategic direction and plan. Your SSAS forms part of what you have rather than being isolated. It is there to be deployed in concert with other resources, relationships and assets you may have available.

This clarity of action and purpose is further heightened in importance for those who have more than one SSAS member trustee particularly if they are from different family groups. It is important to set clear and agreed points of reference, ensure all are in accord with the direction and the mechanics of the SSAS.

An important document for you to consider, create and review with your fellow Trustees is a Statement of Investment Principles (SoIP). This will enable you to clearly document what your strategy is, and why, and enshrine the plan for achieving your jointly agreed goals.

A robust SoIP may include the following areas:

- Introduction
- Governance
- Investment objectives
- Investment beliefs
- Delivering the investment objectives
- Day to day operations
- Responsible investments
- Communication, reporting and transparency
- Compliance with this SoIP
- Appendices

This book will help you understand and debate what part property plays within your SSAS plans.

1.6 ASSETS

There are generally seven recognised types of assets and each one, or a combination of several, have the basic foundations to create substantial wealth which will compound powerfully over time:

- Business
- Property
- Pensions
- Intellectual Property
- Investments: Stocks and shares

- Home equity
- Joint ventures

With few exceptions, a SSAS can affect and enable most of these, directly or indirectly. Each asset class can form a key part of your over-arching wealth strategy. It is the interaction between assets that can create a very powerful accelerant to your plan, if used strategically.

Personally, I have experienced this and whilst I have many further plans evolving, some of the progress of interacting assets include the following and you can create this type of structure as well:

- A SSAS used to acquire commercial property
- Large property developments funded by SSAS trustee investors
- Businesses make contributions to SSAS
- Created intellectual property by writing multiple books on SSAS and commercial property
- Created and invested in a business (www.SSASAlliance. org) to help others explore SSAS
- Mentoring business (www.EquaAcademy.co.uk) to support people in property development, business, SSAS and life
- Use cash-flow from businesses to invest in other businesses
- Use SSAS to invest in businesses
- Use cashflow from businesses to acquire more property
- Have joint ventures with multiple partners

Take a moment to reflect on your assets, both now and the future, and start to shape your wealth strategy that will take advantage of the power of assets and compounding over time.

How will you create your own circular economy?

1.7 STRATEGIC ACQUISITION OF PROPERTY ASSETS

Nobody came out of the womb wanting to own property, I am pretty convinced of that!

It is what property provides that is important. Identifying HOW each property acquisition has a larger purpose, is crucial. Greater than the sum of the parts - creating a recurring model or interlinking jigsaw of elements that builds a multi-purpose, dynamic and compounding cluster of assets.

It is a vehicle to get you to where you want to go and once that is fully understood, then we have empowered ourselves with a clear hunting license to operate.

I find that the first stage of freedom is understanding who you are and what your plan is.

As Socrates said, "To know thyself is the beginning of wisdom".

Having a clear remit of a plan often lifts a huge burden from people. They are then free from procrastination, uncertainty, 'shiny penny' syndrome and overwhelm. They now understand what they need and how it delivers them the value they need. A large millstone has been removed from their shoulders.

The *aha!* moment is often the understanding that your SSAS isn't in fact the strategy - it is a tool in your toolbox to enable your strategy.

We generally don't look to acquire a property in our SSAS. We will look to acquire a great property deal and then look at how best to structure it, to deliver the results we need.

What is your focus for your SSAS in property?

- Invest to hold long term
- Invest in a developer deal
- Invest in business
- Invest in a fund
- Loan to others
- Loan to your sponsoring company
- Minimise your return on time invested
- Invest for future development potential
- Buy your own business premises
- Enablement but never own
- Sale and lease back
- Land development
- Planning gain
- In specie
- Rebase leases
- To optimise tax efficiency

The list is long and the options almost endless and we will be exploring the strategy and tactics YOU can deploy in the pages ahead.

1.8 CONTROL NOT OWN

Recent years have seen continuous tax changes which make holding property in one's personal name less and less attractive for most. Clause 24 is a recent example where mortgage interest rate relief has now been predominantly removed. There are some positives to take from this and highest on the list for me is the professionalisation of the property industry which, given some of the practices I have seen over the years, did need to happen.

"The secret to success is to own nothing, but control everything" - John D Rockefeller

This quote is very relevant and certainly makes us think why and how we are owning property assets and how best to structure them, without creating personal burdens of responsibility unnecessarily and optimising tax efficiency.

A good example is the limitation on liability that one has if a property is owned in a trust, limited company or limited liability partnership. This level of protection is not available if you hold the asset in your own name.

Your SSAS plays a hugely important role in providing you yet further options to structure, shelter, fund and operate certain assets classes in a highly efficient and protective manner. Used wisely a SSAS can be an incredible enabling vehicle – a compounding wonder!

Here is an example where controlling but owning can create value and reduce risk through structuring.

John identifies a property that he thinks will work for his strategy. It is on the market with a commercial agent and is a small office that is currently vacant with the tenant having gone out of business recently. The property has an asking price of £280,000.

John runs the numbers through his EquaDA deal analysis tool and completes his due diligence and is in a position to make an offer at £250,000, which he understands may be acceptable to the vendor. The vendor has made it very clear that they will not accept a lease option and wants to see proof of funds.

John has a SSAS with circa £375,000 in cash in its bank account, having just been transferred from his workplace pension. He has been mulling over whether to use his SSAS to buy the small office, however, his primary strategy is to get Permitted Development Rights and convert to residential. He is aware that residential property cannot be held in the SSAS so he will have to sell eventually out of the SSAS when almost complete, at latest.

John decides to structure his offer in an innovative way:

Offer made by:	Johns SSAS Pension
Offer price:	£250,000
Deposit:	£10,000 fully refundable
Conditionality:	Subject to gaining Permitted Development Rights
Additional provisions:	Assignability clause

The conditionality or 'subject to' is a great way of protecting your downside risk whereby you are not having to buy a property with the risk of getting, or not getting, planning and being left with a building that cannot be used for your intended purpose.

John will exchange contracts and pay a fully refundable deposit. John uses his SSAS bank account statement as proof of funds.

The offer is duly accepted and work progresses for contracts to be exchanged. Once contracts are exchanged John uses his SSAS to engage a planning consultant and architect to do a measured survey and produce plans and a submission for permitted development rights for five apartments. This process takes three weeks and the submission is then submitted to the local authority.

The permitted development process in this case takes 48 days (usually upto 56 days) and John received notification that the submission has been successfully determined.

The date of this letter changes the conditional 'subject to' exchanged contracts to one of now unconditional, as the condition of permitted development rights for what John was looking to achieve has now been fully met.

NOTE: at this stage, often a top up deposit is required to the full 10% amount which would be a further £15,000. However, John had the foresight to negotiate this part out, along with making the deposit fully refundable – a great example of working with a great mentor. This reduced capital at risk and also an unwelcome impact on cashflow.

John then decides that he would like to acquire the building in a Limited company rather than within his SSAS. He uses the assignability clause and 'assigns' the exchanged contracts to his limited company who then acquires the property.

John puts in place an agreement between his Limited company and his SSAS to confirm the value of the enhanced property (now with permitted development rights for five apartments) and secures a Red Book Valuation to confirm it is a fair market valuation. John's SSAS can recoup its fees and take a margin for its hard and tenacious work from the uplift.

John has a certain degree of choice to decide where the enhanced value is held – in the SSAS or Limited company or possibly another operating company.

The principles at large here are of value creation and destination whilst remaining compliant. Does John want to:

- Maximise the increase in the fund value of his SSAS Pension?
- Create a modest return for the SSAS's resources and function in the transaction?
- Ensure his strategy is clear at the outset on where his risk parameters sit and his end destination for the asset

KEY POINT: When acquiring or selling a property involving a SSAS, it is important to know that a formal Valuation will need to be conducted. Given that this will almost certainly be involving a commercial property, this will be a RICS Red Book Valuation – see later chapter in this book.

1.9 WHERE DO YOU WANT THE VALUE?

A question we debate with our mentees is 'where do you want the value?'. This is a crucial question in enabling maximum traction for you achieving your goals. Some may want to leave their job or create additional income to have choices on where and what they work on, how they spend their time and how they can afford certain targets.

If considering your own SSAS to acquire commercial property, you should consider if you want the value within the SSAS or outside where it may be more accessible in a liquid form.

The answer to the question lies in structuring to ensure the right balance is achieved between tax efficiency and accessibility of return. Mapping out a clear plan and the steps required to use the resources at your disposal, to achieve the goals, is a key step in the process. It is no good working really hard on a single strategy to create income to leave a job if that income is then difficult to access without punitive tax charges.

I can't stress this enough – structure is everything!

My expertise over 30 years in business has been finely honed in this area; yes I have made the mistakes and yes I have learnt from them - quickly!

Structure, structure, structure.

A question often overlooked at the beginning of a property acquisition is where do you want the value to sit? By starting with the end in mind and working back we have an excellent opportunity to ensure the property assets serve you in the best way possible, taking advantage of all the benefits available.

Considerations will include but limited to:

- What benefits do you seek – reduce tax, increase income, long term capital growth etc
- When do you want the benefit – are you looking for income from assets immediately or looking to reinvest and compound over time?
- Tax efficiency
- Shareholding and distributable value through dividends
- Cashflow
- Effective use of Capital allowances and other tax efficient initiatives

- Limitation on liability
- Use class
- Business interests
- Availability of funds – funds within the SSAS or external to the SSAS
- Security options – which may come in to play if you are considering loan backs for instance
- Compliance
- Your age
- Risk appetite
- Asset protection
- Lifetime allowance levels and your position along with your family
- Legacy – what are you creating, why, for whom and do you want them to become involved
- Other wealth

A brick on its own has no strength and left to be kicked around or exposed to the elements will get worn down, broken and eventually turn into dust.

A brick in a wall laid with the right bonding pattern and carefully mixed mortar will form a structure which will remain solid for centuries, sheltering the occupants and retaining its strength and value.

Each of your assets forms a brick in the wall of your family's financial fortress.

Define your plan and start building.

1.10 SSAS CORPORATE TRUSTEE MANDATE

There is a caveat to your ability to execute your strategic and tactical consideration as a SSAS Trustee. It will, in no small part, be dependent on the mandate that your SSAS Corporate Trustee operates within.

There can be a wide-ranging level of acceptance, interpretation and internal policy rulings which can enable, or frustrate trustees, depending on their strategy. The reality is that not all SSAS Corporate Trustees are the same and as you are responsible for your strategy, you should ensure that the SSAS Corporate Trustee you select is able to support you in your compliant strategic objectives.

Some of the areas that I have seen raised by Trustees over the years as being challenged by their Corporate Trustee include:

- Only a first charge security on property acceptable on third party unconnected loans
- No loan allowed if counterparty cannot produce three years of audited accounts
- Certain investment structures by developers for fund raise not permitted
- Debenture security not allowed
- Only a first charge security on property acceptable for Loan Backs
- Security not acceptable on a residential property even with a security trustee in place
- Enhanced wariness for investment in businesses
- Inconsistency in allowable Loan Back purposes

The purpose of this list is not to decry these stances necessarily, but to merely enable you to have an 'eyes wide open' approach to selection of your professional team to assist you in enabling YOUR strategy.

If you find that your SSAS Corporate Trustee does not offer the type and style of mandate that you require for your strategy, first stop and ask why. There may be very good reasons for this that are preserving your compliance.

The phrase 'walk a mile in another person's shoes' is a favourite of mine and for good reason. It has served me well in years of negotiation around the world and in finding the win-win in enduring relationships.

Organisations that provide SSAS trustee and administration services may also provide services for other pension related activity such as SIPP's. They will be affected and have policies which govern how their business operates and may make decisions on the best interests of their shareholders, as well as clients. They will have Professional Indemnity insurance to protect themselves to certain degree. This insurance product has become extremely expensive for businesses over recent years and when they consider risk v reward, it is easier to see how many adopt a risk averse mandate in the trustees' opinion.

Some of the areas considered by the corporate trustee may include:

- Level of fees and profit for services provided
- Availability of suitably qualified and experienced staff
- Market size and potential
- Risk of providing services and advice
- Increase in litigious culture in society

- Level of Professional Indemnity insurance required
- Duration that claims may be made and therefore insurance needs to stay in place – this could be decades potentially
- Interpretation of HMRC rules
- … and of course, their overall strategy

Feedback that I frequently get from corporate trustees is worth noting for any SSAS trustee. There is sometimes a sense of frustration that corporate trustees and administrators place many caveats behind their opinions and fall short of providing advice. It is important to note that they will stand behind the services they provide – however, what they almost certainly will not do is underwrite your investments. That is not their role.

After considering all the pro's and con's, if you feel that changing to another Corporate Trustee might widen the mandate to better serve your SSAS, and wider strategy, then you are able to do this through a process called a SSAS takeover. I cover this extensively in my book, 'SSAS Pensions: Creating extraordinary levels of compounding wealth', in the chapter 'SSAS Takeover'.

1.11 RESOURCES

A short note on the resources of a SSAS and those available to it. In essence the SSAS has three assets:

a. Cash as its primary resource

b. An 'investment license' by being approved by HMRC

c. The skills of the trustee(s) to use leverage

If you do nothing with it, the SSAS fund value will erode against inflation and fees, and rot away.

Of the thousands of SSAS trustees I interact with and know, one thing I never hear from any of them is "I want a full-time job managing my SSAS pension!!"

We can take the 'glass is half empty' approach and say the SSAS has limited resources so we need to work really hard, or we can adopt the 'glass is half full' approach and see the SSAS as having an unlimited access, to best in class advice and support, from an almost unlimited pool of expertise.

You can employ whatever resources you require to meet your investment strategy, directly from your SSAS. This can include, but not be limited to:

- Solicitor
- Commercial agent
- Planning consultant
- Surveyors and valuers
- Building contractors
- Lettings agents
- Tax advisor
- Security trustee
- Independent Financial Advisor
- SSAS administrator
- Builders
- Accountant
- Insurance
- Commercial property agent
- Commercial funding broker
- Health & safety/CDM

- Project manager
- Private investors
- Monitoring surveyor
- Banks
- Commercial manager
- Design team
- Interior designer
- Structural warranty provider
- VAT specialist
- Stockbroker
- Fund manager
- Capital allowances surveyor

A SSAS trustee should never feel isolated or exposed. They have a huge array of expertise, wisdom and counsel available to expedite their strategy. Compliance, governance and support are essential for any organisation and a SSAS is no exception.

Applying business acumen is essential to ensure your SSAS remains compliant, efficient and therefore sustainable and growing.

2. FUNDING & INVESTING IN PROPERTY

2.1 PEER-TO-PEER LENDING /CROWD FUNDING

Peer-to-peer crowd funding across all4 sectors has seen a huge increase in popularity over the last five years and property investing through these platforms are becoming ever popular. For SSAS trustees this is a compliant form of investing and is highly time efficient with equity or debt returns available, based on differing levels of security.

So, what is peer-to-peer lending/crowdfunding?

Peer-to-peer crowd funding sites enable small businesses to raise funds from investors, 'the crowd', who all invest fractional amounts in the business. It started as a way to fund creative projects such as expeditions, films, theatre projects and music recordings. Over recent years its growth and popularity has dramatically increased and it is now a recognised platform for many organisations to raise money in a compliant manner.

Property developers became naturally drawn to its flexibility and there are many platforms now which enable property investment fund raises through peer-to-peer crowd funding.

Generally, crowd funding does not allow you to withdraw your money when you want; once you have put money in, it can be tied up for a long time.

Whilst crowd funding is a generic term and can be utilised to raise funds from everything from charitable, business start-up seed capital to community-based schemes, we are focusing on SSAS and property and there are a number of variant themes.

Each crowd funding platform will have its unique product and approach and may concentrate on different parts of the funding capital stack including:

- Debt with first charge – taking the place of traditional bank funding
- Debt with second charge – mezzanine funding
- Equity – variable security levels available

Within this investment sector you have the choice of selecting a wide array of investment choices, or if you are looking to raise funds, a number of alternative routes to raise funds.

It is perfectly possible in theory for a SSAS to raise funds through a crowd funding platform. The SSAS would need to ensure that all lenders are unconnected third parties (this would be done via the crowd funding platform) and of course all external borrowing must be limited to a maximum 50% of the fund value of the SSAS, at the time of borrowing. This is calculated in the aggregate and would also include any other borrowing that the SSAS had taken.

Most crowd funding is authorised and regulated by the Financial Conduct Authority and your capital invested is at risk and not covered by Financial Services Compensation Scheme (FSCS).

Returns can vary depending upon security and the deal. However, the spread would be typically mid to high single digit through to mid to high teen % return, 7% - 15% being typical of what is seen.

However, as mentioned before, the level of security and therefore risk you are prepared to accept will be an important consideration and probably noted in your Statement of Investment Principles (SOIP) discussed earlier.

Finally, the return on time may be important for your strategy. Not everyone wants to spend a large amount of time managing their pension and a relatively hands-off approach may well be attractive too. There are other 'returns' which may also be attractive, such as Earn & Learn where you can invest and also have multiple other returns including meeting fellow investors, learning the processes of property development and interacting with the property developer. We have used this approach of providing EquaEarn & Learn with our business, sharing our 30 years of business experience and it can be a very mutually fulfilling and beneficial proposition.

2.2 TRUSTEE CASE STUDY: VOON FUI LAI - Strong Returns with Impactful Outcomes

2.2.1 Introduction

A warm greeting to you, dear reader! My name is Voon Fui Lai. I have over 20 years' experience in the corporate and SME sectors. My professional career began as a project manager, architect and urban planner with the international award-winning consultancy, Gensler. I was responsible for a number of Global/EMEA business divisions, whilst acting as Development Manager and Sustainability Advocate in leading integrated teams to deliver large scale urban regeneration and mixed-use communities across the globe.

I have since left the corporate world to focus on being a private investor. I have applied my entrepreneurial approach, corporate governance and risk management skillsets to my investments in property, stock markets and private equity.

In that time, I have also discovered the world of SSAS and became a Member Trustee in May 2018. One of my first undertakings was to develop my personal investment mandate. Drawing upon my experience in placemaking and revitalising communities, I have developed a liveability framework of themes relating to work, live, play, learn and wellbeing to nurture resilient communities of the future. My mandate seeks to reinforce positive liveability consequences whilst securing risk adjusted commercial returns. In summary, 'strong returns with impactful outcomes'.

My SSAS journey was indeed a steep learning curve, albeit a thoroughly enjoyable one. I would like to share the following lessons learnt. Please note none of the following constitutes financial recommendation. Please seek professional advice for your own personal requirements.

2.2.2 Investing with a SSAS

Since becoming a Member Trustee, I have undertaken some specialist SSAS Trustee training modules on Commercial Property, Loan Back and Bridging in order to understand the intricacies of SSAS investing. As a Member Trustee, I constantly check in with my SSAS Administrator/Corporate Trustee on any tax charge risks on the investment opportunities that I evaluate.

2.2.3 My Initial Steps

Having set up my SSAS, I have partially transferred funds from my Hargreaves Lansdown SIPP to my SSAS and invested in:

- an equity deal for a 25 unit eco-homes development, Oxfordshire

- an equity deal for a 12 unit detached homes development, Gloucester
- a third-party loan on a 4 unit detached homes development, Cambridgeshire
- a third-party loan on a 48 apartments Commercial Conversion project, Crawley
- a third-party loan on a 24 unit Serviced Accommodation Conversion project, Cumbria

The security provided for the loans varied across Debenture, Second Charge and Personal Guarantees. The investment ranged from £25,000 to £100,000 per project. Some of the projects were direct relationships with the developers and some through crowdfunding platforms. As an investor in the projects, I try to advocate for liveability themes to be incorporated, wherever possible, into creating resilient and inspiring environments.

I have just transferred a second tranche from my SIPP to invest in a few First Charge and Second charge loan deals and opened an AJ Bell SSAS account to invest in ETFs, shares and funds. I have kept a modest amount in my SIPP to keep my pension wrapper options open.

In this case study, I will elaborate further on my experience with Crowdfunding.

2.2.4 Crowdfunding/P2P Funding

There are two types of funding platforms for property projects. Crowdfunding which focusses on Equity and Peer-to-Peer (P2P) which focusses on Debt. However, Crowdfunding platforms are increasingly offering Debt deals. Thus, the distinction has lately become blurred. To gain access to deals, one has to self-certify as either a High Net Worth or Sophisticated Investor. Due to recent high-profile investment scams, the government is increasingly barring retail investors from accessing crowdfunding platforms. Hence, the self-certification requirements to ascertain that the investor is sufficiently experienced and knowledgeable of the risks involved.

One should be aware that any investments cannot be redeemed at any point before the project completes. It can also result in the investment capital being put at risk, should the project generate losses. Any losses are not covered by the FSCS. As most of the deals are development or commercial conversions, which result in habitable residential units, most investments are covered by the platform's Security Trustee to avoid any potential tax charges, should the project face difficulties in exiting. It is important to verify that the platform has a Security Trustee in place.

The benefit of using a platform, compared to investing directly with a developer, is that it is a more structured and collaborative experience. The projects tend to be larger hence there is more margin for error. The developers also tend to be more experienced and have significant skin in the game. As there are more investors involved, one can compare due diligence perspectives with other investors. The platforms themselves also do their own due diligence on the projects before uploading the deals for investors to peruse.

2.2.5 Due diligence

On due diligence, one should evaluate the platforms from the outset. Do the platform operators have significant property experience? What were their success or default track records? How do they deal with worst case scenarios? How often do they provide investor updates, monthly or quarterly? Do they organise site visits throughout the life of the project? One should not be rushed into deals. Take your time to ask as many questions as you need.

If it is a debt deal, always enquire about the security offered. First Charges are the most secure followed by Second Charges, Personal Guarantees and Debentures. Some platforms provide Charges with Developer's Personal Guarantees as well to cover the investors' capital and interest.

One should also consider the Term or Timeframe of the investment. Most platform projects will have already secured planning permission or permitted development rights. Nevertheless, do consider if the construction and marketing/sales period are sufficient.

An important consideration is the Exit. Are the developers planning to sell or to hold the project at the end of the Term? The more prudent projects will have multiple exits in place.

One should never take the Gross Development Value (GDV) at face value. Check the sales comparables of recent sold prices and take local agents' estimates with a healthy pinch of salt. Most platforms will be able to provide a copy of the Independent RICS (Red Book) valuation sourced from the developers.

Another point to review is the Construction or Conversion Cost. Try to ask the platform for £/SF benchmarks of local areas in order to review against the project's estimates.

Questions to ask about the Delivery Team include: Developer - what experience and skin in the game? Contractor – what is their financial exposure/risk of bankruptcy? Consultants – what relevant experience and Professional Indemnity Insurances are in place?

The location of the project will also have a bearing on its potential successful exit. What are the fundamentals of the local area - e.g. Amenities, Demography or Rate of property sales.

The Loan to Value of the project can range anywhere from 50% to 80% of GDV. The higher the leverage, the riskier the project is should any potential adverse incidence occur – e.g. market correction, cost escalation, etc.

Finally, on Risk adjusted Returns, indicative benchmarks for Mezzanine and Equity investments are as follow: First Charge Mezzanine loans offer 8% to 12% annualised, Second Charge Mezzanine loans offer 15% to 18% annualised and Equity profit share investments are anything above 20% on capital invested (not annualised). There are also hybrids with a combination of secured debt and profit share.

2.2.6 Managing Risks

To mitigate risks in the topsy turvy world of property, diversification is key. One should invest across multiple platforms, project typologies and locations. My own preference is to invest about 5% to 10% of my SSAS portfolio on each project. Some platforms have minimum investment levels. Thus, we might need to invest higher percentages on occasion.

The economic or property cycle will have an influence on whether to choose equity or debt investments. In a rising market, equity investments are lucrative as a hot market could bid up sale prices, resulting in higher exit GDVs. Conversely, in an uncertain or falling market, secured debt investments are preferable, as any delays or cost overruns will not materially impact annualised returns.

2.2.7 Conclusion

Investing on the platforms provide unrivalled opportunity to gain knowledge of different geographical markets, identify trusted joint venture partners and establish long term relationships.

Over time, the SSAS investor could refine his or her risk management and due diligence skills towards being a more secure, prudent and diversified investor and potentially leave a legacy for loved ones.

I hope that the reader will embrace and enjoy this collaborative and immensely rewarding journey as much as I have.

Wishing you every success in your SSAS and investing journey!

2.3 IN SPECIE TRANSFERS

'In specie' is a Latin term meaning 'in the actual form'. Transferring an asset 'in specie' means to transfer the ownership of that asset from one person or company or entity to another person or company or entity in its current form, which in essence means without the need to convert the asset to cash.

In a SSAS pension context 'in specie' can come in two forms:

- **'In specie'** transfers: this involves a transfer of assets between two pension schemes
- **'In specie'** contributions: this involves the transfer of assets from an individual or company to a pension scheme

'In specie' transfers can take the form of shares and property for instance, as well as funds in certain circumstances.

Generally, there will be no dealing costs. However, either or both of the ceding and receiving schemes could charge for the work involved in the transfer. Assets involved need to be properly valued and assessed for suitability by the receiving scheme.

The transfer of the ownership of the assets from the ceding entity to the SSAS happens by re-registering the assets in the name of the SSAS.

This succeeds in getting the assets transferred into the new pension scheme but does not count as a contribution and therefore there is no tax relief. Neither does it count against the annual allowance.

As the assets are not being bought or sold, there are no dealing costs. However, the SSAS administrator might charge for the work involved in changing the ownership of the asset and there could be two charges - on the way 'out' of the existing scheme and on the way 'into' the new one. There may also be solicitors' legal charges, depending on the nature of the asset in question.

An 'in specie' transfer can often occur when a member of a pension scheme has started a new SSAS and wishes to transfer existing assets from their old pension scheme to the new SSAS. Both the existing pension provider, and the new SSAS administrator, must both approve the transfer of assets from a compliance and administrative perspective.

2.3.1 Shares

Whilst the focus of this book is on property and SSAS it is important to understand that stocks and shares can also be transferred 'in specie'. The process for transferring shares from one pension to another is fairly straight forward. Firstly, the receiving SSAS must request an 'in specie' transfer of assets from the old pension vehicle, via a specific application form that your SSAS administrator will have. This gives the SSAS administrator permission to approach the old pension administrator to request the transfer.

The old pension administrator will then arrange for the share assets to be re-registered in the name of the new SSAS scheme. The process should take somewhere between 3-8 weeks on average.

2.3.2 Commercial Property

The transfer of commercial property commences in a similar way to shares whereby the SSAS Trustee must make a formal transfer request, via an application form, to the SSAS administrator to facilitate the transfer.

Commercial property is a fairly complex asset class, and a property solicitor will need to be formally engaged to change the title of the property and document and register the transfer of ownership with Land Registry. The solicitor will ensure that the receiving SSAS pension will have the due diligence covered, including all conveyancing searches and checks in an identical way as they would if they were purchasing the property. This will ensure that the correct bank grade due diligence process is undertaken, ensuring that the asset is valued correctly, has no flaws in the title, any leases are structured correctly and that no concerns are prevalent in the property.

The commercial property transaction process can take typically 4-12 weeks to complete, depending on the complexity of the asset.

The transfer of an asset to a SSAS as an 'in specie' contribution is usually subject to Stamp Duty Land Tax (SDLT) because although the transfer is for nil consideration, it is a transfer of value all the same. Any Stamp Duty Land Tax payable will be calculated on the open market value of the asset, on the date of the transfer, as verified by an independent specialist valuation. For commercial property this will require an independent valuation from a qualified Royal Institute of Chartered Surveyors (RICS) valuer, normally through what is known as a Red Book valuation.

Capital Gains Tax may be payable by the transferor depending on its structure and the history of the original purchase. This could be from a company, partnership or individual making the contribution.

Some other additional considerations are important in transferring a commercial property asset into a SSAS, including:

- Joint or multiple ownership of the asset
- Who is the beneficiary of the asset in the event of death
- Capital Gains Tax may be payable if there is any increase in property value on disposal
- VAT and Stamp Duty Land Tax (SDLT) tax issues must be carefully considered
- Annual allowances
- Asset type/class
- Existing and new leverage on the asset

Taking the last point on leverage, any existing mortgage provider must be consulted, and permission and terms sought to transfer the property asset in to the SSAS. Some providers will not allow this, and a refinance may be required with costs being incurred as appropriate.

2.4 LOAN BACK

How would you like to be the bank and deploy your investment funds in a manner that suits your strategy?

Well with a SSAS you can – it is a wonderful gift provided exclusively for SSAS Trustees by HMRC and it is called a Loan Back. In return for this exclusive gift, HMRC provide a few rules that we must abide by to ensure the privilege is not abused and preserved for us all to enjoy.

By knowing these rules, we provide ENABLEMENT for our personal economy.

There are many advantages to a SSAS. However, one which isn't available with other types of pension is a connected-party loan to your sponsoring employer and this can be a highly beneficial investment.

A SSAS can make authorised payments to its sponsoring employer, often referred to as a Loan Back. Any payment made outside of the rules, set out in The Pension M5anual, is an unauthorised employer payment and subject to penalty tax charges.

Put simply, this loan option – which is available to any participating employer in the pension – provides a source of business funding without having to seek investment from a third party, such as a bank. And the beauty of it is you have control and security.

There are five key tests that a loan must satisfy to qualify as an authorised employer loan (Loan Back). If a loan fails to meet one or more of these tests, it may be classified as an unauthorised payment.

The five key tests are:

1. Security
2. Interest rates
3. Term of loan
4. Maximum amount of loan, and
5. Repayment terms

A loan to a person connected to a member, or sponsoring employer, and who is not a member or sponsoring employer, is treated as though the loan were made to the sponsoring employer and must comply with the five tests.

2.4.1 Security

When a SSAS makes a Loan Back to a sponsoring employer, the amount of the loan must be secured throughout the full term as a first charge on any asset either owned by the sponsoring employer, or some other entity. At the time the loan is made, the security used must be of at least equal value to the face value of the loan including interest.

So, what does a First Legal Charge mean?

If a first charge on a property at Land Registry (CH1) was the first thing you thought of then you wouldn't be alone, and you would be correct. However, we can also think more laterally and explore a number of options including:

- First legal charge at Land Registry on an unencumbered commercial property
- First legal charge at Land Registry on an unencumbered residential property
- First legal charge at Land Registry on the asset you are acquiring, in a company or privately
- First charge on a share portfolio
- First charge on the Intellectual Property Rights
- First charge on a guaranteed/securitised income stream
- First legal floating charge on assets of a company, often referred to as a debenture

For any of the above to be compliant and prudent it will require a professional to assess the value of the asset to ensure adequate security is in place. This might be a RICS valuer for property or an accountant for valuation on a company and its assets.

Your SSAS Corporate Trustee may have a view on the following, depending on their mandate, however, so firstly make sure you check you have a Corporate Trustee to serve your compliant strategy and secondly the trustee will support you in exploring the right options to protect your SSAS and its compliance.

Note that there must be no other charge on the asset that takes priority or indeed is 'pari passu' (of equal standing) over the charge made by the scheme, hence first legal charge is key.

If the asset used as security is replaced by another asset, the value of the replacement at the time the security is placed must be at least equal to the lower of:

- the market value of the asset it has replaced, or
- the amount of loan outstanding (including interest)

The role of the security trustee is important in insuring you have a robust and protective structure in place, making sure that your SSAS does not incur a penalty charge by default. Please see the chapter on Security Trustee later in this book.

2.4.2 Interest rate

All Loan Backs made by a SSAS must charge interest at least equivalent to the rate specified in The Registered Pension Schemes (Prescribed Interest Rates for Authorised Employer Loans) Regulations 2005. This is to ensure that a commercial rate of interest is applied to the loan.

The <u>minimum</u> interest rate that a scheme may charge is calculated by reference to 1% above the average of the base lending rates of the following six leading high street banks specified in the regulations:

- The Bank of Scotland plc
- Barclays Bank plc
- HSBC Bank plc
- Lloyds Bank plc
- National Westminster Bank plc
- The Royal Bank of Scotland plc

Being prudent is important as a SSAS Trustee, hence the average rate calculated should be rounded up as necessary to the nearest multiple of 0.25%.

A registered pension scheme may make a loan at a fixed rate of interest as long as that interest rate is at least the rate specified. As long as the terms of the loan remain unchanged, there will be no requirement to alter the interest charged on the loan during its life.

2.4.3 Term of loan

The repayment period of the loan must not be longer than five years from the date the loan was made.

An unauthorised payment occurs when the repayment period for a loan is longer than five years from the date the loan was made, unless the loan has been rolled over in accordance with the requirements for Rollovers.

2.4.4 Maximum amount of loan

A SSAS is restricted to the amount it loans via a Loan Back to 50%

of the aggregate of the amount of the cash sums held and the net market value of the assets within the SSAS immediately before the loan is made. So, in simple terms that equates to the net assets of the SSAS.

If the Loan Back is made and it is found to exceed the 50% limit, the amount of the Loan Back in excess of the 50% limit is an unauthorised payment and could attract a penalty tax charge.

2.4.5 Repayment terms

All Loan Backs must be repayable as a minimum, in equal instalments of capital and interest for each complete year of the loan, beginning on the date that the loan is made and ending on the last day of the following 12-month period. This is known as a loan year.

The amount of capital and interest repayments payable, by the end of each loan year, must not be less than 'the required amount' – however, it can be more which is perfectly acceptable.

The Loan Back is calculated as follows:

[(L+TIP) / TLY] x NLY

Where:

L is the amount of the loan

TIP is the total interest payable

TLY is the total number of loan years

NLY is the number of loan years in the period

2.4.6 Rollovers

Rules for Loan Backs does acknowledge that on occasions the

sponsoring employer may encounter issues with making the repayments. Where an employer is having genuine difficulties making repayments, and there is an amount of capital or interest outstanding at the end of the Loan Back period, the Loan Back period can be extended or "rolled over" for a period up to a further five years.

A loan may only be rolled over once. If a loan is rolled over more than once, then the Unauthorised Payments tax rules will apply. The rollover loan will not be treated as a new loan and therefore any existing security may continue, even if the security is less than the face value of the loan. Any increase to the original loan will be treated as a new loan. The 50% limit will only be re-tested in the event of a new loan being taken out.

Example – First Charge

Let us take an example of Mr & Mrs Arnold who have worked their entire adult lives watching the pennies and saving. They have contributed into a combination of state and company pensions and are now retired, living off a monthly annuity pension amounting to £220 in total.

During their working life they purchased their family home and always harboured the ambition to pay off the mortgage which they duly achieved before they both retired.

Their daughter Jane is a SSAS Trustee and property investor having left her legal career at the age of 40. Jane wanted to enable her property company, which is also the sponsoring company of the SSAS, to borrow £150,000 via a Loan Back from her SSAS. In order to provide the relevant security for this, Jane's property company needed to provide a first charge at Land Registry which it did not have as the portfolio had mortgages on (the first charge being taken by the respective mortgage companies).

Jane's parents had indicated to her that they were struggling to live the life they wanted to, due to monetary constraints. They wanted to travel, to see parts of the world they had always wanted to see; they had taken up hobbies and needed more cash in their personal economy.

In summary they were asset rich and cash poor and didn't know how to change their financial outlook.

Jane suggested that the available first charge on her parent's house, with a current market valuation of £300,000, was something that would be useful to support her business and in return could provide a return for her parents.

Jane discussed this sensitively with her parents, whom she had enjoyed a long and trusting relationship with. Jane had plans that the £150,000 would be used to invest in the next stage growth and working capital requirements of her business. She did her calculations and offered a £200 fee per month in return for the first charge, for a period of five years which was the duration of the loan back. This fee would be payable via a contract between Jane's property company and her parents.

Jane decided that the overall cost of the 'fee' for the first charge facility of £12,000 plus a small amount of legal costs to establish the first charge and to remove it at the end of the term, was great value for her to secure the Loan Back.

This is how the final transaction played out:

Property value: £300,000

Security for Loan required:	£150,000
Max Loan to Value:	75%
Security required:	First charge at Land Registry
Beneficiary of first charge security:	SSAS Trust
Maximum loan security possible:	£300,000 x 75% = £225,000
Actual loan security achieved:	£150,000/£300,000 x 100 = 50%
Property company fee to parents:	£200 pcm = £2,400 pa = £12,000 over 5-year term

From Jane's property company perspective, they would be entering into a Loan Back contract as sponsoring company to the SSAS Trust based on a 5-year term where they would be paying capital, plus interest back each year over the term.

Jane explained to her parents that the initial loan to value security on the property, whilst commencing at 50%, would technically be reducing over the following five years until the first charge is removed, once the loan is repaid in full at year five. This is shown as follows:

- Year 0   Loan to value 50%
- Year 1   Loan to value 40%
- Year 2   Loan to value 30%
- Year 3   Loan to value 20%
- Year 4   Loan to value 10%
- Year 5   Loan fully re-paid and first charge removed

Note: Loan Back interest was agreed at 3% in line with HMRC

approval guidelines of a minimum of 1% above the average of six high street lenders' base rates. The interest exposure has not been calculated, however, in reality, you would include that as a liability also, until fully repaid.

2.5 CASE STUDY: TOBY SPANIER - Return on Integrity

The multiple layers of return that can be achieved through a SSAS Loan Back.

The most important ROI, for any investment, is the return of your investment. However, I believe the most rewarding ROI, is the Return on Integrity. I define Return on Integrity as doing the right thing at the right time and for the right reasons.

In this short chapter, I will explain the multiple layers of return that can be achieved through a SSAS Loan Back and the additional rewards that acting with integrity delivers.

I have two property examples from this calendar year which show the layers of return facilitated by a Loan Back. I set up my SSAS last year, and in November arranged a Loan Back of £175k to my limited property company. Fortunately, I had another property in my portfolio to provide a first charge security for the Loan Back, which was just over a third of my total SSAS pension pot.

So, in January I purchased a five-bedroom house in Corby in the Midlands, using my Loan Back funds, for £120k. Although this was the first time I had ever purchased a property in cash, I still wanted a RICS surveyor to give me a valuation of the property at the time of exchange. Unbeknownst to me, this same surveyor had valued the same property at £150k for a previous buyer who had then failed to complete. Clearly this put her in a bind, because I was buying the property at £120k, its market rate was obviously £120k, but this was 25% less than her previous valuation.

So, she settled for a valuation of £130k, stating in her report that the £120k purchase price was for a 'quick cash sale'. I have had several previous down valuations, but this was my first 'up-valuation', and meant that the day I purchased the property, it had effectively increased in value by £10k! This instant creation of equity was entirely due to the Loan Back, which had enabled me to be a cash buyer, and purchase an unmortgageable property at a significant discount.

Having spent £120k on purchasing the Corby property, I had £55k left from the Loan Back. I wanted to open up a second investment area and was looking for houses down South which I could convert to a House of Multiple Occupation (HMO). I used £42k of the remaining Loan Back funds for the deposit on a three storey Victorian terraced house in Folkestone. I purchased the property £167k, using a mortgage to fund the remaining 75% of the sales price.

I planned to convert the property into a seven bed, six-bathroom HMO. Working closely with my architect, I had worked out a way to stay just within the Council's minimum room size rules for HMO's, which would allow me to create additional bedrooms without having to extend the footprint of the building. I had effectively spotted a loophole in the HMO licensing rules, which would have meant that the Council couldn't have legally prevented me from putting more HMO bedrooms into the property. The plan was to technically comply with all the HMO licensing requirements, although I would be essentially breaking the spirit of what those requirements were intended to achieve.

www.EquaAcademy.co.uk

The purchase completed on Monday 23rd March, just after the Covid 19 restrictions had taken effect. At the time I was extremely concerned that if I started a major HMO refurbishment on the property, I might not get to complete it, if any further restrictions on building work were implemented by the government.

I would then be left with a large mortgage, an unfinished house, zero rental income, and no real exit from the situation. Although the government never did bring in Covid 19 restrictions on undertaking building work, at the time I thought this was a likely scenario. Even if I did go ahead with the HMO conversion, I knew that building suppliers would soon run out of supplies, which would further delay, or stop, the conversion.

I didn't know how Covid would turn out, but I knew it was something major and hard to predict. I decided to pivot from my HMO scheme, and on Friday 27th March I got in touch with Folkestone Council to see if they had a need for emergency housing.

Although the property was in a shocking state, I figured I could very quickly restore it to being a good quality four-bedroom family home, and that even if letting agents were shut down, due to Covid, the Council would have a ready supply of tenants, and dispensation to house them throughout the crisis.

I also thought that emergency housing status would give me priority with acquiring scarce building supplies, which certainly did turn out to be the case. I knew I could also massively reduce my refurbishment outlay from £70k to £25k, as I didn't need to convert the property into an HMO, move any walls, or add any bathrooms.

Six weeks after starting the refurbishment of the property, my new tenants moved in. They were a homeless family of seven, who had

66

previously been living in a one bedroom flat above the public toilets in the centre of Folkestone. There was an issue with rat infestation at this building, and hence the Council were extremely keen to find suitable housing for the family as soon as possible. Obviously, the family were absolutely delighted and felt that all their Christmases' had come at once.

It was then in retrospect that I realised my previous plan to convert the property to an HMO and squeeze as many bedrooms and bathrooms into it, was not the right thing to do. The strategy would have technically worked, at least initially, but over-developing a family house would have created a cramped HMO, where tenants would be unlikely to want to stay for the longer term, so was unlikely to be a sustainable model for the long term.

The HMO market in the area was not mature, and so there was also the danger of over-capitalising the property and not being able to realise the refinance valuation I needed to recycle my funds. And of course, I would have been operating at the limits of the Council's HMO requirements and effectively breaking the spirit of their space standard rules, which were designed to prevent overcrowding.

In short, I realised that had I gone down the route of the seven-bedroom HMO, I would not have been doing the right thing with the house, and I wouldn't have been acting with the highest of integrity, as I would have effectively forced the Council to grant an HMO licence on a property it would deem to be overcrowded (regardless of its compliance with the letter of all space standard requirements).

The property was a terraced family home in a street of terraced family homes. I realised that the right thing to do with the property was to reinstate it as a family home. This is what I call acting with integrity – doing the right thing, at the right time, and for the right reasons.

So how did acting with integrity result in the most rewarding Return on Investment?

Well firstly, I did actually feel really good that I had done something to help a family in dire need of a home. For one of the first times in my property career, I actually felt proud at what I had done as a property investor. I was also proud with what I had achieved in such a short period of time. The house really did look fantastic after what was effectively a light cosmetic refurbishment.

In addition, the refurbishment of the property had supported 21 different trades (and their families) during the height of the Covid crisis, as I had paid for the services of plumbers, builders, painters, electricians, architects, carpet fitters, damp specialists and many others.

The Council were delighted that I had also taken a family off their homeless list - because I had done the right thing by them, I actually financially benefitted in a number of ways.

Firstly, the Council gave me a £1,500 incentive to let to a family on their emergency housing list, which was paid on the day the family moved in.

Secondly, because I was housing such a large family, and housing benefit is paid according to the number of bedrooms required, the Council were able to pay me £900 a month, rather than £730 a month. As the private rental market rent in this street was £750 a month, I actually ended up with rent 20% above the market rate, and 35% above the market rate once the £1,500 incentive was factored in (although this would only apply to the first year's rent).

Thirdly, the Council were happy to set up the rent payments to be paid to me directly, and so I would have no rent arrears. Given the

Council were paying the family's rent, I can't see why the family would ever want to leave, so effectively I have a guaranteed rental income for decades (my tenants are a very young family!).

Fourthly, the Council had effectively become my letting agent, but at zero cost!

Lastly, and this is the pièce de résistance, the Council also gave me an interest free grant of £25,000 to undertake the refurbishment works. This was because the property had been vacant for a long time, was is a very poor state of repair, and was the worse house in the street. The interest free loan covered the full cost of the works, which have increased the property's value from £167,000 to £225,000.

As a 75% Loan to Value mortgage would raise £168,000, this deal was effectively a Money-In-Money-Out deal. The deal has also allowed me to recycle my funds in just over six months. I still need to pay back the loan, but have three years to do this, and can pay for it out of the rental profits. I then have a house that has cost me nothing and which gives me a rental income forever!

Had I not set up my SSAS, the £175k of funds which became my Loan Back would have been invested in pension tracker funds delivering at best 4% a year after costs (i.e. £7k a year), if we ignore the volatility of the stock market (which is a big if!).

Instead, my Loan Back allowed me to purchase two investment properties, which I otherwise could not have bought. I was able to recycle my funds from the Folkestone property within six months, ending up with a 'free' house (or rather a house with none of my money left in it). I also converted the Corby property to a six bed HMO, at a refurbishment cost of £30k, and then mortgaged the property at £180k valuation, raising a mortgage of £135k.

So, I was able to recycle my purchase Loan Back funds and half my refurbishment costs on the Corby property. Across the two properties I have created £118k of equity, recycled my Loan Back funds, and only left £15k in of my own money. And I have done good as well and delivered positive social value in both investment areas.

I think you can now see why I believe that Return on Integrity - doing the right thing for the right reasons at the right time - is the most rewarding ROI, both emotionally and financially!

2.6 UNCONNECTED THIRD-PARTY LOANS

A SSAS can lend money to the sponsoring employer (i.e. a SSAS member's company) and also to third parties that have no connection with the SSAS. I cover the former in the Loan Back chapter.

SSAS schemes can make loans to unconnected unquoted UK companies but loans to members are not permitted, other than a loan by a SSAS to a sponsoring employer. Loans to any company (other than the sponsoring employer) that is controlled by a SSAS member, or relative of a SSAS member, are not allowed either.

A simple way to check if you connected in any way is via these two tests:

1. In Blood: are you related through family – brother, sister, husband, wife, children etc?

2. In Business: co-director or shareholder at the time of the loan

Where a SSAS Loan is made to a company, it must be a trading company and the loan must be for a genuine trading reason. A SSAS loan to avert a company from becoming insolvent is not a genuine trading reason.

The loan can be for any amount and could in theory be upto 100% of the fund value and is unaffected by the 50% cap on Loan Back. This is an important point as there is often confusion that a third-party unconnected loan is limited to 50% or needs a first charge security. It is not.

Whether you deem it a correct strategy for you to loan a high percentage to other parties, with a low level of investment diversification, is entirely your choice. Equally so is the level of security you agree to. This could be the weight of the legal loan agreement on its own, it could be personal guarantees, debentures and charges on property. We cover this in much more detail in the chapter on Security.

The loan must be made on the basis of:

- Commercial: Must be a trading company and the terms must be on a commercial basis comparable with others found in the market
- Prudent: Be based on sound due diligence and not be overtly 'edgy' on risk. These are pension funds we are talking about!
- Secure: Must be some level of security albeit HMRC and TPR leave the measure of that security to SSAS member trustees to define. Note the title word here is secure, not first charge security

Your corporate trustee, depending on their policy and mandate, may have restrictions on what you can do and have tighter rules than are defined by HMRC and The Pension Regulator. Make sure you understand what your strategy is likely to be ideally before you select your corporate trustee to ensure they are the right fit and enable, rather than restrict your strategy, subject to compliance rules.

I have seen corporate trustees place restrictions well beyond what the legislation tells you can be done, such as:

- Percentage of funds that can be loaned
- Covenant strength of borrower
- Borrowing entity must have been trading for a minimum of three years
- Borrowing must provide three years' audited accounts
- If the loan is being used for residential purposes, then non allowable
- They will not allow security to be taken on residential property
- Duration of loan restricted
- Interest terms annually as a minimum

The reality is none of these are correct in principle. You can, in theory, disregard all of these. Whether you should, however, is of course a matter for you, your fellow trustees, corporate trustees and your strategy.

Example

Jack has a property development company that has been running for four years. Their strategy is to acquire commercial property on a fully conditional basis, subject to gaining permitted development and occasionally full planning permission, for conversion to residential apartments.

They have a requirement for £100,000 as a working capital loan into their holding company.

They are approached by a SSAS Trustee, Stephen, whom they have known for many years and respect. Stephen has had a SSAS for five years and is currently in liquid cash funds of £175,000.

Stephen is keen to lend £100,000 to Jack's business. They have no connection in business with no shareholding or directorships together. They are also unrelated. This is a prerequisite to determine if they are unconnected, and on this basis they are and the loan may be permitted, without breaching rules and creating a penalty charge from HMRC.

Stephen and Jack agree on terms of 10% per annum interest rolled up to the end of the 18 months loan duration. They include a long stop provision of 24 months and a penalty interest clause of 20% per annum, should the loan not be paid back on time.

Stephen is keen to explore what options exist for security of this loan. Jack explains that all the company assets have mortgages on them and a first charge on a property at Land Registry is not available. However, they would be able to provide a second charge on a residential property with sufficient loan to value coverage to enable security for the loan. Jack confirms that the existing first charge mortgage provider is happy to allow a second charge on the property, although there will be costs incurred.

Stephen hears the word 'residential' and is immediately concerned that there must be no event that would trigger his SSAS ever owning a residential property and consults his SSAS Corporate administrator. They suggest placing the security in the hands of a Security Trustee which would mean that in the event of a default the Security Trustee would invoke the charge and ultimately repatriate cash and not the residential property back to the SSAS should funds cover this in full. For more details see the chapter on Security Trustee.

They agree on the loan and a solicitor is instructed to draw up the terms of the loan and to process the second charge on the property.

Loan amount: £100,000

Interest: 10% per annum

Term: 18 months

Long Stop: 24 months

Penalty interest: 20%

Security: Second charge

This is an example of one of many ways that a loan could be structured. There are a huge array of options available. The key is to make sure that all parties, with their professional team, find common ground that establish SSAS compliance, a formalised legal agreement and terms that are mutually agreeable.

2.7 TRUSTEE CASE STUDY: CHRIS & TRACY HENRY & CHRIS PATON - The Joy of Joint Ventures

This is the story of one of our SSAS loans through the lens of Chris & Tracy Henry as investors and the developer Chris Paton.

2.7.1 The view from the SSAS trustees

MindYerBusiness Ltd SSAS was set up in August 2014 with my wife Tracy and I as Trustees.

The initial purpose of the SSAS was to fund the purchase of a Business Coaching franchise using our redundancy received from leaving Lloyds Bank after 24 years.

Once we understood more fully the power of SSAS, in terms of generational wealth and legacy, as well as weighing up the potential risks, we took the decision to transfer out from the bank our two Final Salary Pension Schemes. Not for everyone and a decision which requires professional advice.

SSAS...trategy

Our goal at the outset was to generate a passive monthly profit (*Note: nothing is ever entirely passive*) of £7,500. Just having a number gives you a reference point for a plan.

This profit would come from both within the SSAS and from activities outside of the SSAS. The initial priority being wealth creation within the SSAS, due to the absence of tax, and therefore faster compounding opportunity.

We achieved the goal after three years using the following strategies:

- Loan Backs from MYB Ltd SSAS to our two companies (up to 50% of the SSAS Net Assets)
- Leveraging the SSAS by borrowing money (up to 50% of the SSAS Net Assets)
- Acquiring a portfolio of HMO's in the North East
- Lending SSAS funds in a measured way to trusted/ experienced third-party property developers
- Syndicated lending where multiple SSAS' joined together to fund a bigger development
- Inviting four other trustees temporarily into our SSAS, again to create leverage and to act as an incubator for them before they move into their own SSAS
- Investing in commercial property developments in Scotland
- Deploying surplus SSAS funds into shares and management funds in between projects

For us and our family the SASS has been a complete game changer.

We have a daughter with Cystic Fibrosis which is a debilitating life shortening disease, and SSAS has allowed us to help her live the life she fully deserves.

Northern Wealthbuilders - Changing Lives

One of the keys to success in life, and in business, is connection and collaboration with good people - ideally people who have the same values and who have a Win-Win mindset, and where there is a synergy. What they have in terms of skills and resources complements what we have.

We were fortunate enough to have met a superbly talented young property developer - Chris Paton - in 2015 and he has been central to our SSAS journey.

We have gathered a group of investors around him, close trusted friends and contacts and most of Chris' project are now funded by the group.

The beauty of the relationship is that Chris can call on the group and, based on a regularly shared view of collective cash flow, know when and if funds are available – a win for us as investors and for Chris as the developer.

Funding approach

Number 42 Heaton Rd is the most exciting we have been involved in so far. The funding of the purchase and the refurbishment was entirely using SSAS funds. Three SSAS's were involved in the syndicated (joint) loan which totalled £425k. The beauty of funding the full project was the ability for us to take a first charge, which has always been our policy.

A ranking agreement was also included to ensure that none of the lenders ranked above any other upon receipt of sale proceeds, in the event of any default.

The transformation from a Doctor's surgery to a high quality five bed Service Accommodation was incredible to see.

Quarterly visits were undertaken to see the project in progress, really bringing our investment to life and, finally, a major party and an overnight stay as guests in the property rounded off an amazing investment for both us, and our very good friend Chris Paton.

2.7.2 The view from the developer- Chris Paton

Acquisition of the building

Prior to the acquisition of the building, a derelict Doctor's surgery, we submitted a pre-planning application in order to obtain a firm grasp of the realistic potential of the site. Once we received a positive response, we moved ahead with the purchase.

The building was acquired in one of our limited companies, Aspire North East Limited, with the SSAS loan taking first and only charge over the property. On completion, we immediately applied for full planning permission for the creation of five apartments and had the building delisted from business rates by the Valuation Office Agency.

The Vision

Our goal was to create five bespoke premium apartments which consists of two x studio apartments, two x two-bedroom apartments and one x three-bedroom apartment. These apartments would then be let out as serviced accommodation. The building, dating from around 1875, had some history attached to it and one of our primary goals was to create an end product of character which takes inspiration from its past, with a firm nod towards the future.

The Numbers

Acquisition & Development

Purchase price	£275,000
Total Acquisition Cost (Inc Fees)	£281,000
Building gross internal area (GIA) once developed:	3,125 square feet
Development Cost (Inc furniture)	£230,000
Loan Interest paid to SSAS	£72,000
Gross Development Cost (GDC)	£583,000
Gross Development Value (GDV)	£665,000

Ongoing Running

Annual Revenue Ex VAT	£114,000
Annual Operating Costs	£23,000
Annual Mortgage Payments	£20,000
Annual Net Profit	£71,000

The Exit

Once the building was complete in June 2019, our primary intention was to rent the building out as serviced accommodation. Once we found a suitable mortgage product for serviced accommodation, the property was then title split creating five separate leasehold apartments, each with a 999-year lease. These were then sold to a subsidiary SPV of the original holding company for tax efficiency reasons. The holding company retained the freehold and receives a small ground rent each year. We chose this strategy as it allowed the creation of leasehold apartments, which has a greater value collectively, than the single commercial valuation of the building.

2.8 SSAS COLLABORATION

One particular feature of SSAS that many hold dear, is the ability to collaborate with other parties. This wide-ranging feature is prized by those that connect with others, enjoy the entrepreneurial spirit and are prepared to be accountable.

Collaboration takes many forms and can include:
- Family members
- Friends
- With fellow directors
- Your Business
- Other Businesses
- Other SSAS's
- Involving the children/next generation
- Connecting with your passion

Over the many years I have had a SSAS, and the thousands of SSAS trustees I have got to know, it is incredible the diversity of business and life experiences. Almost every conceivable profession, skill and trade and background is present. It is quite possibly one of the most diverse and knowledgeable communities there is. That is what makes SSAS so special - the enablement of combining highly accountable, knowledgeable people who have decided to take control of their personal economy with diversified investment decision making and entrepreneurial and enterprise structuring.

One word of caution, however, before we all link pinkies and walk off into the sunset!

As passionate as I am about what can be achieved by a SSAS in the right hands, I also understand the risks. A SSAS is not for everyone – it needs planning, management and accountability. For 20 years of my career, I was a corporate trouble shooter and have seen during this time, as well as subsequently in the property investment world of networking meetings and property education circles, that deep perils can loom for the unwary.

Where money exists, sharks will smell blood in the water and descend, looking for the vulnerable or gullible. Equally, some potential partners get so consumed by the positive emotion of the thought of doing something together that they fail to ask the tough questions in the good times.

These may include:
- Compatibility
- Roles
- Strategy
- Age
- Risk appetite
- Location
- Aspiration and goals
- Duration of relationship

- In-equitability
- Integrity
- Honesty
- Track record

In my trouble shooting role I have had to unpick the sad debris of failed joint ventures and resolve, often in very unpleasant acrimonious circumstances, the aftermath. Common traits over the years have emerged such as lack of agreements, misunderstandings and lack of long-term planning to name just a few.

So, collaboration can be, and is, extremely powerful and enduring relationships can be created as long as proper diligence and critique is performed.

2.9 TRUSTEE CASE STUDY: ALEX IMPEY - The 'Loan Back Ranger'

"A fiery horse with the speed of light, a cloud of dust and a hearty, 'Hi Yo Silver!" OK, so I may not be the legendary lone ranger from our childhoods, and I definitely do not have a horse which can break the laws of physics, but I do hope to explain some pretty innovative ways in which you can utilise the 'SSAS Company Loan Back strategy' in order to create your own cloud of dust and leave everyone else in your wake.

As you may have guessed already, book writing and comedy may not be my forte. However, I have spent the last 12 years as a Mechanical and Project Engineer and this has taught me an appreciation of the detail and building repeatable systems to help generate success. It is my belief that the SSAS company Loan Back is the single most effective way to deliver your financial success, both inside and outside of your SSAS.

The SSAS Loan Back strategy is probably the most widely known advantage of having a SSAS. However, at the same time, the nuances of this strategy and how it can truly be used to your advantage are probably the least explored of all the options. I am a strong believer that the only way to explain these nuances is through story, so I'm going to give you an example of a recent Loan Back which I employed to my own sponsoring company, which wraps up three techniques into one.

In this case study, I will cover the consolidation of existing loan backs into one single Loan Back, within the sponsoring company. We will look at how you can use an asset, which is not owned by yourself, in order to satisfy first legal charge SSAS requirement. Finally, we will then also look at how we can use this Loan Back to deliver some great returns to your SSAS and your sponsoring company. All of this whilst protecting your projects from expensive senior charge financing and providing savings for both your investors and your own project - oh and did I mention all of this was on a residential development? So, firstly, let's set some context - as Simon Sinek says, "always start with WHY?"

Stoneywood Gate: XUSA Development

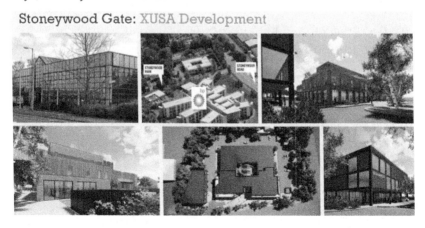

So, what were the original motives for this Loan Back? In this case my business, XUSA, was looking to fund the initial seed capital needed to cover costs of acquisition and finalise planning for one of our new mixed-use developments, of which a brief overview can be seen below:

Sponsoring company: XUSA

The Project: Stoneywood Gate

Location: Aberdeen

Project Headlines:

- £10M GDV
- 50 apartments (one and two bedrooms)
- 18,000sq.ft of commercial

We had initially agreed to a mix of finance to help us with the primary phase of this project. This included senior charge finance, by way of a bridge loan from a well-known commercial institute, as well as private investor funds. I have shown the structure of this deal and amounts for your benefit: (opposite)

We had originally planned to use the first charge senior funder as a bridge to help us acquire the property. This is a strategy which we use regularly with our developments and the commercial debt runs alongside private investor money, in case of any last-minute private investment issues. The commercial bridge headlines of the loan were as follows:

Commercial Bridge Headlines

- 11% p.a. interest on the principal (£150k) paid monthly = £1,375 interest charges p/m

- Total Fees of 4% on principal (£150k) = £6,000
- Cost of lenders solicitor = £1,500
- Cost of RICS Redbook Survey = £4,000
- Total term = 12 months
- Total cost of loan over term = £28,000

Development - Corporate Structure

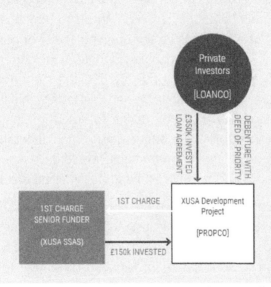

As we all know, commercial bridges and seed capital loans are super cheap, very secure and very quick to deploy! Hopefully you sensed my sarcasm in that last sentence, as although we had organised everything, had funding agreed and credit backed terms in place, it turned out the finance company didn't have any of their ducks in a row, which delayed the injection of funds for purchase. Just after purchase, we then again tried to draw down the funds as capital seed for the project. However, at this point in time, the world had already gone into a COVID-19 meltdown and a worldwide lockdown ensued. We were told that our loan was on indefinite hold until the 'picture became clearer'.

A clear picture looked to be the least likely outcome in April 2020, and although we had sufficient capital to continue our project, we were unable to provide our typical level of bank grade operational reserves for our one year 'rainy day' scenario. At XUSA we look at all the potential outcomes of a project and look to cover all scenarios with additional operational reserves - this is to the benefit of both the project but also to ensure the ongoing safety of our investors' contributions. With the banking situation looking unlikely to resolve itself anytime soon, I put my thinking cap on in order to try and secure some capital at 'reasonable terms'. Initially I looked at the private equity and debt market to raise the funds, but even then, many investors were either going into hibernation or the offers which were landing on the table would have made even the toughest loan sharks seem like a beautiful smelling orchid.

It then occurred to me, when I was out one day, "Why couldn't I use my SSAS to support this instead?" The only issue I had was that I already had one Loan Back outstanding for £50,000 and which was in its second year of running. I was due to repay the entire loan within the coming months, due to a smaller project terminating and the sales proceeds coming through. However, by taking an additional loan for £150k (to cover the original bridge) this would have pushed me beyond the 50% max requirement for a SSAS. Rather than allowing this to scupper my plans, I decided to ask my corporate trustee whether they would allow a Loan Back consolidation. This meant taking out a new loan of £150,000, but simultaneously paying back the original Loan Back of £50,000 with the proceeds. Let's have a look at the figures:

Consolidation Loan Overview

- Total SSAS value = £320,000
- Total allowable Loan Back of SSAS (50% of value) = £160,000
- Amount already used by SSAS (Original Loan Back) = £50,000
- Total max allowable Loan Back with current loans (£320k - £50k / 2) = £135,000
- Total loan consolidation requested = £150,000

Total redemption to account = £150,000 - £50,000 = £100,000

Now I can hear those maths savvy readers shouting at me, "But you need to lend £150,000 and if you go ahead with this consolidation you only have £100,000". You are 100% correct. In reality there were two options available at this time:

1. Repay the total original Loan Back of £50,000 and consolidate or

2. Payback part of the Loan Back and consolidate

With option two, as the max available Loan Back available at this point was £140,000, I needed £10k more (which would have meant paying £20k to my SSAS), so by paying £20k back into my SSAS, I would have had enough to take the new Loan Back. However, on this occasion, I choose to pay the full capital amount; Here's why:

1. The annual capital and interest charges were due for this loan, which would have meant I would have needed to have paid approximately £11k back to my pension, along

with another £11k to the SSAS in order to reach the total qualifying amount. This would have taken £22k from my personal economy and cashflow

2. I was already due to receive the proceeds from a recent finalised project, which allowed me to repay the entire Loan Back (£50,000)

3. The reason why we were taking this money was to provide operational reserves cover to a project, which was already funded, and the total amount was not required in one whole amount

It is worth taking a pause here to discuss the benefits of the Loan Back consolidation as it may not be initially apparent. Imagine you have two existing Loan Backs of £50k value each - with capital and interest you would be paying approximately £11k+ (depending on your interest rate) every year to service each of these loans. Imagine the repayment dates were in September and December - that means in the last quarter of each year you would need to find £22k+ from your personal economy to pay the debts. If you are banking on a property transaction liquidating in order to pay off part, or all of these loans, then you could be carrying a lot of risk, should that property transaction not finalise. With a consolidation Loan Back, you could arrange for this in say August or September of the following year, thereby removing the obligation to have to pay back £22k of capital and interest needed for both of the Loan Backs. Instead with the consolidation you could then defer your interest/capital by an additional year. This could be very useful in your own project, especially where cashflow is essential.

Let's go back to my example with the Stoneywood Gate project - now is probably a good time for us to refresh ourselves with the original corporate structure and point out that in this new structure the senior charge lender has now changed, from a commercial lender to that of my SSAS. However, we should also note that the same security requirements (a first legal charge over a non-movable asset) is still required, along with the same obligations to investors - see below:

Development - Corporate Structure

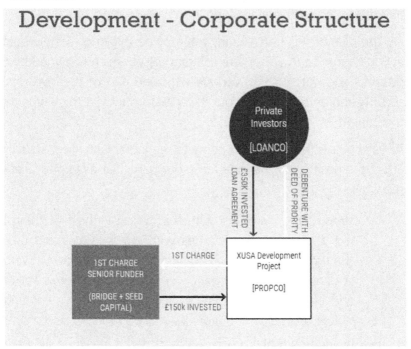

Why am I reminding you of this? Well, it's important to know that as a developer I still have obligations to the company, shareholders and also our investors and without their approval this strategy would be simply resigned to the scrap heap. As you are no doubt aware, a SSAS needs a first ranking legal charge in order to execute a Loan Back and in our case the investors have a debenture in their favour over the development company and its assets, as part of their security.

Furthermore, in this case, the asset sits within the development company and so I do not have personal control of it. However, this is not an issue so long as the controlling and interested party/parties agree to this. For the development company, the financial benefit is quite obvious, which we will demonstrate shortly. However, it may not be so easy for the investors to see this. That's why transparency and dialogue are essential, along with a clear vision.

On the face of this transaction, you may be thinking - why would anyone agree to this? You are using an asset which is owned by a business and not yourself, you are removing part of the investors' security and on top of this, your SSAS will profit from this - where's the benefit?

All valid points, but as we will come to see, none which will actually affect the position of the investor in our particular examples. Let's see why:

- When I first came up with this concept, the first thing I did was to discuss this idea with our investors and take the time to explain the situation. They knew that we were searching for operational cover (£150k) which was above and beyond the normal project capital requirement and would be used in the project's unlikely worst-case scenario

- In addition to this, I also demonstrated that even if we were to remove £150k from the total security, due to the existing levels of collateral, IP and building value, there was still well in excess of the £350k available within the debenture, thus covering all of their individual interests comfortably. The debenture was also attached with a deed of priority which meant that only the asset was at risk, nothing else, as part of the debenture

- Instead of having a corporate commercial entity administering the loan with inflexible terms, there was now a common party who was making decisions for the best of the project. This would have not been the same case, should the commercial lender have been used

- All of the loan (£150k) to cover the operation cash reserved would be available for use within just a couple of months of approval

- By using the SSAS, we would be able to acquire this capital at a very reduced rate. Instead of 11% p.a. this was replaced with a 4%/8% p.a. structure. This means that 8% would be charged, only if money was actually drawn down by the Development company for use. If the loan remained unused (either part or in full) then that unused principal would only be charged at 4% upon until the point of exit

- Assuming that the reserve stays unused (4% interest charge) then this will provide a total savings to the Development company of £16k, in comparison to the commercial loan (see headlines below). On top of that, interest is not paid monthly but annually, providing significant cash flow savings

- This saving ultimately also helps improve the returns for the investor upon existing their equity positions as this is money saved and should the project run as expected

SSAS Loan Headlines:

- 4% p.a. interest on the principal (£150k) paid annually = £6,000
- Total Fees = £500
- Cost of Lenders solicitor = £1,500

- Cost of RICS Redbook Survey = £4,000 (Original Redbook Survey used)
- Total term = 12 months
- Total cost of loan over term = £12,000

Comparison Table of potential loan costs

Loan Provider	Interest P.A (%)	Total Set-Up costs (£)	Total Cost over term (£)	Total Savings (£)
COMMERCIAL	11%	£11,500	£28,000	-£16,000
MY SSAS	4/8 %	£6000	£12,000	+£16,000

It is clear to see the benefits to the investor in this case and why therefore, we were also able to go ahead with this strategy. At every stage of the dialogue, we always looked to put their interests first and show how we were protecting them at every moment - Win!

Now, normally, this would be the point that I would mount my trusty Steed and ride off into the sunset, but that's not the end of the story. Not being content with just one 'Win', we were able to create a cycle of wins for five different parties:

Win 1 = My SSAS is able to deploy considerable amounts of capital and take a small, but solid return, of 2% from the sponsoring company

Win 2 = My sponsoring company is making a modest profit through means of arbitrage (it lends from my SSAS at 2% and charges the Development company 4%)

Win 3 = The Development company has saved £16k in loan costs and also has a flexible lender working in the best interests of the project

Win 4 = Our Investors improve their position in relation to their investment and security

Win 5 = My personal economy did not have to take a hit of between £10k - £20k during the middle of an economic crisis in order to repay back the outstanding original Loan Back, and the success of the development company will hopefully provide a benefit for my personal economy once complete.

There we have it folks! By my own admissions I am no 'horse riding vigilante', but that said I do come armed with a SSAS, an inventive mind and a corporate trustee who listens. With these three things

you can turn even the most 'straightforward' of SSAS strategies into a very powerful tool, which has the ability to support your own projects as well as provide a fantastic waterfall of financial returns for all within it. I hope you enjoyed this case study and that this gives you inspiration with your own SSAS - *'Hi Yo SASS'*.

3. SSAS AND PROPERTY STRATEGIES

This chapter will focus on the exciting array of opportunities that are available to property investors, developers and SSAS trustees using SSAS to enable, own and/or liberate additional value from property business transactions.

This can be a complex area and great advice will be needed at every step of the way from your professional team and mentor to create assured outcomes wherever possible.

Each transaction is different and should be treated on its own merits. It will not only be the property aspects that will vary each time but also the circumstances including the buying party, the funding methods, the ownership and control structuring, to name but a few.

3.1 PROS AND CONS OF COMMERCIAL PROPERTY IN A SSAS

Those that know me well will understand my passion for SSAS and commercial property is always balanced with risk adjusted review of the pros and cons. Here is a list of some of the advantages and disadvantages to enable you to consider what is right for you and your personal circumstances.

<u>Advantages of commercial property in a SSAS:</u>
- No Income Tax on any rental income
- Wealth falls outside of your estate when considering

Inheritance Tax

- No Capital Gains Tax on the sale of the property
- Business cashflow enabling by unlocking capital back into the business
- Assets are protected and therefore not accessible to creditors in the event of business or personal bankruptcy
- SSAS can use leverage, via commercial mortgages, to borrow up to 50 per cent of its fund value to acquire commercial property
- Assets can be sold at any time
- SSAS can collaborate and purchase in conjunction with other SSAS members and Trusts
- SSAS is independent and there are no individual or business liability on any SSAS loans (unless alternative guarantees are entered into)
- On the passing of a SSAS trustee assets can be transferred in a tax efficient manner

Disadvantages of commercial property in a SSAS:

- It cannot be used as collateral for any loans to the business
- The business in occupation must pay market rent, even if it's your own business
- The SSAS administrator is obliged to chase rent, even if it's your own business
- Regular revaluations may be required, which could incur cost
- SSAS loans tend to be short term, which can make them expensive

- Interest on any borrowing doesn't qualify for tax relief
- Property expenses will be due, whether or not a tenant is in place
- If it's the primary asset of the SSAS, it could leave the investments poorly diversified
- It's generally an illiquid asset, which could take months or years to sell at the right price
- Lenders to a SSAS are fewer than for mainstream Limited company lending, therefore interest rates and terms may be less favourable
- SSAS is highly tax efficient anyway and therefore cannot take advantage of capital allowances and other extended tax efficient schemes (See chapter on capital allowances)

Let us bear these in mind whenever we evaluate our strategy to ensure we have the right property, in the right structure, using the right funding, with the right risk profile and delivering the value where intended.

3.2 ACQUIRING LAND

Land is classed as commercial property and is an asset class that can be owned by a SSAS.

Land with planning can also be owned by a SSAS. Planning permission in itself does not change the use class, it merely provides permission to change the use class of the land (or building). Afterall, consider what happens to planning permission after 3 years – the permission lapses if not proceeded with.

What will happen though is the potential valuation of the land increases with planning, which opens up a whole host of opportunities for a SSAS, or indeed collaboration with a SSAS.

Here are some areas that can be possible with a SSAS enabling land acquisition:

- Land to new build residential
- Land to commercial
- Agricultural land to offices
- Brown field land to industrial sheds
- Demolition of existing property and rebuild using new permitted development rights or full planning
- Car parks which could be a cash-flowing asset
- Title splitting land from a residential garden
- Acquire land in SSAS whilst gaining planning
- Use SSAS for a purchase option agreement
- Acquire land with existing cash flowing use and work on securing planning uplift for the future
- SSAS enabling commercial property acquisition to secure capital allowances in the right structure for tax efficient off sets

3.3 OVERAGE/UNDERAGE

How can a SSAS create substantial value from converting commercial property to residential, or even land to residential, without having to be concerned about the physical construction or ownership hazards of owning residential?

Well, one area that could be considered is creating an overage clause in the contracts between the SSAS and the acquiring party.

What is an overage agreement? Also known as claw-back or uplift, an overage is an agreement that the buyer will pay additional to the purchase price, if and when certain trigger events occur. A common reason would be when increases in the value of the land happen by obtaining planning permission.

Overage payments are typically a percentage of the uplift in value derived from the granting of planning permission for a particular development, or if triggered by a sale of the property by the buyer at a profit - the difference between the price received by the buyer and the price originally paid to the seller.

The Valuation process will identify the value of the land, the enhanced value of the land with planning and then the final GDV of the finished development. An overage clause can be agreed so that the SSAS is compensated for further additional value that is created and is paid upon completion of the development, by developer, to the SSAS.

This represents a further example of where wealth creation can be distributed in numerous ways to suit personal circumstances.

It is possible for the reverse to happen where an underage clause is inserted to protect a perceived over purchase of the property. These can be more complex as they can require clawbacks and often escrow accounts may be used to protect parties.

3.4 LEASES

Commercial leases are a necessity for pretty much every commercial property and, if structured correctly, can add a very significant amount of value to the property valuation. Alternatively, with just a few lapses of concentration or poor advice, a very substantial amount of value could be lost in the eyes of a funding valuation.

A commercial lease is a legally binding contract made between a landlord and a tenant who is usually a business. The lease provides the tenant the right to use certain demarked property for a predefined business or commercial activity. This right will be governed for a period of time in exchange for a financial consideration paid to the landlord.

The lease outlines the rights and responsibilities of both the landlord and tenant during the lease term. Commercial leases are deemed to be between knowledgeable businesses rather than potential less knowledgeable residential tenants. The parties to a lease are the lessor, or landlord, and the lessee, the tenant.

One of the most commonly used leases is a Full Repairing and Insuring lease (FRI) where all costs of maintenance and repair and the cost of insurance are the responsibility of the Tenant.

Key components of a commercial lease would include the following:

- Name, address and use type of the property
- Type of business that may be operated on the property
- Term of the tenancy
- Whether the tenancy is a fixed term or renews periodically
- Arrangement for security/damage deposit
- Amount, frequency and timing of rent payable
- Ownership of leasehold improvements
- Break clauses
- Arrangements for lease renewal
- Tenant improvement responsibilities
- Ability for tenant to assign or sublet the property
- Notice for termination of the tenancy
- Insurance provisions

The covenant strength of the tenant can have a substantial impact on the rental terms agreed and therefore the valuation received on the property. However, high financial covenant strength organisations are fully aware of their strength in negotiation and will usually be able to agree much more favourable terms.

From the landlord's perspective they will gain the benefit from a much healthier valuation on securing funding.

It is important for a SSAS trustee to master commercial lease negotiations and details and most will use a solicitor and a commercial agent to undertake this on their behalf.

3.5 LEASEHOLD & FREEHOLDS

A SSAS can own leasehold as well as freehold properties - as always, the devil is in the detail however in principle this is possible.

This question may be posed in a number of scenarios:

- Restructuring an existing asset that you hold - this could be a commercial property such as your business premises. You may choose to sell or transfer the freehold to your SSAS

- Acquiring a leasehold commercial property – a commercial property could be acquired by the SSAS directly

- Restructuring - the SSAS may hold a commercial asset which it is developing, however, part of the development will include residential units which must exit the SSAS prior to them becoming technically 'residential use class'. Consideration in structuring would include enabling lowest cost of funding and avoiding flying freeholds - see chapter on Commercial to Residential Conversions to understand this important aspect in detail

- Sale and leaseback - the SSAS may do a sale and leaseback whereby it sells the freehold of a property and leases back part of the property, on say a 999-year lease basis

- Affordability - the SSAS may not be large enough to acquire all of the property being sought. Upon legal completion a Limited company might acquire the freehold of the property and simultaneously the SSAS acquires part of the property owned on a leasehold basis

Property investors are always looking to add value and a particular niche strategy is to acquire short leaseholds and then negotiate the extension, or to acquire the freehold thus adding significant value. This clear and intended strategy would need to be set out when presenting the acquisition plan to your SSAS corporate trustee for compliance checks. It may well also require an initial cash purchase, or bridge, before bringing more vanilla commercial finance leverage, once the lease has been extended or freehold acquired.

This particular subject again reminds us how important it is to seek qualified advice and counsel. However, having said that, it is our tenacity and skills that are required to identify potential properties, scenarios and structures and to create the ideas for our professional team to then become additionally creative and to test if what we suggest is in the art of the possible. Then together you evolve the solution to create the final structure that is assessed to be compliant and acceptable to all parties.

One question that does come up frequently is, can a SSAS own the freehold of a block of apartments? In short, the answer is no. This would be too close to holding an interest in a residential asset class and therefore would attract a penalty tax charge from HMRC.

Starting with the end in mind however, if the strategy of your organisation was to acquire freehold interests then one might be inclined to explore how a SSAS could 'enable' rather than 'own' the freehold interests of say blocks of apartments.

Could the Board of the sponsoring company identify that it requires working capital to seek further business growth and in order to do this structure a Loan Back from the SSAS to the sponsoring company with a first charge on assets. This could then enable the business to continue its growth strategy. Clearly the detail would need to be scrutinised. However, the point is well made that your SSAS is a powerful tool within your overall toolbox of wealth and can be a primary, or indeed a secondary, enabler if thinking strategically.

Considerations for a SSAS holding a leasehold on a property would include:

- Lease duration - any lease which is lower than 60-70 years remaining starts to become termed as a short lease and may start to become a concern

- Ground rent - levels of ground rent have been a topical issue for a number of years now with Government seeking to address some of the terms of leaseholds deemed unfair. This generally relates to 'unfair' escalation and indexation levels over time for ground rents which can lead to unparalleled and unserviceable levels of per annum rents thus essentially making the properties economically unviable and therefore rendering them extremely difficult to mortgage/re-mortgage

- Mortgage qualifying - mortgage companies may lend up to 25 years and they will have a keen interest in knowing that you will be able to refinance the asset with a further mortgage of say up to 25 years, hence the likelihood is that anything without a 25 years + 25 years + X years may mean a higher interest rate on borrowing and less options available

Example:

A scenario might be a business owner has found a new property on the market in their local town. The property is being offered on a freehold title basis and consists of a retail space at street level with a residential flat above.

Both the flat and the retail space are empty and the director plans to move in to use the premises for their business.

The property is valued at £400,000, and the valuation supports a 40%/60% split between the residential and non-residential parts respectively.

In its current form, the SSAS cannot purchase this property due to the residential part, which is not permitted as a pension asset, and would incur a penalty charge. The SSAS can only purchase the non-residential part.

So how can the SSAS effectively enable the acquisition of the property asset?

The solution could be to create a new leasehold title within the existing freehold title using the following steps:

- Offer is made to the vendor to purchase the property for £400,000
- RICS red book valuation is carried out by a surveyor on behalf of the SSAS which identifies:
    - Size and value of commercial element

- Size and value of residential element
- SSAS plans to acquire the commercial elements in cash and lease back to business
- Solicitor is formally appointed by the SSAS to act on its behalf
  - Legal work commences to transfer freehold title
  - Simultaneously the solicitor creates a new 999 year leasehold title on the non-residential part
  - The freehold transfers to the business and leasehold to the SSAS
  - SSAS releases £160,000 to the solicitor, client releases £240,000 to the solicitor
  - Vendor receives £400,000 for the freehold title
- The SSAS enters into a lease with the business and receives rent
- Once the above is in place the SSAS then decides to apply for a commercial bank mortgage on the commercial property with a long-term tenant in place

3.6 TITLE SPLITTING

Title splitting can be relevant to a SSAS in a variety of ways, as follows:

1. It can be an essential method of ensuring compliance in areas such as commercial and industrial conversion to residential ensuring, through correct structuring, that the SSAS remains compliant at all times and not risking a penalty tax charge

2. A sale and lease back where mixed-use schemes including

business premises can be structured to enable a SSAS to own a commercial property whilst retaining income from one of your other business interests in the form of rent. This is an excellent way of keeping costs within a circular economy, retaining value and compounding over many years

3. A great way to finding and securing property, whilst adding value through leasehold and freehold splitting, multiple and also instantaneous purchases where two or more acquisitions happen at the same time for one property

4. Adding value by breaking a freehold into multiple parts by creating leaseholds and selling them to other parties (connected or non-connected) or refinancing across several lenders

Once you have built the experience and knowledge on how to title-split, and the various techniques that can be used, the opportunities of combining a SSAS with your companies as well as extended collaboration become infinite!

Whether the strategy is to buy, develop, sell or buy, develop and hold, the trustee and/or developer must understand how the freehold and leasehold system operates to evaluate the correct strategy to deploy, to meet their goals.

Typically, when approaching a title split strategy, the freehold of the property would be split into a number of leaseholds. Each lease would be usually:

- 99 years
- 125 years
- 250 years
- 999 years

Most apartments are sold on a leasehold basis and typically 125 years would be very common.

The 999-year lease is often referred to as 'virtual freehold' and, while on the face of it, appears advantageous, be aware that the obligations and permissions are where the perils may lie in the future.

For example, imagine a development where you own an office, held on a 999-year lease, that sits above a retail unit on a High Street location.

If you wished to develop the upper office floor levels, you would be required to contact the freeholder on the following elements:

- Approval from the freeholder for changes
- Responsibility for the freeholder's professional fees to consider your application/request
- Bound by the timescales it takes the freeholder to negotiate and communicate
- Pay a fee to freeholder to develop
- Pay all freeholder costs

Many freehold investments are held by large pension companies and quite possibly by offshore legal entities or investors based abroad – so beware of the bureaucracy and timescales that these negotiations can entail if you are considering purchasing and developing a virtual freehold commercial or residential property. It may be wise to add freeholder approval to the conditionality of your offer.

There are a number of key components to freeholds which must be appreciated and four of the most relevant are:

1. Ground rent
2. Service charge
3. Terms of the lease
4. Enhanced value potential

3.6.1 Ground Rents

Freehold buyers are parties who the developer will be looking to sell the freehold interests to and who in turn, will be looking at value extraction in a number of potential areas including annual ground rents over a long period of time, between 125 – 999 years.

For further details we will go into more depth in the following chapter on Terms of the Lease.

3.6.2 Service Charges

Management company and service charge fees will be established within the leasehold documentation. This has strong governance attached to it and is a specialist area.

Consideration may be given towards wider picture economies of scale on the service provision of the freehold provider and the management company. This may include services such as administration, insurance, gardening, window cleaning, overhead efficiency and rebates etc.

3.6.3 Terms of Lease

The terms of the lease may offer additional potential for the freeholder with areas such as long-term escalations and indexation. This is a core area that lobby groups and government are focusing in on, at the time of writing, and this will come under increased scrutiny.

Indexation on leasehold agreements may be in a number of

different formats with the primary methods of tracking indexation being influenced and contracted by:

- Retail Price Index (RPI)
- Consumer Price Index (CPI)
- Bank of England Inflation Rate

However, the issue has been prevailing over the past few decades where seemingly innocuous provisions have made their way into leases which may contract an entirely different indexation structure.

For example, a 125-year lease had a ground rent provision of £250 per annum.

If this is not paid annually by the leaseholder then action would be taken by the freeholder which, ultimately, could result in the leaseholder losing their property. This is highly unlikely to happen for the sake of £250 p.a.

This is why the covenant strength of this type of investment is considered exceptional and the yield will possibly be 3% – 5%.

If the indexation is at 3% p.a. for example, then the £250 would rise to circa £614.21 in thirty years' time.

However, what if a provision had been made in the lease that ground rents would double every five years? Seems pretty minor on the face of it and that is exactly what many thought no doubt when entering into these contracts. However, £250 doubled every five years would mean a ground rent in thirty years' time of £16,000!

An apartment with a ground rent escalation of this level would render the apartment unlikely to be sold and if it is unlikely to be sold, the owners are unlikely to also get a mortgage on the property.

A huge issue for the leaseholder.

This would create a massive dilemma, and this is what is unfolding across the country as a result of 'unfair' contracts that parties have entered into many years ago.

3.6.4 Enhanced Value Potential

This will include extracting additional value from the property through a use of:

- Air space – additional floors
- Loft conversion
- Basement conversion
- Further land development in gardens/car parks
- Efficiency of future expenses
- Long-term relaxation of the planning system enabling further upside

The example earlier in the chapter about the conversion of the offices above a retail unit on a virtual lease, brings the Freeholder 'enhanced value' element into sharp contrast.

When considering title splitting your freehold into individual leaseholds, it is important to understand the key implications of the lease and its specific terms. As developers, we are trying to strike a balance here between favourable terms, which will add value to the freehold sale. We're also looking at terms which are attractive and fair to our purchases of the leasehold parties.

Government is increasingly taking measures in evaluating the fairness of leaseholds. We can expect, in the next few years, a tightening of the governance around the creation of leaseholds in apartments and new build and again, this is a very specialist area where specialist advice must be sought.

We have to strike a balance between creating great value for our freeholder and great security in value for our leasehold purchase, so that:

- Our lenders will be able to fund the purchase
- The buyers will be able to buy
- The freeholders will see value and will acquire the freehold

This represents a win-win-win for the three parties - the buyers of the individual units, the freeholder and ourselves, as the developer.

3.7 SAS CASE STUDY: NIGEL GREENE - SSAS commercial property enablement

In mid 2018, my fellow Trustee, Nigel Greene identified a wonderful commercial property in Colchester, Essex which consisted of five commercial properties under a single title. The property was located in the old part of Colchester, the oldest City in England by all accounts, and was set just off a highly desirable cobbled High Street, popular with boutique retail shops and service industries such as estate agents and café's, all with considerable footfall.

The properties consist as follows:

a. Commercial lease for a café with several years remaining on the lease
b. Tattoo parlour with three months remaining on its lease
c. Vacant shop
d. Vacant dance studio/shop
e. Clothing repair business with two years remaining on the lease

The property was in a position where, with our specialist knowledge of commercial property, we saw the potential to drive significant value and appreciation into this asset.

The two diagrams that follow show how we have secured and developed multiple phases of additional value that will serve our families for decades to come. It really is that powerful!

3 Stage Transaction (after initial purchase)

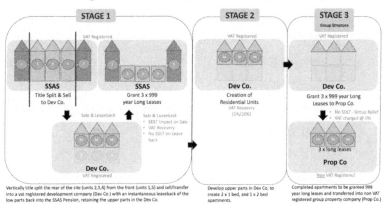

Final Structure and Funding

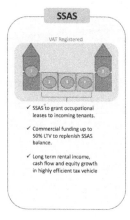

SSAS

VAT Registered

✓ SSAS to grant occupational leases to incoming tenants.

✓ Commercial funding up to 50% LTV to replenish SSAS balance.

✓ Long term rental income, cash flow and equity growth in highly efficient tax vehicle

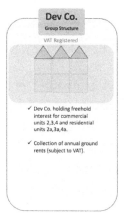

Dev Co.

Group Structure

VAT Registered

✓ Dev Co. holding freehold interest for commercial units 2,3,4 and residential units 2a,3a,4a.

✓ Collection of annual ground rents (subject to VAT).

Prop Co.

Group Structure

Non VAT Registered

✓ Prop Co, to rent out apartments on AST's

✓ BTL lending between 55%/60% to repay all costs.

✓ Long term rental income / cash flow and equity growth.

The following identifies the key steps in the process that complement the diagrams to give you a really deep dive into how knowledge, experience and action can come together to achieve great things:

1. Our accepted offer of £620,000 was fully conditional on securing planning permission.

2. We identified that the three vacant units could have their 'uppers' at first floor level converted to residential units

3. Full planning permission was required, due to the stunning location being in a conservation area, hence Permitted Development Rights did not apply

4. We duly applied for full planning permission which was granted

5. We then completed on the purchase of the property in the SSAS in cash on this particular occasion

6. We then title split units two, three and four and sold them into our Development Company for development into

three residential apartments as well as the three commercial properties below

7. We then sold the 999-year virtual freehold interests of the commercial units back to the SSAS in a quasi-sale and leaseback

8. We then developed the residential units into three beautifully appointed one and two-bedroom apartments. Note that these are now importantly outside of our SSAS, in our development company

9. The development company collects the ground rent for the three commercial units with a 999-year lease each year

10. As a development company it is VAT registered and can therefore reclaim the VAT paid on professional fees (20%) and on the main contractors build costs (5%)

11. Once completed, the residential units were then sold into a Property Company where they will be held long-term. This is a non-VAT registered entity as we do not want to charge VAT to our tenants on AST rents

12. The Property Company raised Buy to Let finance on the purchase of the three residential units

13. Commercial units one and five remain in the SSAS and have 10-15 year FRI leases placed on them, with counter parties, with very reasonable covenant strengths

14. Units two, three and four have 10-15 year FRI leases placed on them, with counter parties, with very reasonable covenant strengths

15. Units one - five were then re-financed on the strength of the improved leases

16. The re-finance replenished the funds of the SSAS and

enabled yet further investment opportunity

17. All freehold and leasehold commercial units, as well as the residential units, are held in their respective legal entities in perpetuity

This SINGLE investment cluster will provide our Trustees and families with:

a. Five commercial units within our SSAS with ever increasingly secured leases for long term cashflow for decades to come

b. Three residential apartments which will be held in our Property Company for strong monthly cashflow and long-term capital appreciation in this desirable area

c. Three commercial unit freeholds held in our Development Company

This asset is a unique and extremely valuable case study of establishing multiple layers of compounding wealth and how a SSAS can be the catalyst for that value creation.

The first layer of compounding sits in the SSAS that has benefitted from driven appreciation through planning permission, sale of the units two, three and four and renegotiating the leases on more favourable terms, as and when they come up for renewal.

The second layer of compounding sits outside of the SSAS but has been directly ENABLED by the SSAS. This represents three residential units and three commercial unit freeholds.

How can you gain FIVE layers of compounding wealth across your portfolio of interests using your SSAS as a catalyst for growth? These may well include, like ours:

- SSAS cashflow

- SSAS asset capital growth
- Property company cashflow
- Property company asset capital growth
- Development company freeholds and their potential

An amazing deal I think you will agree, for 10-12 months of hard effort and a heap of tenacity!!

3.8 SERVICED ACCOMMODATION

Can Serviced Accommodation be held by a SSAS? Well the simple answer is - it depends!

With the advent and growth of organisations such as Airbnb and Booking.com over recent years, a new service industry has arisen, utilising property for short-term stay accommodation, often referred to as Serviced Accommodation. In reality this has been around for decades, however, the technology and booking systems have now allowed a multitude of property asset classes to be deployed now and has brought a whole host (no pun intended!) of new business and property owners seeking to take advantage of this opportunity.

And therein lies the essence of the debate on whether Serviced Accommodation can be held in a SSAS. We need to examine what we mean by Serviced Accommodation and then decide what the asset class is, to determine compliance.

If the property is clearly commercial and used for short-term lettings, such as bed and breakfast and hotel accommodation under a use class of C1, then the answer will be probably. If the property is clearly a residential property, such as an apartment or semi-detached or terrace house that has been repurposed, then the answer is almost certainly a resounding NO!

So, is serviced accommodation a property business or a service business?

There is a trend for undertaking rent to rent contracts whereby the business does not own the Serviced Accommodation but rents it from a landlord. This might be a commercial property, house of multiple occupancy (HMO) or residential as examples. In this case there is no property asset owned within the business. Equally, many Serviced Accommodation businesses, even if the shareholders and/ or directors did have access to owned assets, may well choose to adopt an operating company/property company (OpCo/PropCo) model and introduce, in effect, a rent-to-rent model to create improved structuring for ownership and tax efficiency reasons.

The Serviced Accommodation OpCo may require working capital for the initial cost and outlay of furniture - for example, for a new premises, which might be traditionally through a business loan from a bank or private investor. If the business was a sponsoring company to a SSAS, a Loan Back could be explored, as long as certain provisions were met including a first charge security.

The subject of whether Service Accommodation can be held within a SSAS is probably one of the top three frequently asked questions that usually end up failing compliance checks when interrogated. Please use caution in this area as with all aspects of SSAS compliance.

Two counter arguments are frequently raised when assessing if Serviced Accommodation is SSAS compliant:

1. It pays business rates
2. It has a change of use class to C1

Both of these are tests for commercial property and will be used in your assessment with your professional team. However, it will not sway HMRC if the property in question is a 3-bed semi-detached property in suburbia which clearly is of residential stock and a penalty tax charge may well arise.

As I have mentioned before, HMRC have provided a great opportunity with a SSAS, which I refer to as enabling trustees to 'graze in a large lush green meadow'. Why would we then try to head to the boundaries to 'graze in the barren shady ground close to the barbed wire fence' risking serious investigation?!!

3.9 ACQUIRING RESIDENTIAL PROPERTY

"Can my SSAS own residential property?"

This is one of the most common questions I get asked. The simply the answer is **No** - unless you want to incur a very substantial tax charge of 55% + to your fund!

However, of the thousands of SSAS Trustees that I know, and the many more who are interested in exploring SSAS, I do not know anyone who intends a SSAS to be everything they have got – they have other investment interests.

Asking the right question is crucial.

As Tony Robbins said, "Successful people ask better questions, and as a result, they get better answers."

A SSAS is just part of your investment plans. Your bigger 'Why' and vision are the key driver. Having absolute clarity in your game plan is crucial.

If one of your goals is to own more residential property, then maybe your question could be reworded to:

"How can a SSAS enable me to own residential property?"

A few subtle yet fundamental word changes, have now transformed this to an open question designed to provide a host of options - because there are many ways and this book explores numerous methods which you can consider.

Let's get a point of reference here. Regardless of how a property was purchased, or how it is run, the view of HMRC is a property is classed as a residential asset if:

- Any related land that is wholly or partly the garden for the building or structure
- Any related land that is wholly or partly grounds for the residential property and which is used, or intended for use, for a purpose connected with the enjoyment of the building
- Any building or structure on any such related land
- Any building specified in Regulations as residential property

So now that we are clear that SSAS cannot own traditional residential property in any way, we can consider the other alternatives. SSAS can enable the acquisition and holding of residential property in many ways including:

- Loan back to a sponsoring company that has residential property as its purpose – did you know you can have multiple sponsoring companies?
- Third party unconnected loan from a SSAS to your company
- A SSAS invests capital in a company that acquires residential property
- Third party unconnected loan from a SSAS to fund a commercial to residential conversion
- Tax free cash from your SSAS at age 55

So, the question doesn't start with "Can a SSAS....", it starts with "How can a SSAS be part of enabling my strategy...".

3.9.1 Example of a clear plan

If your three-year plan is to have a monthly cashflow from buy to let residential property of say £6,000, and let's say cashflow per property in your area was £400, here are two examples of how this could be achieved:

Example 1

Total properties by end of year three = 15

This could be five per year which is roughly one every two-and-a-half months

Your plan could be based on buy, refurbish and rent enabling significant equity to be created through the refurbishment and development phase.

If each property requires private capital of £75k - £100k, then you may only require 3-4 SSAS investors to deliver on your plan and create shared value returns to the investors at the same time.

Example 2

We could achieve this by delivering two commercial to residential conversions delivering a total of 15 apartments. Allowing a six - nine month period to gain the necessary education and practice to find your first deal and then with a 15-18 month build, refinance and hold, you could have the first tranche of apartments in your property company, cash flowing within two years.

Whilst doing the first development, maintain the commercial agent relationships and build on the traction created and secure a second development one year after finding the first deal.

This would enable you to create your target plan of 15 units in three years.

The funding of these developments could come from commercial development finance from banks and also from SSAS investors on a third-party unconnected loan basis.

At the time of writing, we are in the process of holding circa 50+ units in this financial year from our commercial to residential development business. Your aspirations may be at a different level, but it is possible.

One of our mentees on our *Equa*Mentorship programme has secured 14 units in just under two years whilst another is on the third development in a year which will result in 20+ new houses.

A famous quote by Henry Ford springs to mind, "Whether you think you can, or you think you can't – you're right!"

If you set a target to find <u>three</u> buy-to-let's in the next three years – do you think you could?

If you set a revised target of <u>thirty</u>, do you still think you could?

The answer often lies in the way you think and tackle a challenge. In this case the same level of thinking will not deliver the same results. You have to challenge yourself to think in an entirely different way, possibly even running two strategies.

You can succeed, you will succeed – it is possible! The mindset on setting goals then acting on a clear plan is critical and transformational to many and you may also find that working closely with a mentor will help you expand your knowledge, ambitions and unlock your goals.

If you set your angle of your trajectory too low, you may run the risk of never finding what you are capable of and unable to live the life you deserve. Having a SSAS or working closely with those that do can help you achieve this and buy-to-let residential property is one of the most powerful and widely adopted ways of achieving this.

3.10 TRUSTEE CASE STUDY: TATIANA PREOBRAZHENSKAYA – High Street retail and office conversion

3.10.1 A little bit about myself

I am an investment actuary with vast corporate experience in a financial sector, where I used to develop and implement capital management solution for global insurers and pension funds across the globe. I am a mother of two beautiful children and ever since I had them, I started to look for opportunities to rebalance my life to spend more time with my family. This is where I realised that the best way to do this was to take control of my personal economy and develop a strategy around by personal goals, the same way we do in business.

I started my property business in 2015. My company, Land Matters, pursues residential development opportunities (new builds or conversions), where value can be added through the planning system or a restructuring process. SSAS pension is indispensable to our funding strategy; I use my own SSAS and SSAS of my investors to fund suitable parts of the development, which creates attractive returns for everyone involved.

In this brief case study, I would like to show how SSAS and restructuring could help add value to your development.

3.10.2 Original case brief

The original proposal was to purchase an office block at

Leatherhead High Street arranged over six floors with prior approval for conversion into eleven apartments. Although the planning for eleven apartments was secured, only nine could be converted since one of the floors was still occupied by a commercial tenant.

Deal priced @ 20% profit on costs on that basis and secured shortly after the auction.

3.10.3 Value adding components:

1. Negotiations with the leaseholders

- Commercial tenant occupying the premises agreed to surrender the lease. The discussions can be very painful at times, but in this case was straightforward since they knew that the building would be undergoing renovation and were worried about the ongoing noise and dust. This enabled us to add two more residential units to our development appraisal.

2. Planning uplift

- Optimising the floor plans and sweating every meter helps to further drive value into the project. A small extension at the basement level enabled us to add an additional unit. Creating dormers within the roof space increased the top floor units making them two-bedroom instead of one-bedroom apartments. As a result, the scheme turned into a 12 units scheme with all units, except one, exceeding 35 sqm floor area and double bedroom units exceeding 50 sqm.

3. Restructuring

- The last part of our value enhancing strategy was restructuring the unit, which involves two steps:

  a. Separating the non-value-adding areas from the rest of the development. In our case the Ground Floor unit was occupied by a café. This unit will remain commercial throughout. Since this was a tenanted unit, which was expected to remain unchanged, the cost of funding on this unit should be lower. In addition, 70% loan to value could be achieved (as opposed to 65% loan to GDV)

  b. Finally, using SSAS to fund part of the development could help achieve the following objectives:

     - Reduce the costs of funding for the SSAS portion of the debt (i.e. arrangement fees could be brought close to zero, interest could be set at a lower level depending on the desirable profit flows)

     - Reduce the level of required equity since SSAS borrowing could fund up to 100% of the unit value, which helps to increase the leverage whilst keeping control over both equity and debt tranches

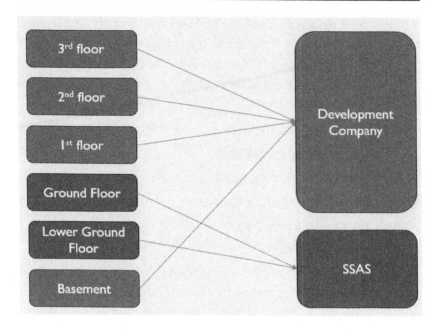

In our case two long term leases had been created:

- Ground Floor (Commercial Unit not subject to conversion) was bought directly into our SSAS. SSAS leveraged 50% of its net asset value for the acquisition at 7% p.a. whilst purchasing the unit at 10% discount to the market value. SSAS has also entered into an option agreement with the developer, giving it the right to sell it back in twelve months' time at full value.

- Lower Ground Floor is being converted into two units. To avoid any tax implications SSAS has advanced a Loan Back equal to 50% of its net asset value, which, in our case, was nearly 100% of the value of the unit. This helped to relax the leverage constraint and further reduce the level of equity required.

- As a result of this strategy, SSAS investments had secured the return of circa. 12% p.a. However, the developer is expected to pay 10% in line with the remaining credit lines - the difference is achieved through third party leverage of the commercial unit.

The developer achieved the following benefits:

✓ Decreased project costs

✓ Reduced the amount of equity required

✓ Relaxed leverage constraints

✓ Kept control over part of the debt

✓ Improved all KPIs

✓ Contributed towards saving the High Street by converting the abandoned office block in Leatherhead conservation area into attractive and desirable homes for young professionals looking to get on the property ladder.

3.11 RESIDENTIAL HELD IN A SSAS

Your pension scheme cannot hold residential property – at least not without incurring tax penalties.

A SSAS, as we know, can work well with commercial property. However, it may be possible to have residential property within a SSAS, in theory, in certain cases, provided certain very specific criteria are met. I want to really stress that this is a highly specialised area.

Possible SSAS compliant residential areas to consider:

- Staff accommodation above a public house
- School caretaker accommodation
- A home, or other institution, providing residential

accommodation for children as a dedicated children's home

- A hall of residence for students. This does not include normal houses or flats let to students
- Nursing and care homes with care worker accommodation
- Supported living with live in carers
- A home or other institution providing residential accommodation with personal care for persons in need of personal care by reason of old age, disability, dependence on alcohol or drugs, mental disorder etc
- Properties with occupation as a condition of employment

The last bullet point, 'Properties with occupation as a condition of employment' is the key here. There would have to be a very robust case and audit trail, including employment contracts, to substantiate the case for holding this asset within a SSAS.

Irrespective of whether one of the aforementioned can be structured within a SSAS, it is forbidden that any member trustee or connected party can occupy any of the residential related assets.

The case of J & A Young (Leicester) Ltd v HMRC 2015 is a very interesting and relatively recent example of case law which clarifies some of the important aspects and lays out clearly the criteria required. You may be able to avoid tax penalties if you can prove that the dwelling is used to house employees as a condition of their employment.

The company in 2006 purchased a residential property into its SSAS, which was used to house foreign employees when they came to work in the UK, under the terms of their employment. HMRC took the company to tribunal arguing that the SSAS had an interest in a residential property that was taxable under FA 2004, s 174A.

The taxpayer argued that the property was not taxable because it was a condition of employment that the employees lived there (para 10(2)(c)). Alternatively, condition B applied because the property was used in connection with the business premises, held as an investment, in the pension fund.

The First-tier Tribunal said that the employment contract did not require employees to live in the property and therefore it could not be described as a condition of employment, Condition A was not satisfied.

The judge agreed with the taxpayer that condition B was satisfied. He said the use of the property as accommodation for the foreign employees working in the yard was a "sufficient connection" for the purposes of para 10(3)(b). It was bought for that reason and used only by such employees. The arrangements were not artificial and there was a direct connection between the property and the yard.

WARNING NOTE: Having a SSAS should be considered a privilege as I have mentioned before. HMRC have presented us with a unique and highly tax efficient opportunity and the penalties for abusing that privilege are substantial. This particular chapter will be highly emotive - and it should be!

I considered whether to include this at length, conscious that some will stray too close to the boundaries. However, in the interests of advancing each of our awareness, knowledge and accountability, I decided to include it. It was the clear legal record of this case that provided the substantiation to include it as it distilled it down to clear evidence. The reality is that it will be an extremely rare case indeed where a SSAS actually proceeds on a compliant basis with this type of investment. There will be undoubted interest, however, I would have thought few SSAS corporate trustees will be willing and able to sign this off.

Whilst J & A Young (Leicester) Ltd were successful in their appeal, it is probably safe to assume that the entire legal process took many years, countless hours of stress, huge application of resources including management time and cash, very substantial legal fees and many years of broken sleep patterns. Ask yourself if you would have the appetite and resources to fight a concerted tax investigation from HMRC?

The following is a more detailed exert from Croner-i of the J & A Young case study and can be found at https://library.croneri.co.uk/cch_uk/btc/2015-tc-04771.

The First-tier Tribunal (FTT) allowed an appeal against an unauthorised payment, scheme chargeable payment and sanction charges imposed by HMRC in relation to a pension fund, finding that a property was not a 'taxable property' for the purposes of Finance Act 2004 ('FA 2004'), Sch. 29A.

Summary

J & A Young (Leicester) Ltd ('the Company') was the administrator of the J & A Young (Leicester) Ltd Retirement Fund ('the Fund'), a small self-administered occupational pension fund for the benefit of certain employees of the company (members of the Young family). The Fund owned the yard from which the company carried on its plastics packaging operations, but not the factory in which the plastic was processed. The employees involved in packaging worked outdoors in the yard in all weather conditions but because of the difficulty in finding employees willing to tolerate these conditions, the Company had begun to use employees from Eastern Europe, who worked exclusively in the Yard. Owing to difficulties in finding suitable accommodation for them, resulting in lost working time, the Fund purchased a residential property ('the Property') to house them. Their contracts of employment provided that accommodation would be provided (subject to a weekly charge) as a term of their employment and must be immediately vacated if the employment ceased. Occasionally an employee subsequently found alternative accommodation and the employment contract was then amended by letter.

The company and members of the Fund appealed against the unauthorised payment, scheme chargeable payment and sanction charges imposed by HMRC under FA 2004, s. 174A, s. 185A and

s. 239 on the grounds that the property was not a 'taxable property' for the purposes of Sch. 29A, either because it was occupied by an employee, as a condition of his employment (Condition A of Sch. 29A, para. 10), or because it was used in connection with business premises held as an investment of the scheme (Condition B of that paragraph). The FTT considered that Condition A was not satisfied because the occupation of the property by the employees was a term, not a condition of employment (although they rejected HMRC s argument that the term 'condition of employment' should apply only to circumstances where occupation of a particular property was an essential requirement of the job). However, they found that Condition B was satisfied because the phrase 'in connection with' was sufficiently wide to cover the use of the Property to provide accommodation for employees working in the yard.

Comment

In reaching their decision, the Tribunal considered both the statutory purpose referred to in the Technical Note on the proposed legislation that enacted Sch. 29A (being to prevent pension funds from investing in holiday or second homes and other prohibited assets for the personal use of members of the fund or their families), and the more restrictive wording of the previous legislation from which Condition B was derived ('in connection with the occupation by that person of business premises held as an investment by the scheme') and found that both supported their wider interpretation of the existing Condition B.

3.12 B&B'S, GUEST HOUSES AND HOTELS

Bed and breakfast establishments, guest houses and hotels can be treated by HMRC as commercial property. They all share a common aspect, generally that they also provide commercial food preparation and service which tends to make them distinct from serviced accommodation, although this is not the only test to differentiate.

Due diligence is required to check if the investment meets the qualifying definition of a hotel. If the property is offering nightly accommodation and meals to residents, it would likely be a hotel.

If the property was doing this for three beds for instance, it may not pass the tests for being commercial. However, most establishments will be 8-10 beds and above.

The test of food preparation and service is not an isolated area of scrutiny and must be undertaken in conjunction with other questions to avoid non-compliance. For example, a restaurant may have a residential apartment above it, and being treated by HMRC as residential property would result in a penalty tax charge.

Provided the ownership criteria is satisfied, bed and breakfasts, guest houses and hotels can be a perfectly viable and tax efficient SSAS investment.

The SSAS could hold 100% ownership of the hotel or it could be a part owner with the sponsoring employer of the SSAS as an example.

However, if the hotel or hostel comes with rights for you to use the property – for example, through a timeshare – it may lose the exemption rights to hold within your SSAS, without incurring a penalty tax charge.

3.13 SSAS CASE STUDY: LOUISE RIGHTON: Enabling success in peer-to-peer property development loans

Louise is a Property Investor, SSAS Trustee, Author of *SSAS Superstars! How Ten Entrepreneurs Unlocked Their Pensions – Without Waiting to Retire.*

From the time of establishing my SSAS, my first investments were into secured third-party property development loans. Why did I choose this route first? Well, quite simply, peer-to-peer lending tends to provide investors with higher returns than traditional investing via financial institutions or the stock market, secured often with a first charge on the property being developed. This drives growth in my SSAS in a more dependable way than investing in the stock market, or relying on deposit interest, in my experience.

I have made a range of secured third-party property development loans, always as one of a pool of lenders, often called multi-lender loans or crowdfunding. Although I have loaned to a range of platforms and developers, the approach I took could be described as one of two strategies:

-   Loans direct to developers that I have developed a trusted relationship with, and
-   Loans to developers via per-to-peer (P2P) platforms, also known as crowdfunding

There is a third route, of making loans via agents, which to date I have not leveraged, but I may do in the future.

Loans direct to developers have worked well for me, and I have focused on getting to know, and trust, a small pool of seasoned property developers, investing in a couple of projects at a time with each, so as not to over-expose my SSAS to one developer. The importance of due diligence on the developer, the principals and the project cannot be underestimated when one is going direct to the developer with a loan. I have enjoyed spending time getting to know these developers, delving into their plans and attending site visits and investor days to receive updates on progress. These investor days provide an opportunity to network with other investors as well as the developers, and to share experiences and learn from each other.

I particularly like P2P platforms, also known as crowdfunding platforms. This space is very innovative, with several leaders emerging in this space over the past few years, offering high quality projects with great returns and first charge security for lenders. I particularly appreciate the fact that the platforms are run by experts in their field – they are not so much financial institutions as experienced developers who have expanded into lending platforms to fund their projects. This means the projects have already gone through a rigorous due diligence stage before they even reach the platform.

The high returns are possible, not because the loans are risky, but because the crowdfunding business model is completely different to the high street bank lending model. The leading platforms today have built infrastructures to lend efficiently and effectively. They utilise technology to offer efficiency to the investor, who can log on to watch a project launch, pledge an investment and receive regular project updates on their loans, all through the technology platform. The leading platforms are underpinned by property development experience, meaning only robust projects make it to the platforms for investors to invest in, with riskier projects filtered out by the experience and diligence of the platform analysts and decision-makers.

The leading platforms have given me the confidence to invest quickly with developers I didn't know personally, although I have later got to know some of them and invested with them for a second or third time. I only invest in the platforms that offer first charge security to investors. Why is this so important to me? It's because, by the very nature of investing via a crowdfunding platform where projects are launched which can fully fund in days, hours or even in some cases in minutes, I have less time to do my own due diligence on the project and the developer. The first charge security with a few other checks and balances gives me the confidence I need to invest decisively.

My very first secured property development loan was a particular success story which gave me the confidence to continue with my investing strategy. I made a loan to an experienced development team, via one of the leading crowdfunding platforms, with whom

I now have an established relationship with, as an investor and ambassador. The developers were raising £1.1 million for the purchase and development of an attractive and historic four storey office block into fourteen self-contained apartments in a well-established and upmarket English seaside town. The exit was sale of the apartments into the developers' SA business to be used as holiday lets, but there was an alternative exit of sale as holiday apartments on the open market.

The LTV was only 57% of the GDV which met my investing criteria – meaning, if the project failed to meet its financial targets, there was sufficient headroom to return capital to the lenders. I typically look for less than 70% LTV, meaning the borrowers have sufficient 'skin in the game' to make the project a success; in fact, the majority of P2P platforms will not fund-raise for projects with riskier LTV profiles than this. The borrowers had also ensured that should a sale not be completed in time, then a refinance would be utilised to ensure investors' capital and interest could be repaid as per the terms. At the time of the raise, the borrowers had already approached refinance lenders and held advanced talks to ensure this was viable.

Despite the limitations of Covid-19, the development was completed ahead of plan, and actually paid back in 12 months rather than the forecasted 18 months – a terrific result! With a 12% return on my investment, always backed by first-charge security, this project represented a great example of a low-risk way to drive high growth in my SSAS. My conclusion - if I can grow my entire SSAS fund at this rate, I will more than beat the residual performance of my previous pensions, one rising in line with inflation, the other subject to stock market volatility; both outside of my control and with no engagement, enjoyment or self-development, all of which are offered by investing in secured third party property development loans.

I currently have around half of my SSAS invested in third party property development loans. I have spread my investments across platforms, developers and geographic areas as well as project types, encompassing commercial to residential conversions, commercial to SA conversions and simple residential refurbs and flips.

The returns I've achieved so far have been impressive, typically 8% at the low end to 14% at the top end of fixed returns, then as part of equity deals, heading for the 20% plus return figure. I find that P2P works so well because it represents the most efficient matching of supply and demand in the lending market with its niche audience of investors – although investor numbers are growing rapidly as the word gets out about the solid returns with well secured risk.

When selecting a P2P platform to invest with, check that it is authorised and regulated by the FCA, that it is an HMRC approved ISA/IFISA manager, and that it understands and can accommodate SSAS and SIPP Pension investments. Finally, remember the importance of first charge security, not every project or platform offers this. The first charge gives you the top priority in case of the developer's default – nothing can protect your money better.

3.14 HOLIDAY ACCOMMODATION

Holiday accommodation can come in various forms. For serviced accommodation, bed and breakfast and hotels refer to the specific chapters on these areas.

Other forms of holiday accommodation may include:

- Campsites
- Caravan parks
- Residential outward-bound centres

- Glamping sites
- Activity centres

Each of these is a very specialist area and would require thorough examination to establish compliance.

3.15 STUDENT ACCOMMODATION

HMRC are yet again our default point of reference as to what is deemed acceptable as student halls of residence for the further of SSAS investment. Large HMO's are not acceptable to be held in a SSAS, even if they are for the purposes of student accommodation.

HMRC are clear that in order for a student hall of residence to be an acceptable asset class, it must be connected to, and dedicated to, serving the educational establishment that it is engaged with. These tend to be on-campus halls of residence for a specific college or university.

Furthermore, the accommodation must generally be based on a communal living model with separate kitchen facilities and lounge/living areas with each bedroom NOT being self-contained living. As such, whilst en-suite rooms are acceptable, studios and any rooms with integrated cooking facilities would not be acceptable as this would fall into a residential category for personal enjoyment.

If I think back to my first student accommodation back in Sheffield in 1988, the 'halls of residence' were specifically for that educational establishment, had separate toilets, bathrooms and kitchens independent from the bedrooms and had communal lounge and eating areas. There would be no way that accommodation could be sold off by specific 'apartment'.

In summary, for a property to be a 'student halls of residence' thus avoiding a penalty tax charge from HMRC, it would need to meet the following:

- The students living within the halls of residence must be being educated from the educational establishment
- The individual rooms within the property cannot be acquired or disposed of separately
- The educational establishment engaged must be involved in the placing of their students in the accommodation for the purposes of attending their courses
- There must be an educational establishment connected by association to the halls, identifying the accommodation as a hall of residence related to them
- The layout cannot be configured or adapted to residential self-contained apartments
- There must be communal kitchen and living areas for the use of all of the students

Whilst this model is technically possible for a SSAS to own, the reality would almost certainly be that SSAS trustees may invest in a business that has this asset class as their business model.

3.16 RENT TO RENT MODELS

In recent years property investment circles have seen a rise in rent-to-rent models where an intermediary rents a property and then sublets that property to others. This has been used in the buy to let, Serviced Accommodation and HMO markets predominantly, all of which are unable to be held directly within a SSAS (note the chapter on Serviced Accommodation).

It is certainly possible to have the ability to sublet commercial property as long as the necessary documentation and clauses are in order. The challenge with rent to rent and a SSAS is that mostly it is not a property investment strategy but more using leases to provide a trading platform of a business. It may be possible to include option agreements (see chapter Lease & Purchase options) in rent-to-rent agreements as a way of securing the asset, during or after a lease term.

Many will be attracted to the Loan Back option enabling their SSAS to loan to the sponsoring company, possibly to then fund this type of business, however it is important to note several points:

- Your SSAS Corporate trustee will want to understand the purpose of the Loan Back and each may have a slightly different view on compliance and their willingness to sign it off
- A Loan Back will require a first charge on an asset (usually on property, however not necessarily)

It may be possible for the SSAS to own the commercial property and lease the property to an intermediary, who will then let the property to others. Certain property assets may lend themselves to this scenario.

3.17 OFFICES AND CO-WORKING

Offices are a use class that are permissible by HMRC and can be acquired and held in your SSAS. They are often use class B1a which makes them also part of permitted development rights, in many areas, which is a potential area of increase in added value.

It is the extensive use of permitted development that has, in some part, played a role in removing a large swathe of office stock from many areas thus increasing scarcity and driving prices higher. Certain areas have seen office space acquisition costs higher than developers would pay for conversions levels.

The potential exists for acquiring office space and holding with a lengthy lease for income whilst also building a longer-term value adding an array of options such as additional floors, extensions, change of use and conversion restructuring leases. One might also repurpose the office space for the increasingly popular co-working space phenomena.

As part of delivering almost 4m square feet of infrastructure over the last 30 years with 25% of it being office space, I have seen many trends on how office space has been designed and used.

- Early 1990's: cellular office for individuals with managerial status a core factor
- Mid - late 1990's: open plan office space increasing collaboration all with assigned desks
- Late 1990's and early 2000's: hot desking becomes more popular with food and drink stations integrated and work benches
- Late 2000's – early 2010's: real focus on collaboration areas and huge decline in any individual office. Group meeting rooms with collaboration software, interactive whiteboards and video conferencing
- Mid 2010's – early 2020's: the rise of flexible working. No longer do organisations prize the expensive real estate in cities which incurs lengthy and expensive commutes for employees. Greater focus on productivity, home working and co-working

- Early 2020's onwards: with Covid 19 the world has changed at an unparallel level with working patterns arguably changed forever. Organisations have been forced to operate differently with lockdowns and isolations and are having to adapt to constantly volatile changes and ensuring that business continuity remains constant. Home working has increased dramatically, however businesses recognise the need to bring teams together and provide flexible accommodation at convenient locations and this is seeing the continuing rise of co-working offices

Co-working is the provision of high-quality flexible working accommodation where individuals and small, medium or large businesses can rent office desks, rooms or entire floors on a range of tariffs ranging from daily, weekly, monthly or annually.

These co-working offices focus on community working where different organisations co-mingle across a common office area with food, beverage, printing facilities, high speed broadband and all modern office requirements. The tenant clients pay rental costs with none of the capital expenditure, like a normal office, and can spread their locations much wider to attract, enable and inspire and retain their very best members of their team in local areas to where they live.

SSAS investors are becoming increasingly aware of this commercial asset class to either acquire and lease to co-working organisations or to invest in these organisations as a business investment.

3.18 AIRSPACE

In the UK, if you own the freehold of a property, you not only own the ground that the building sits on, you are also the owner of a certain amount of airspace directly above the property.

Does this mean you own a column of space vertically of infinite height? Well, no, not in England as this would impede or complicate air travel etc. Generally speaking, airspace can be divided into two layers:

- lower stratum – This would include the area immediately around your property which you have the right to take enjoyment from and where the activities of others would infringe upon that enjoyment and right
- higher stratum – This is the height at which others may use the air space and deemed to not affect infringe on your rights. According to Section 76 of the Civil Aviation Act 1982, the upper stratum is approximately 500 to 1000 feet directly above the property

Airspace rights are part of the asset value of a building. These may vary from zero to millions, depending on the purpose one is looking at. Think telecoms masts, roof top patio through to complete additional floors on buildings. Recent liberalisation on planning permissions rules have brought this decades old potential to the attention of the masses now and is creating this additional emerging asset class which can be sold separately.

Restrictions and complication may exist when considering actual roof tops suitable for air space development and these may include:

- Existing leases on roof space
- Existing options on roof space
- Sky and television aerials
- Advertising boards

- Light wells
- Telecommunication antennas, equipment cabins and towers
- Microwave dishes
- Lift shafts
- Utilities risers and housings
- Specialist surface water drainage systems
- Existing usage and rights by current tenants

I was involved in the mass acquisition design and construction of the 2G and 3G wireless mobile base station infrastructure throughout the 1990's and back then there was a high level of interest to acquire roof top rights to place telecommunications equipment. If you consider the technology, we were looking for high points on the landscape which had unrestricted line of sight to the next installation location (for point-to-point microwave transmission) or for local coverage of high areas of mobile usage. We would actively deploy surveyors and search agents to acquire large volumes of roof space suitable for these installations.

Our approach at the time was to target not only individual building owners, but to also identify multiple landlords and negotiate nationwide rooftop rights. Organisations such as BT were prime targets as they owned large volumes of real estate, ideally suited in areas of high population.

The volume of suitable buildings in the UK that are potentially available to be used for air space development is estimated in the hundreds of thousands and with the new permitted development rights enabling development permissions to be gained much more readily, there is a very healthy increase in interest in this strategy.

Freehold ownership is a specialist area of property asset historically seen as low risk, long term with a low yield reflecting its security. Economic returns would typically come in the form of ground rents, service charges and also the future potential for enhancements. These might include:

- Extensive refurbishment
- Extending the building outwards
- Creating basement space
- Extending into air space

Freeholders will be actively reviewing their portfolios with new permitted rights emerging, knowing that they have a reservoir of potential for redevelopment awaiting in many of their assets.

From a practical perspective there will be a number of considerations which will affect time, cost and viability on potential, including:

- Structural capacity of the building to take the additional load
- Access to the roof
- Right to light of those in the surrounding area
- Building control requirements - access, egress, fire evacuation etc
- Existing construction of the existing upper levels – may be a flimsy roof with residential directly underneath
- Ability to strength building whist under occupation
- Rights and uses of existing roof space
- Constructability – consider cranage, scaffolding, temporary works, noise, vibration and oversailing etc
- Services - availability and design of services to high rise building levels

3.19 HOUSES OF MULTIPLE OCCUPANCY (HMO)

HMO's are deemed as C4 accommodation and many now have mandatory licensing requirements to the local authority. From an HMRC perspective they are considered a residential asset class and hence will almost certainly NOT be able to be held in a SSAS.

HMO's are a very popular property strategy. The question many will be looking for are what are my options for enabling HMO's by using SSAS Pensions?

Here is a summary of some of those main options:

- Use a Loan Back from your SSAS
- A third-party unconnected loan from another SSAS
- Mixed use scheme of commercial and HMO (for example a shop with uppers) where freehold and HMO uppers is held in a limited company with the commercial being sold leasehold to your SSAS (or someone else's for that matter)

A SSAS may use an HMO as a first charge security at land registry for a Loan Back or third-party unconnected loan. However, care must be taken in the structure of the security given the HMO's residential status (refer to the chapter on security trustee later in the book), as a SSAS cannot own the HMO even by default if it had to call on the security charge.

An HMO can be mortgaged on commercial finance terms, however this does NOT have any bearing on making it a commercial asset and SSAS compliant in any way.

3.20 COMMERCIAL TO RESIDENTIAL CONVERSIONS

In every survey or poll that we undertake in EquaAcademy and

SSAS Alliance amongst SSAS trustees, without fail, commercial to residential conversions comes top of the list of the most aspired too, and popular strategies.

If your strategy is to find commercial property to then acquire and convert to residential units, then your SSAS can become a true gamechanger with a multitude of ways that it can assist.

- It can add value through:
  - Buying at the right price
  - Enhancing value through change of use
  - Powerful use of low-cost commercial finance leverage
  - Delivering the conversion process to create the new apartments and homes
  - Sell the units to homeowners or retain for long term cashflow
  - Retain commercial units as part of a mixed-use scheme, either within or outside of the SSAS

I have been involved in commercial to residential strategies extensively involving SSAS on numerous occasions over the last 5 years including:

- Our development business, EquaGroup, developing large 10,000 – 30,000sq ft commercial properties into 20-60 apartments. We frequently work with SSAS trustees and high network sophisticated investors to fund these developments
- We hold Buy-to-Let apartments resulting from our commercial conversion developments, within limited companies

- We use this strategy for our own SSAS where we create a powerful double compound curve of acquiring commercial property in the SSAS and converting the uppers to residential, and holding them outside of the SSAS
- We mentor SSAS trustees and property developers involved in all aspects of commercial conversions, raising funds as well as other strategies in this book
- Loan Backs to enable funding for a development

The blend of adding value and funding options provide a highly attractive spread of opportunities and benefits for you to create value in the SSAS as well as outside of it. True enablement!

In this book we will not have the time to focus on the specifics of the process of converting commercial property, but fortunately you can start to master this subject by immersing yourself in my dedicated book on the subject – *'Commercial to Residential Conversions: The essential manual for property developers'* available on Amazon.

The crucial part of converting commercial to residential when engaging with SSAS is the 'residential' bit and for this we must be acutely aware of the rules and parameters that we must operate within.

Structuring is essential to ensure that you can safely deploy your conversion project and maintain compliance at every stage. The structuring of your development must be thoroughly considered at the start of the process to ensure you have encompassed the best advice, counsel and wisdom in all areas including tax, funding, SSAS compliance, investor security, timing, refinance and exit etc.

As you are ultimately creating residential units, these must never reside in the SSAS, not even by default. So, let us take a look at the timing of when a commercial property becomes a residential property and what aspects need to be in place. The following is a list that covers many parties' views on what completion looks like and we must have exited these units from the scheme well before all of these are in place to avoid an HMRC investigation.

So residential would be at the point of a Certificate of Habitation. The trouble is no such certificate exists! It is the combination of many aspects draw together, all held within an audit file. So, the asset would become residential when, for instance:

- Bathroom and kitchens installed – the property must be mortgageable
- Planning permission is received, and all planning conditions are satisfied
- Utility connections made – electricity, gas, water, communications
- Gas Safe and Electrical test certificates provided
- Building control sign off
- Structural warranty certificates
- Final handover pack of all test and product literatures and manuals
- Legal signing, approval and payment of any Community Infrastructure Levy, S106 agreements, Affordable Homes levy, SANG and any other related requirements to the development
- Any other specific aspects relating

It is important that your commercial property held in your SSAS does not end up inadvertently holding residential property. If the sales of your units were delayed, or refinance or sale process held up your strategy, none of these would be an excuse to HMRC and a penalty tax charge would result which could be 55% or higher!!

Careful planning and consideration will help you to de-risk this from ever happening.

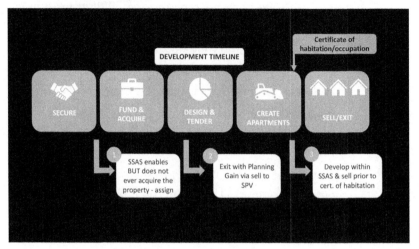

This image shows three stages during a typical conversion development where your SSAS could be involved in a safe manner whilst enabling the huge added value that can reside in these developments.

1. The SSAS enables but never owns: as we have mentioned numerous times in this book, a SSAS can enable just as powerfully as it can own. Your SSAS could establish a lease option, or a condition contract that is assignable, and secure the planning permissions required. It could then utilise the assignability clause and a limited company could purchase the development and proceed

2. Exit with a planning gain: the SSAS acquires the property and once planning is approved, sells the property to a third party (could be your development company for a planning gain) who

would develop it, typically in a traditional limited company

3. The SSAS acquires the property, gains planning and then develops the conversion to residential – however, then sells the units BEFORE they become residential units (as defined by the list above). The challenge in this scenario, whilst technically possible, are namely:

   a. You would be selling a partially completed asset. Have you ever tried refinancing or gain commercial finance on a building site?!!! Not easy! This method would best be served by buying in cash if you have the facility to do this

   b. The risk of gaining funding to sell out of the SSAS in a timely manner. Any delays in the timing of the sale may mean you have to halt or delay construction, which could incur extension of time delay costs and damages from your builder

   c. There is a risk transfer of incomplete assets which are untested and uncertified which are likely to be of concern to your new funder

   d. And finally, you can never put a price on 'putting your head on the pillow and sleeping easy'. Think, is it really necessary to run the risk of not having a timely exit and the worry of bringing funding at the right time to enable the exit? Most of us did not get a SSAS to bring stress and pressure unnecessarily

3.21 TRUSTEE CASE STUDY: JON DALE - Project Cowell Street

JAG Property Investments Ltd is owned by Jon Dale and Gavin Williams and we invest in property full time. We have a buy-to-let portfolio that we are constantly building, and we buy, renovate and sell houses. JAG has developed and sold new build projects and is now doing a commercial conversion.

We are both SSAS trustees and have been involved in IFA businesses since 2010. A lot of trustees use their SSAS to build their pension pot and invest into theirs and other investment projects, allowing them control over their pension. We've been attempting to utilise the advantages of building assets, inside and outside the SSAS, as we have residual income from our buy-to-lets, new builds and other projects, and so we were looking at ways to keep our hard-earned money within our wealth bubble and to avoid giving it away via taxes and fees. The benefit for us, both personally and within the business, is that we can pay profit into the SSAS and it becomes tax free as we can off-set it against corporation tax. Once the money is in the SSAS, we can then access it in various ways to continue building wealth, both inside and outside the SSAS.

We believe this real-life case study (that did not take millions of pounds to get over the line) is a great example of how one can utilise the advantages of a SSAS. We used the SSAS to help make more money, with the exit of this project, and create residual income both within the SSAS and our business, JAG Property Investments Ltd.

3.21.1 The Property:

This is a commercial unit with four stories based in the centre of Llanelli, South Wales. The commercial unit was an old sunbed shop and above was an unused storage area. It looked as though it was previous living accommodation as it has multiple old fireplaces and ceiling roses throughout.

3.21.2 Start with the Exit in Mind:

After viewing this property, it was very obvious from the start that

the best plan for us, as a business, was to keep the commercial unit as retail and convert the upper floors to flats. With that in mind, we contacted our professional team. We first spoke with our architect to see what we could do with the upper floors: four flats agreed. We then spoke with our structural engineer to confirm what we needed to do with the floors and strengthening, etc. We then used our QS to give estimates on pricing. Once we knew our build costs, we could make our offer whilst working out the best way to pay for it.

We considered cash, mortgage/bridge finance, investors and using our SSAS. After working out all the cost and savings, we initially were looking at investors and using our SSAS, but after working through all the figures we came up with our decision.

3.21.3 The Plan:

1. Purchase for cash giving us lower costs and greater bargaining power as we are ready to complete ASAP

2. Keep the retail unit and split the title on the upper floors

3. Get planning permission for the flats

4. Use development finance for the conversion of the four flats

5. Move a tenant into the retail unit on a good, long, solid internal repairing lease – adding value

6. Re-mortgage the flats and rent them out, adding four more units to our portfolio

7. Finally, interspecies transfer of the commercial unit split 50/50 ownership between our two SASS's at full market value

3.21.4 Benefits:

The commercial unit would be worth a lot more than what we paid for it and the flats, after all the building costs, would leave very little money left in the deal once re-mortgaged. Thus, we would be able to add a retail unit to the SSAS, creating an unencumbered asset that produces recurring income from the rent. Thereby allowing JAG Property Investments Ltd to pay less tax as it has made a pension contribution.

3.21.5 The Outcome:

Since buying the property, the rules have slightly changed regarding interspecies property transfers. They are not allowed, but it hasn't affected us too much as we can buy the property from the money within the SSAS. Then we can make a pension contribution from JAG Property Investments Ltd into our SASS. As a business, we can then offset the contribution against corporation tax – the same result, just a different execution.

We have gained planning for the flats and are currently out to tender for the conversion. Since buying the property, we have also invested in an estate and letting agent's business which has worked out well as they are now going to occupy the retail space as it is right on the main thoroughfare next to other agents. We have also had very positive talks with the local council who will look to take all four flats from us on a long, fully repairing lease once finished. This will mean that we will be fairly hands-off and can therefore concentrate on more projects, while the cash rolls into both our business and our SSAS.

3.21.6 The Figures:

The property was on the market for £75,000–£80,000 guide price. It had just had a sale fall through. After negotiation, planning cost, legal cost and other professional fees, the total cost of buying and getting the plans and tender in place ready to start will be £40,000. The cost to convert the upper floors into four flats is going to be around £200,000. The finance cost £22,000 based on high street borrowing, including legal, set up and exit fees plus interest payments. The total cost of the whole development with be £262,000. Each flat will have a minimum end value of £65,000 and the commercial unit £80,000, giving a total GDV of £340,000. Once we re-mortgage the four flats at 75% LTV, we will have £195,000 back upon completion. We will sell the commercial unit based on a full valuation to the SSAS at £80,000, giving JAG a £40,000 profit based on purchase price. We will then pay £40,000 (split 50/50) into our SSASs. This will save JAG £8,000 in corporation tax. Our SSAS will then have a commercial unit in the SASS, making £7200.00 per month. We have £40,000 extra in our SSAS tax free. Outside off the SSAS, once re-mortgaged, we will have a block of four flats at £27,000 in total, after all costs, and a cash flow, after costs, of around £16,800 per year.

3.21.7 Returns:

We like to work out what the return is on any money left in a deal. Realistically, once the above has happened the end position means we have used £40,000 from the amount within our SSAS, therefore we will be getting the equivalent of 18% return on the money left in. The flats will result in JAG Property Investments Ltd leaving £27,000 in the deal after re-mortgaging the flats, which is a massive 62.2% return on money left in. This is why we greatly benefit from using our SSAS - great returns, great flexibility and full control.

3.22 INDUSTRIAL PROPERTY & CONVERSIONS

Industrial property is commercial and can therefore be held in a SSAS in a compliant manner. There are a variety of ways in which industrial property could be attractive to SSAS and those wishing to collaborate with a SSAS.

With the rapidly changing world of ecommerce and the decline in the retail high streets, there is a huge demand for logistics-based distribution and warehouse properties, typically with great access to motorway and rail networks.

With the ever-increasing rise on consumerism, coupled with city living, out of home storage facilities have grown exponentially over recent years. These are usually industrial buildings which have been fitted out with lockable and 24hour accessible flexible storage from anywhere from 1m2 rising steadily to large rooms. These facilities are low on overheads, often manned with a skeleton staff and providing additional services if required.

Both these examples illustrate the changing nature of business and how location and purpose is important to serve local, national and global markets.

With many choosing land to residential schemes, there is a powerful strategy emerging for taking an alternative approach of gaining planning for land to industrial use classes. This could provide an easier and beneficial strategy where residential may have failed in the past.

Examples include:

- Acquiring land and getting planning for industrial purposes
- Constructing steel portal frame buildings, particularly popular with small engineering and logistics businesses
- Acquire and ownership of existing light industrial buildings
- Heavy industrial buildings are possible; however, given their size and historical uses may be too large for a SSAS to acquire and could have significant contamination and

clean-up costs from an environmental perspective

- Conversion of industrial use classes to residential property
- Acquire a business with property assets within
- Types of industrial could include:
  - Petrol stations
  - Engineering facilities
  - Manufacturing and processing plants
  - Scrap yards
  - Mills
  - Off-site storage
  - Warehouses
  - Land that has previously had any one of the aforementioned uses on it

With historical permitted development rights, approval for light industrial consent to residential, industrial buildings became a very prominent discussion point circa 2017/2018 and whilst some traction was gained, it never really made mainstream practice for developers.

The practical reality of industrial buildings often, means that location can be a challenge as often they are not in residential areas and have heavy vehicular movements of HGV (heavy goods vehicles), require substantial remediation of windows and doors usually requiring planning, and can suffer from poor light into the building and contamination issues.

However, those properties that can be identified by those with the knowledge to assess, can become a very low entry cost for fruitful developments, if planning can be achieved.

3.23 TRUSTEE CASE STUDY: SAM COOPER – Family collaboration

After working in the family business for over 10 years and hitting a turnover of £1.8m, we had come to the realisation that the current business model was broken, and things needed to change. In early 2013 we made the difficult decision to put the business into voluntary liquidation, which was not an easy decision to make. I had started working with Dad in the family business after being a mature student at University and Mum and Dad had the opportunity to purchase a business that Dad had been the MD of as the current owner was looking to exit and retire. They said they would buy the business if I would come on board after my degree course had finished and manage the business, and essentially be their succession plan. They had no cash with which to do this, but this was back in the days when the banks' lending criteria was:

- Does the borrower have a pulse?
- Yes!
- Here's a pile of cash! Oh, and please sign this personal guarantee that means we can take all of your personal assets if you default (there's a whole other story in there!)

Things were going swimmingly up until 2008 when the wheels fell off everything. To cut a long story short, we struggled on to 2012 trying different initiatives and ideas but it was no good - something drastic had to change.

Dad and I studied the parts of the business that had failed, and what was still viable, and set out on a new venture on a 50/50 ownership basis concentrating on the design, marketing and fitting of light commercial vehicle accessories, with one proviso imparted by me - as soon as the business was in a saleable condition, we would market it for sale and move on to other things.

We both successfully exited the business in 2017. Dad has since retired, and I am now concentrating on the property business.

So, what has this all got to do with SSAS I hear you ask?

Well, when we set up the business in 2013, we rented a 2700sq.ft warehouse unit from a local landlord. The unit was brand new and had stood empty for a few years, so we were the first occupants. Whilst negotiating the terms of the lease, and because of some recent property training I had done, we included a 3 year 'option' agreement to purchase the property at an agreed price. After 12 months or so of trading, with the business starting to stabilise, we started to think about how we could exercise the option and purchase the property. After doing a bit of research and some conversations with financial advisors I came across something called a SSAS Pension.

Personally I had not got a pension but I knew Dad had worked for a number of large companies and had built up a pension pot over the years so we had a conversation around this 'thing' called a SSAS and how we may be able to use it to purchase the warehouse. Dad started to make some enquiries and spoke to a local trusted independent financial advisor (IFA) - who also happened to be a bloke from our local pub - I think you can take a guess at how this worked out!

The IFA was not particularly au fait with SSAS's either (believe it or not!) so he did some research and found a company that could act as our provider. After seven months the Family SSAS was set up with Dad and I as trustees, along with the provider, and we went about the process of purchasing the property, which took around a further 10 months to complete.

So why bother going to all this trouble as from the business's perspective nothing changed - after all, the rent had still got to be paid out each month. Well, the key benefit to this is where the rent goes and what tax is saved in the process. We had created a 'circular economy' where the profit being made by the business was directly funding Dad's SSAS, so the money was being retained within the family and not being paid to a third-party landlord. The rent has to be paid anyway so it is a 'no-brainer' to effectively pay it to yourself!

As mentioned, this is also highly tax efficient. When the company makes a profit, it has to pay corporation tax - rent payments for the premises the business is operating from can be offset against the profit so reduces the companies tax liability. Also 100% of the rent is paid directly into the SSAS, increasing Dad's NET wealth. In order for Dad to extract the same amount of money from the business, in a more conventional way in the form of a salary, the company would be subject to Employers National Insurance contributions and the salary paid to Dad would also be subject to National Insurance contributions and Income Tax (either @ 20% or 40% depending on other income). The other method of extracting cash from the business is via a dividend. In order to pay a dividend, the company must have made a profit and will have paid corporation tax and the dividend would be currently subject to tax @ 7.5% for basic rate taxpayers and 32.5% for higher rate taxpayers.

Either way, a significant amount of tax is being paid out.

So, back to the bloke in the pub AKA the financial advisor. We had successfully got the SSAS set up, purchased the commercial property and the rent was now being paid directly from the business into the SSAS which was now increasing in value by around £1100 per month - fantastic!

However, the SSAS was getting hit by some pretty hefty charges along the way. The financial advisor, who was doing very little advising, was now taking a 1% cut per annum of the total value of the SSAS, in addition to their major share of the set-up fees. Our SSAS provider seemed to be generating random invoices and just helping themselves to the cash, without consulting either Dad or I as they were in control of the account.

After trying in vain to get answers to why these invoices were being created, we decided it was time to sack the financial advisor and move the SSAS to a more suitable provider.

After conducting some further research and paying further charges, Dad made the decision to move the SSAS to another professional organisation and we have found them to be very good so far, with fixed transparent costs.

Although we have now sold the business, the SSAS is still holding the commercial property and the new tenants are continuing to pay the rent into the SSAS and now that Dad has retired, it has essentially provided him with a perpetual income stream for as long as the property is rented. On the capital value side, we have recently received offers to purchase the property for 38% more than the SSAS paid for it in 2014.

Needless to say, we are happy with how it has turned out.

3.24 REAL ESTATE INVESTMENT TRUST (REIT)

A real estate investment trust, or a REIT, is a company that buys income-producing real estate assets. They enable individual investors, and other companies, to pool their money together in order to buy properties and profit from any increases in value.

A SSAS can invest directly in a REIT.

A REIT (Real Estate Investment Trust) is a single company REIT or a group REIT that owns and manages property on behalf of shareholders. Since the REIT regime was introduced in January 2007, it has provided a well-established method to structure, collective investment in UK real estate and the ability for investors to efficiently access rental income streams from wide ranging, underlying real estate assets. Key features of REITs include an exemption of corporation tax on rental profits and gains from their UK property rental business. As a result, REITs must distribute 90% of their net property rental income to investors.

A company with REIT status isn't subject to corporation tax. In return,

HMRC demands that REITs distribute at least 90% of their property income to shareholders every year as Property Income Distribution (PID) dividends. The REIT must withhold basic rate income tax of 20% on these payments.

There are over 50 REITs with a market capitalisation of over $70bn listed on London Stock Exchange investing across industrial, office, residential, retail, speciality, hotel and lodging real estate.

3.24.1 REIT Sub sector distribution

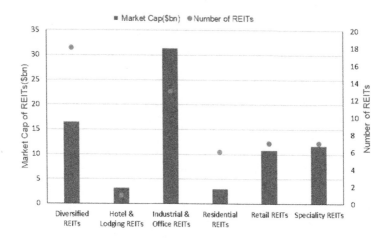

Source: London Stock Exchange, FTSE ICB Sub Sector Data

REIT's are an organisational structure that attracts tranches and pools of investment capital and invests it in:

- Property investment holdings
- Property developments

REIT's are often a highly tax efficient structure, depending on the in-country rules and stimulus available. They operate nationally and globally and are most commonly found in the US. Their approach is usually a high-level reinvestment strategy and usually up to 90% of returns go back to its investors annually, therefore benefiting from tax relief in the REIT and therefore potentially higher returns for investors.

From a fund raise or multiple raises, a REIT will invest often in a broad diversified range of property investments across differing sectors and locations. Due to the scale they can operate, they have access to a large choice of investable asset classes not usually available to retail or SSAS investors.

Investment in a REIT would usually be via a purchase of shares.

A Real Estate Investment Trust (REIT) is exempt from UK tax on the income and gains of its property rental business. Corporation Tax is payable on its profits and gains from any other activities.

As a REIT:

- you'll pay at least 90% of your property rental business income to shareholders each year
- your investors will be taxed on this income as if they've received income from property directly

You're a 'property rental business' when you make money from land for rent. It does not include money made from the occupation of land. This is chargeable as property business income - for example, farming or running a hotel are chargeable as trades so are not classed as a property rental business'.

UK Government confirms that a company, or principal company, of a group can apply to be a REIT if it:

- has an existing property rental business of at least 3 properties, where no one property represents more than

40% of the total value of properties involved

- is UK resident for tax purposes
- is not an open ended investment company

The requirements to qualify for REIT status include setup requirements such the balance of assets test:

1. At least 75% of the UK REITs gross assets must be used in the rental business and at least 75% of the UK REITs profits must be earned in its qualifying rental business

2. Members of a UK REIT may have other activities. Such activities must not involve more than 25% of the UK REITs gross assets, nor generate profits of more than 25%.

3. Only rental profits and gains realised on the disposal of properties used in the UK property rental business will be exempt from tax

4. There must be at least three properties with no one property accounting for more than 40% of the value of the REIT assets

5. Property development by the UK REIT for investment on its own account is permitted and is generally included within the property rental business, unless development costs exceed 30% of the acquisition cost and the property is sold within three years of completion

6. Property trading is permitted, but is taxable, and falls outside of the property rental business for the purpose of the balance of business restrictions

7. There are no restrictions on foreign assets and it may invest outside the UK in real estate wherever located

The main reason why REITs are so attractive is because there is tax relief on rental income and gains from property investment.

REIT's can focus on singular asset classes such as telecommunications, office, retail, shopping malls, energy, industrial, logistics and residential.

Some of the largest organisations we see are REIT's and include:

- Big Yellow Group – the UK's largest self-storage operator
- Digital Realty Trust & Equinix – two of the world's largest carrier neutral data centre providers
- Prologis – global distribution and logistics organisation
- Land Securities Group – often referred to as LandSec; this is one of the largest offices, retail and residential property owners in Europe
- Brookfield Property – owners of student halls, offices, industrial and residential property on a global scale
- Crown Castle International – global owner of fibre networks, radio towers and wireless base station infrastructure
- British Land - one of the UK's biggest property companies and part of the FTSE 100

REIT's often have a very low overhead level and staff requirement as they are often a pure asset management organisation relying on the profession skills of external advisors and supply chain to maintain portfolios and enhance value.

3.25 SUPPORTED LIVING, CARE HOMES AND HOMELESS ACCOMMODATION

What better examples of truly amazing ways to invest AND create shared value in society at the same time than with Supported Living,

Care homes and Homeless Accommodation. This delivers a huge Return of Impact.

Organisations like Cornerstone Place are creating a huge impact in society by bringing together property, commercial structures and capital to enable charities and registered providers with the assets, resources and time to do what they are great at. Providing point-of-need care to those that need it most.

Furthermore, this return of Impact can be, and in my opinion MUST be measurable, as can be seen by the enormous value being created by Cornerstone Place's strategy over the next ten years.

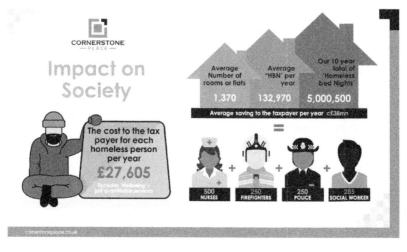

Cornerstone Place's ten year impact goals in the service of society

Categories of specialist support that fall within these asset classes would include:

- Drug and alcohol dependency support
- Sheltered housing
- Homeless hostels

- Assisted living
- Short term accommodation
- Move-on accommodation
- Long term protected living
- Warden supported accommodation
- Elderly supported living
- Social housing
- Care providers
- And other supported living parties

Profile of supported housing by client group and country

Client group	England		Wales		Scotland		Great Britain	
	Units	%	Units	%	Units	%	Units	%
Older people (65+)	395,000	71	30,500	79	36,500	61	462,000	71
People with learning disabilities	38,500	7	3,000	8	6,000	10	47,500	7
Single homeless people (inc rough sleepers)	30,000	5	1,000	3	6,000	10	37,000	6
People with mental health problems	29,500	5	1,000	3	2,500	4	33,000	5
Vulnerable young people (16-25)	19,500	4	1,000	3	1,000	2	21,500	3
People with physical disabilities or sensory impairment	9,000	2	*	*	2,500	4	12,000	2
Homeless families	5,500	1	500	1	2,500	5	8,500	1
People with drug or alcohol misuse needs	4,500	1	500	1	1,000	2	6,000	1
At risk of domestic abuse	4,500	1	500	1	1,000	2	6,000	1
Offenders	4,500	1	*	*	*	*	4,500	1
Others (inc refugees or asylum seekers and others)[43]	13,000	2	*	*	500	*	13,500	2
Total	553,500	100	38,500	100	59,500	100	651,500	100

Source: Local authority survey. Base: 83 commissioners.

There is complexity in this area which can be learned and bring not just property, but a number of important factors together:

1. The need in society
2. Party to provide the care service
3. A fundable structure

4. Suitable property

5. Dependable income stream

6. A contract suite that serves all parties over 5, 10, 15 years or longer

7. Strong leases with strength of covenant of counter parties

8. Funding – institutional and/or private including SSAS

Typically, the property asset class would be commercial and can be held in the SSAS. Equally other structures would enable SSAS to pay a collaborative role in many forms including third party unconnected loan, loan back, property owner etc.

One of the most crucial areas of the structures are the ability to secure long term dependable income streams that are acceptable to any funders (institutional banks or private/SSAS). The security of this income stream will have a very large impact on the level and cost of the funding as it will significantly affect the risk profile.

This area is becoming a more popular investment route, over recent years, due to its ability to create huge shared value to society as well as creating investment grade returns over many years.

There are increasing levels of challenge in society with local authority housing investment relatively minor and there are correspondingly huge increases in alcohol and drug dependency, mental health and suicide rates. Sadly, this area is growing year on year and the public purse simply does not have the depth or impact to create a solution for everyone.

The private sector must step forward to assist in tackling these challenges by bringing scale of expertise, funding and structures to create solutions whilst not preying on a vulnerable sector. Having said that, in order for the solutions to be sustainable, they must be based on economically sustainable models, rather than charitable donations and philanthropy alone.

3.26 SSAS CASE STUDY: RICHARD KENNEDY & DAVID BALL – Cornerstone Place

The vision of Cornerstone Place is to support charities to alleviate street homelessness by 2030. We aim to contribute to this goal by providing high quality, warm and safe accommodation for those in need while also helping the charities they work with to become more sustainable. As a Certified Social Enterprise our objectives around sharing value are baked into the ethos of the company, and this extends to all partners that we work with, including SSAS trustees.

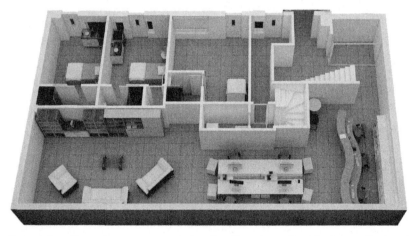

Example of our latest emerging mixed-use product being rolled out nationwide

Cornerstone Place was founded by Richard Kennedy and David Ball. Richard is a SSAS trustee and has spent most of his career in the social sector working with and supporting charities and social enterprises to become more sustainable and impactful and he is passionate about measuring impact. David is a property professional with over 15 years of investing and development experience. A close member of David's family experienced time on the streets, combined with substance abuse issues driving a passion to support others. The combination of hard and soft skills and experience make for a unique blend of complementary attributes that we use to drive the business forward.

In 2020, we were delighted to welcome Mark Stokes and his business partner Nigel Greene to our Board as directors and shareholders. Mark and Nigel provide us with mentorship, guidance, contacts and ideas on a weekly basis.

Cornerstone Place has a rapidly growing reach and pipeline of projects. The combination of structured contracts, acquisitions and connections comes together to serve a dramatically increasing societal need. An example of how our profile is growing was an event that we ran for Local Authorities and charities in Greater Manchester in February 2020, at which Andy Burnham, Mayor of Manchester, delivered the keynote address.

The impact of the Covid-19 pandemic has seen an increase in the number of people at risk of homelessness. Our business model appears to be counter cyclical to the wider economy, so whilst the need for innovative solutions to tackle homelessness were urgent before the pandemic, the need for what we offer is now at critical levels.

One of our operational metrics and outputs is the number of 'homeless bed nights' we are able to bring online. This is similar to how a hotel operates when they measure capacity and performance. Each night of room occupancy is a single chargeable entity. We have adapted this model to measure our impact. Our aim is that by

2030 we will have provided five million homeless bed nights. Every individual night that someone spends on the street is one too many, leaving the individual at personal risk in many different ways. Five million homeless bed nights means there will be five million fewer chances of something terrible happening to some of the most vulnerable people in society.

Example of our latest typical self-contained unit configuration

We rely on a number of stakeholders to help us make progress towards this goal, including SSAS trustees.

Supported accommodation is already an attractive pension investment due to the reliable asset backed revenue streams but this comes with the additional dimension of also providing homes for vulnerable people.

Pensions by their nature focus on long term horizons and therefore are very aligned with investments in supported accommodation which arguably are also contributing to a brighter, more equal and positive future. SSAS investors are able to own certain supported accommodation assets directly in their pension but can also invest through third party loans, amongst other structures.

We call our business model the 'Shared Upsides' model. This is because everyone involved enjoys a share of the value created. This includes the charities we work with, our professional partners, the people we are housing, and the investors who enable the projects to happen.

One of the characteristics of the Shared Upsides model that we hear SSAS Trustees laud the most is that they receive a brand of ROI which sits comfortably alongside the more orthodox measures of Return on Investment and Return of Investment. In this case, the acronym also stands for Return on Impact.

Our focus on measurement means it is possible for SSAS Trustees to understand how each £10K that is invested or loaned to a project results in a proportion of the homeless bed nights over the term of the lease with the charity. There's a direct and quantifiable correlation which sits alongside the financial Return on Investment, which many find compelling.

To get in touch with Cornerstone Place please email info@cornerstoneplace.co.uk

3.27 LAND FOR RESIDENTIAL

Let us consider a SSAS buying a plot of land, obtaining planning permission and carrying out a residential property new build development. Is this possible within a SSAS? The simple answer, in theory, is yes – however, structuring and making sure you do not cross over the HMRC lines of concern is crucial.

If the land is currently being used as a residential garden, then you will need to make sure that your SSAS is never deemed to hold residential property if the land is brought into your pension scheme.

A straight-forward solution would be to fence off the piece of land in question and title split it at the point of purchase. Make sure you have highways access and the necessary approvals if you are doing this strategy though, as ransom strips tend to be expensive!

If the land has a previous non-residential purpose such as a car park, derelict building or other structure on it that is not classed as of residential use, then HMRC may not deem this to constitute residential property.

3.28 TRUSTEE CASE STUDY: IAN KAVANAGH - Land to Residential in Haynes

I consider myself very fortunate to have been introduced to the wonderful tax efficient benefits of a SSAS pension fund many years ago in 1986, when we set up our SSAS with our family run mailing and distribution business linked as sponsoring employer. With my parents, brother, two sisters and my wife all working within the business, the growth of our SSAS, over many years of compounding growth, has served us all incredibly well.

Our SSAS was first used to fund the development and lease back of a 30,000 square feet warehouse and office commercial property, which became the headquarters of our business for many years. With our business paying rent to our own pension fund over many years, this ensured excellent growth to ultimately provide financial security for our family. At times, having a family SSAS behind us feels like having our own bank, which creates great confidence and enables us to make positive investment decisions within our property development business today. I see our SSAS pension as pivotal in helping to successfully transfer financial security to our family's future generations.

Our latest property development project involved us purchasing an end of terrace three bedroomed cottage in the popular Bedfordshire village of Haynes. The property was on the open market and needed a complete refurbishment and extension to maximise the value of the existing cottage. However, the real value of the project was to come from us successfully gaining planning consent and building a three bedroomed detached house in the former garden of the cottage. We always surround ourselves with experts and our planning consultant provided us with great confidence that we would succeed with our planning application for the new build house in the large garden.

To fund the purchase on this occasion we arranged a loan-back from our SSAS to our development company Front Row Developments (UK) Limited and were able to provide a first charge over the property being purchased. We funded the cottage refurbishment using our own funds and repaid our SSAS loan, following the sale of the cottage, with an interest rate of 5% per annum. Once planning permission had been granted, we arranged a title split to separate the land for the new house and undertook the new build funded by one of our private investment partners.

The economics of the project are as follows:

Purchase price: £340,000

Build costs: £230,000

Other costs: £30,000

GDV: £725,000

Profit: £125,000

The new house was put on the market for sale in March 2020, unfortunately just as the country went into lockdown due to the coronavirus pandemic. However, we were delighted to agree a sale at the beginning of June once the property market opened up again.

In summary, our SSAS provided the funds to enable us to purchase the cottage in need of a complete renovation. We saw the opportunity to achieve a planning gain and build an additional house in the back garden to provide a good return. Although there was a small degree of risk, we had a breakeven fall-back position to rely on. Our SSAS made a return of 5% on the funds lent and our development company is on target to make a profit of some £125,000 over a period of less than 18 months. The project also enabled us to provide a return to one of our private investment partners of 10% per annum on funds lent. The support of our SSAS pension fund once again allowed us to make a decisive offer to secure the purchase of this development opportunity.

3.29 WHEN DOES A DEVELOPMENT BECOME RESIDENTIAL?

HMRC deem a property to be residential once it becomes:

- habitable
- the structure is complete
- utilities are connected
- When it has received a certificate of habitation file

There is an audit pack of information required to determine this point and these will include, but not be limited to, the following:

- Building control certificate
- Planning conditions satisfied
- Mortgageable with banks
- Bathrooms installed and plumbed in
- Kitchens installed
- Electrical certification

- Gas certification
- Utilities connected and metered
- Structural warranties

The question often comes up on commercial to residential conversions and we will cover that more in that section; however, up until the point in time that these items above are outstanding, then technically, the property is still commercial and not yet residential, therefore in theory can be developed/held in a SSAS. The challenges come with transferring/selling the property from the SSAS just prior to this point, where in reality, the property is a building site. If you have ever tried to finance a purchase of a partially completed property then you will understand the complexities, significant costs and very low loan to values that will inevitably arise.

3.30 LAND FOR COMMERCIAL

Gaining planning permission from green field or brownfield land can be a great way of adding significant value. In many areas the planning constraints mean it is difficult to secure residential planning on many plots of land, however an alternative strategy might be to adopt a different approach and to seek planning permission for new commercial premises.

This could be:

- Distribution sheds
- Industrial premises
- Offices
- Hotels
- Care homes
- Retail units

- Supported living
- Sports facilities

Each of these can also benefit from a wide range of use classes, leaving lots of flexibility for different commercial tenants seeking leases.

A powerful case can be created addressing the significant needs in society, ranging from bringing employment opportunities to the area through to addressing challenging societal issues. This supporting evidence can have a very positive and favourable effect on your planning application.

Opportunities could be sought in the SSAS for fresh land opportunities, with no planning history, as well as land that may have been declined planning for residential in the past. A new and compelling planning case could be constructed which may enable significant value to be created.

Your SSAS can pay for these planning and investigation fees, as well as purchasing the land. An alternative strategy discussed in a separate chapter in this book, is to avoid taking the risk of buying land and hoping planning can be achieved, but to instead agree an option agreement on the land or conditionally exchange contracts on the purchase, subject to securing planning permission.

This does not necessarily have to be a high-risk strategy and great opportunities exist for joint ventures, managing risk and preserving and minimising seed capital where-ever possible.

3.31 MIXED USE

The term 'mixed use' covers a wide variety of permutations of property. A SSAS is a very useful tool to have in your toolbox when considering how best to structure property deals and this additional resource can enhance your tenacity significantly if you understand deal structuring.

As we have mentioned repeatedly, if part of the mixed-use property is residential, it cannot be held in the SSAS. However, there is no reason why the residential element could not be bought as a freehold in a separate legal entity, such as a limited company with the commercial being sold leasehold to the SSAS.

We have deployed this model with our own SSAS to great effect enabling the creation of assets and value within the SSAS, as well as outside of it.

3.32 SSAS CASE STUDY: GARETH & HELEN ALEXANDER - "The Christian Home for Young Women"

Over the last couple of years, my wife and I have talked about how to ensure that our future finances are secure and that we can provide a legacy for our children to take forward.

I left my corporate job several years ago and like many people, I would only look at my pension statement briefly once a year (Mark Stokes mentioned this same thing in a webinar and it resonated with me) and I would think to myself, *it's too early to worry about my retirement and take much interest in my pension as my retirement date is 2044!*

In 2019, my wife and I decided we needed to put a plan in place to create the financial security we wanted - this included taking control of our pensions. We watched a lot of videos about SSAS pensions, read a lot of information, started to build relationships with other SSAS trustees and I attended a couple of SSAS Alliance events.

After completing substantial research, we decided we wanted to pool our existing pensions and set up a SSAS and use this as a method to invest in property and help us create financial stability. We took the plunge and started our SSAS journey at the end of 2019. We engaged with an IFA, found suitable SSAS administrators and corporate trustees and started the process.

Number 12 Story Street, Hull was our first purchase. I first viewed the property in February 2020 and after completing the initial due diligence, we submitted an offer, on condition of planning approval. The offer was accepted and so the journey began! A planning application was submitted to convert the commercial building into a mixed-use property. A commercial unit (A1, soon to be Class E) in the basement and four, one-bed self-contained flats on each floor. All the units have access to a private secure courtyard.

86. *Story Street from Albion Street, 1888*
(Acc. No. 131.1929)
This sketch shows some of Hull's elegant Georgian houses designed and built between 1788-1803 by E. Story, joiner (left) and A. Bennison, mason (right).
The building on the right, now the Chinese supermarket, housed the Caxton Institute, Typographical Society and Hull Shorthand Writers' Association in 1888. The large house with the pediment further along was the Children's Hospital, established here in 1873 and moved to Park Street in 1891.
Many of the houses on the left were 'apartments' in 1888. No.12 was the Christian Home for Young Women.

But first, let me give you some background about the property. The property was built between 1788 and 1803 in what was known as the Georgian Quarter of Hull. Very few of the buildings in this area still exist today. The reason is not because of the Luftwaffe in World

War Two (Hull was the most bombed city, apart from London, during World War), it is because in the 1960's the local council decided the buildings were no longer fit for purpose and demolished them in favour of warehouses and carparks - they were different times!

Number 12 Story Street is the last remaining building on the street that still has the original Georgian door casings, Georgian basement and Georgian bow windows at the rear. The only reason I know this is because the Hull Civic Society objected to my planning application. Fortunately, this was not upheld, and planning was approved. I reached out to the chair of the Hull Civic Society, invited him to the property and explained our plans, objectives and how we wanted to retain as much of the Georgian appearance as possible, and improve the overall appearance of Story Street. The chairman of the Hull Civic Society wrote to the council planning team to say "the owner of the property should be congratulated for the design and supported the application".

The lesson learned for me is to engage and build relationships with people who have an interest, or are going to be impacted by the development, and don't always assume it will be negative. Yes, you are going to encounter objections, but if you can walk a mile in the other person's shoes, you have more chance of getting a resolution that benefits everyone.

We have learned so much from this property and there are lots of things we would do differently in the future. We have also documented the process and timelines and implemented a 'due-diligence' approach, to ensure we are better prepared for our next development. The mantra of 'measure twice, cut once' was drilled into me when I was an apprentice in the Aerospace industry. That same approach is essential throughout the entire life cycle of property development.

These are some of the key areas of knowledge and experience we have gained since starting the project; read and understand the local authorities Strategic Housing Marketing Assessment plan - this gives a fantastic insight to the local area plans and helps with your planning application; the exit strategy (including having a plan A, B, C & D); how to structure a deal; finance options and the pro's and con's of Bridging finance; RICS valuations; understanding capital allowances and how to maximize them; section 106 and how to make sure you are not paying more than you have to; underestimating planning application process timescales; the importance of having a good architect; working with a QS to estimate build costs and bills of quantities (BoQ); the importance of detailed due-diligence; selecting a prime contractor using a tendering process; not to dwell on mistakes or errors and finally, learn from them and move on.

I'm sure there is a lot more we have learned and will continue to learn in the future. But there is no such thing as a 'get rich quick scheme' and property is a marathon, not a sprint. I have also learned, 'beware of false idols' - there are a lot of people who can tell you how to do it but have never actually done it themselves. We have found it's important to surround yourself with trusted people who all have the same goals and ethics as yourself.

I have watched several videos, listened to various webinars, and read several books that talk about the power of the SSAS. Once you start to learn to understand how it can be used, the possibilities are fantastic. I want to explain how we are using our SSAS and other people's SSAS to help with this development.

We agreed to purchase 12 Story Street for £80,000. The refurb was costed (including contingency) at £130,000. Based on the RICS survey, the overall GDV is £280,000. This was based on a commercial unit value of £60,000 (based on a 9% yield) and £220,000 for the four flats.

The property would be purchased by our property development company, Blue Swan Properties Ltd. We had planned to purchase the property and complete the refurbishment using Bridging Finance. We would then exit via a combination of splitting the title and selling the commercial unit (on a leasehold) and retain the residential units (on a freehold) in Blue Swan Properties Ltd and refinance to release the equity and rent out the flats as corporate lets.

A SSAS (and it just so happens to be our SSAS) agreed to purchase the commercial unit on a leasehold. We agreed to a 999-year lease and agreed on the service charge and ground rents. A lease option contract was drawn up by our solicitors. The contract stated the SSAS would pay 50% upfront and the remaining amount would be paid over stages, with a final payment on completion of the commercial unit. This had a positive effect in several ways:

- It removed the headache of trying to find a buyer for the commercial unit
- It will create a recurring income into our SSAS to increase its value
- It provided Blue Swan Properties with upfront cash flow and provided certainty surrounding the exit strategy
- It allows the new owner (SSAS) to start to market the commercial unit and attract a tenant
- It provides the finance company/investor with confidence that their investment is secure because the property is already providing an income

As I mentioned before, we had planned to use Bridging Finance for the purchase and refurbishment. But at the eleventh hour, the Bridging company decided the solicitor we were using was not suitable for their insurance purposes (the Bridging company decided any Law firm involved in the transaction needed to have a minimum of two partners - my solicitor only had one) and they required us to use a different solicitor. At this stage, we had completed all the legal aspects of the purchase, we had exchanged and planned to complete in a few weeks' time.

In most cases, this would have been a showstopper, but we are now in the process of obtaining SSAS investor finance, using a third-party loan to part-fund the purchase and refurb of the property, as an alternative to Bridging finance. This proves the importance of having different strategies in place to mitigate the risks and unforeseen circumstances.

(Note: at the time of writing this, the third-party loan from a SSAS investor has not been secured, because we were only informed of the Bridging company issue, via our Broker, on the 11th August 2020. Our fallback position is to purchase the property using our SSAS to secure the sale).

This property has shown us the importance of SSAS learning, networking and education and also surrounding yourself with fellow SSAS owners who share the same ethics and goals as yourself. This has helped us to understand what a SSAS is capable of and the importance of due diligence, planning, and risk mitigation.

3.33 BUY-TO-LET

Of all the strategies we encounter, Buy-to-Let is probably the most common for those wanting to hold assets long term. It is a powerful way to combine added value through extensions, refurbishment and other improvements with refinancing and long-term dependable income streams cash flowing nicely with the opportunity for capital growth.

A SSAS cannot directly own residential property and therefore a Buy-to-Let residential property would be non-permissible and attract a penalty tax charge from HMRC if held in the SSAS.

A Buy-to-Let property could be used as security on a third-party unconnected loan, subject to a security trustee being in place, to ensure that upon a default scenario, the SSAS would never inadvertently own a residential property. The type of security for this type of loan could include:

- First charge at land registry on an unencumbered property
- Second charge at land registry
- Debenture on company that owns the property

A Buy-to-Let could be the enabling security on a loan back which could take security, via a first charge, at land registry on the unencumbered property.

Buy-to-Let strategy has many other advantages in addition to adding value, cash flow and capital growth. They represent a very agile and tenacious asset class that I refer to as **'pockets of liquidity'**. Let me explain.

If you wanted, or more to the point if you needed, to sell a seven bed HMO it would probably be to a property investor who would want a great deal, offering at wholesale prices rather than retail; with commercial finance the acquisition may take two-four months.

With a Buy-to-Let you have many different options hence **'pockets of liquidity'**, including:

- Let the property on an AST
- Lease the property over five - fifteen year term
- Sell it: typically, four - six weeks
- Place in auction: typically, six - eight weeks
- Aggregate property in a portfolio
- Refinance quickly to release equity
- Cross collateralisation options

This strategy needs careful thought if you are looking to collaborate with your own SSAS or someone else's to create a Buy-to-Let portfolio. It definitely won't be held in your SSAS for compliance reasons; however, working with your corporate trustee you should be able to establish a clear operating model to enable this.

Taking an alternative view, one could use the proceeds from a Buy-to-Let portfolio held in a limited company to make SSAS pension contributions each year to the allowable levels. Again, yet another different angle to consider.

3.34 PLANNING GAIN

We have touched on planning gains a number of times throughout this book as a SSAS can be a very powerful tool in your toolbox to approach gaining control, acquiring and adding value to property acquisitions. It can assist you in raising the capital, operating at speed and harnessing collaboratively all the other aspects required to secure commercial property in today's ever competitive markets.

Here are a few areas to consider as you decide on your property approach, combining the power of a SSAS:

- By using purchase option agreements, a SSAS can utilise its resources to fund the taking control of a property yet retaining the option to assign to another entity later in time

- A SSAS can pay for the professional and planning fees required to gain planning permission

- A SSAS could take control of a property, say with conditionality subject to planning, and your limited company undertake the planning at risk. Upon successful planning approval the limited company, which has undertaken the work, could secure a win fee from the SSAS thus providing a fair return inside the SSAS, as well as outside, where the risk and resource was taken

- A SSAS can move quickly with liquid funds to secure deals where time is important and can hold whilst planning is secured

- A SSAS could pay a substantial down payment on signing an option to acquire the commercial elements of a mixed-use scheme. These funds can help your development raise funds for the purchase or development phase

There are many permutations in securing planning gains and the important part to consider is where you want the additional value to be - inside the SSAS, your sponsoring company, another connected company or an unconnected company etc. This 'start with the end in mind' philosophy will open up so many doors for you to secure the right terms and structure to suit your circumstances.

3.25 SSAS CASE STUDY: NIGEL GREENE & MARK STOKES – SSAS enablement for a planning gain

One of our first property transactions within our SSAS was to acquire a commercial property which consisted of three x five storey Edwardian terrace offices in a row in Kingston upon Hull.

The property had been owned by the partners of a legal practice that had been acquired by a larger national practice and the original partners kept the property separate from the business acquisition and retained it. After three years of being vacant, and on the market for circa £500,000, we placed a fully conditional offer for the SSAS to acquire the property in cash for £310,000 which we duly exchanged on. The conditional offer was based on full planning permission for change of use to eighteen apartments. The acquisition took place in 2016 and the building was a B1A office building which normally would have enabled us to use Permitted Development Rights to secure change of use. However, this particular property was Grade II listed and an important surviving period building in Kingston upon Hull that lost many local buildings, following significant carpet bombing in World War II.

There was a long stop placed in the contract of just over a year and we successfully secured full planning permission for the eighteen apartments well within this period, and legally completed on the purchase.

It was possible for the SSAS to pay for all seed capital to manage the planning permission process. On this occasion we entered into a contract with one of our operating companies (OpCo) which took the risk of capital in securing the planning permission for the property and provided all the expertise and resources.

Upon securing planning permission we established a special purpose vehicle (see chapter on SPV's) which, for the purposes of the illustration below we shall call DevCo, made an offer to acquire the property for £450,000. Upon the sale of the property from the SSAS to the Dev Co, the SSAS also made a success-based payment to fulfil its contract with the Op Co.

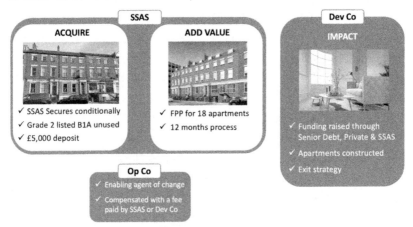

This produced a great win:win:win for the SSAS, OpCo and DevCo including:

- The SSAS made a handsome return on the use of its capital for acquiring the property
- The Op Co made great use of its knowledge, skill and resources to gain planning permission
- The Dev Co made a sensible offer to the SSAS which

the SSAS validated through a RICS Red Book valuation and went on to successfully develop the commercial to residential scheme

On this occasion our SSAS took a very opportunistic view on securing a property and whilst also considering commercial opportunities in the area, decided on this course of action following a small deterioration in the local market in commercial property which corresponded with an increase in appeal for residential property. Care must be taken to ensure that the SSAS does not become a trading entity by frequently repeating this process as this would draw attention by HMRC and could result in a penalty charge. Care should be taken to gain great counsel and advice from your professional team to ensure no surprises and maximum compliance.

3.36 PERSONAL PRIMARY RESIDENCE

Your SSAS can never own a residential property of any description and that includes your own Personal Primary Residence.

Your home may be used as security to support a Loan Back from a SSAS. Thinking laterally this could be security for your Loan Back or from someone else's SSAS, although I think it would be fair to say that you would have to know that person very well indeed – when I have seen this happen it has almost always been between family members.

Remember that the Loan Back does require a first legal charge registered at Land Registry, hence the property would need to be unencumbered from a mortgage or charge.

3.37 PROPERTY ABROAD

Can a SSAS own property aboard?

Yes, in principle a SSAS can own a property abroad; however, there will usually be certain circumstances which may need to prevail including:

- Will your scheme administrator allow it?
- Is English the primary language?
- Dependent on the type of property ownership rules and structures in the country
- Are UK trusts and trust law recognised and accepted in the country
- Does a similar land registry system exist?
- Systematic review of the obligations and liabilities of owning the property
- Consider complexity of legal agreements
- Do tax agreements exist between the UK and the country where the property is purchased
- May require the appointment of in-country solicitors to acquire and also to manage any ongoing obligations
- Local tax regimes may mean that the investment is not tax free
- Purpose of the property – is it an investment or for personal use
- Appointment of a professional team to manage the asset

3.38 WORKING CAPITAL

Any business requires working capital to exist. These costs can be many and varied and alter over the maturity curve of a business's growth. A friend recently acquired a very substantial building and converted it into a large HMO. Each room, including the common areas, required furniture to be bought and installed at an up-front cost of over £25,000. This is a significant initial cash outlay for the business pre any income. It is a classic 'catch 22'. I should say at this point that there are ways to finance furniture costs with specialist providers – however, that is outside of the demise of this book.

This can be a challenge to many businesses particularly when acquiring, in this case, a depreciating set of items (such as furniture). Part of the answer lies in the underlying business case of how this particular cost supports the generation of the income stream and how these costs can account for, thus transforming it, to a key enabling investment for the business.

The list of working capital requirements would be too long and exhaustive for this book – however, with property specifically in mind, here are a list of some of the areas that working capital may be required:

- Furniture packs for HMO's, Serviced Accommodation, hotels and B&B's
- Seed capital for option agreements for legal fees etc
- Seed capital for conditional offers (subject to planning for instance) including legal fees, deposit etc
- Planning fees for architects, designers, local authority fees and surveys
- Permitted development fees for architects, designers, local authority fees and surveys
- Overheads
- Expansion of business

This list is far from exhaustive, however it is meant to get you thinking and exploring what may be in the art of the possible for you.

There are a number of ways that could be considered for collaborating with a SSAS to fund these costs, including:

- Loan Back
- Third-party unconnected loans
- Share acquisition
- Sale and lease back of assets
- Using assets as security for a loan

3.39 PROTECTION CASE STUDY: MARK STOKES - commercial to residential conversion

Weybrook House was a circa 10,000 sq. ft B1a office building which our development company, EquaGroup, identified as having great potential to be converted in to 22 apartments in this tranquil riverside setting. At the time of purchase, it was a B1a commercial property in the leafy market town of Godalming, just outside Guildford in Surrey.

Having identified the building as having great potential, we approached the vendor with an offer to acquire the property.

If we had acquired the property, then applied for the necessary planning permissions and failed at planning, we would have been left with a vacant commercial property and little or no upside development potential. The dilemma was how to protect the downside. This is what we have grown a reputation for – being conservative with risk, as good as our word, high levels of integrity and optimum deal protection through structuring on the way into the deal.

This is what happened.

We made an offer to acquire the building on a conditional basis, subject to gaining Permitted Development Rights determination for 22 apartments.

Following a short period of negotiation, we agreed Heads of Terms to acquire the property for £2.2m on a conditional exchange of contracts. The conditionality was a 'subject to' offer. In other words, we would exchange but only have to legally complete if we secured the necessary permissions to convert to 22 apartments.

The conveyancing and funding process took about nine weeks to get to exchange of contracts.

In parallel, we commenced the permitted development process which included full measure of the building, architectural drawings, full flood risk assessment survey and external ground level survey and then submitted our Permitted Development application via our planning consultant.

We did spend a little more time and seed capital on this application due to the location of the property, next to a navigational canal. While the risk was low, due to this being a specific navigation canal, we wanted to make sure that the application received a positive and swift outcome.

Sometimes a few weeks extra at the front end saves many months in the long term. After all, this is what we are looking for – anticipating what it takes to create assured outcomes.

The outcome:

- We successfully acquired a great property in Surrey and converted it in to 22 apartments
- We took barely any planning risk at all as the vendor paid for the permitted development application, as part of our negotiation, although we retained approvals on design
- We conditionally exchanged with a £15,000 deposit on a £2.2m property (0.68% !!!)

- The deposit was on a fully refundable basis – if we did not get the planning we needed, we would get our deposit back
- We used approximately £5,000 of seed capital for successfully securing permitted development rights determination
- Successful legal completion followed and the building then went into its development phase, creating 22 beautifully appointed riverside apartments

TOP TIP: One important tip I will leave with you is the conditionality based on 'subject to planning' is NOT enough to ring fence your risk. We specifically provide a schedule of what we want planning for. This would literally be based, in this case, on 22 apartments each with a very clear Net Internal Area (NIA) as any deviation from this will alter the economics of the development. The conditional contract would only become unconditional once we secure everything we have requested, or alternatively the price may be renegotiated.

Photo of commercial office purchased

CGI of planned Conversion

Completed Conversion

3.40 OPPORTUNITY OF CHANGE IN PLANNING RULES

Over recent years the government has outlined a swathe of new planning laws which, including permitted development rights, enable a much-needed stimulus to the economy and a transformation of planning bureaucracy, enabling new homes and amenities to serve a currently under served residential market.

Some of these recent changes, or planned changes, will be of high interest to SSAS trustees and those keen on taking advantage of new rules to enable them to create society serving assets.

Areas of interest include:

- Airspace rights
- No permission required to demolish and rebuild unused buildings
- Allow homes and commercial and retail properties to be quickly repurposed to help revive high streets and town centres
- Property owners will also be able to add up to two additional storeys to their home to create new homes and living space
- More advantageous use of land
- Commercial to residential set to increase
- Retail to residential enabling inner town/city dwellings
- Increased speed and lower levels of red tape
- Reduced costs
- A wider range of commercial buildings will be allowed to change to residential use without the need for a planning application
- Increase in types of commercial premises with total flexibility to be repurposed to other sue classes

New regulations will give greater freedom for buildings and land in town centres to change use without planning permission and create new homes through the regeneration of under-utilised, poor performing and vacant/redundant buildings.

3.41 LEASE AND PURCHASE OPTIONS

A SSAS can actively pursue purchase lease options on land and property and being party to these contracts is acceptable in principle.

Lease or purchase option agreements allow you to take out a contract with the vendor to lease the property for a period of time for a pre-agreed consideration. Usually, a rent will be paid for the property for that period with an option, rather than an obligation, to buy at a predetermined price or pricing mechanism.

So, the SSAS could enter into a lease option agreement on a property, have a 5-year period of renting and could use that time to gain planning permission to significantly add value. Once the planning has been approved, the SSAS could acquire the property at the agreed price.

There are many different permutations on this model with the SSAS acquiring the property, assigning the lease to a limited company who then acquires the property.

The acquiring party could gain bank funding on the basis of the new planning permission and the intentions moving forward, rather than at the purchase price level. This can provide huge advantages in mitigating risk, reducing costs and maximising leverage.

If the land/property in question has potential for becoming residential through planning, permitted development and conversion for example, then it would be prudent and wise to include in the purchase lease option contract, a provision for assignability as one may not wish to acquire within the SSAS.

Once planning has been achieved for example, and any conditionality falls away, leaving an unconditional contract, it may be that the most appropriate structure for the asset may not be in the SSAS. This way you are leaving a wide array of structuring options to consider to assign to another legal entity.

So, it is possible for the SSAS to utilise its funds to be a prime enabler of assets – however, if at a future point in time the strategy were to alter, and the asset or contract was best placed in another company structure for example, it could be easily and efficiently facilitated.

The SSAS could pay for the legal and planning costs for this type of property transaction.

3.42 AUCTION ACQUISITION

There can be some great opportunities available through the auction process. The speed of the auction process with typically four weeks to review the auction lots and 21-28 days to legally complete, once the gavel goes down, post successful auction, means that those with cash can certainly gain an advantage through speed, less dependency in the buying process and reduction in costs.

For larger purchases bridge finance may be used in conjunction with cash to also enable swift transaction efficiency.

Other advantageous auction scenarios could be to acquire pre auction or post auction on unsuccessful lots.

- **Pre-Auction**
  If you can assure a swift acquisition process with cash, it is very possible that some vendors may choose to sell pre-auction.

The decisiveness of a cash buyer, such as a SSAS, can increase your potential of snapping up some very quick assets before they go under the hammer. Remember though that you may well be held to the auction house rules for legal completion and due diligence should not be cut short as perils can exist for the unwary or careless.

- **Auction**

The traditional route would be to formally register as a bidder at auction and enter the room or bid on-line.

- **Post Auction**

Not all auction lots meet their reserve at auctions and remain unsold. It is perfectly possible to approach the auction house post auction and make an offer for these unsold lots. As before, auction house rules may still apply – however, negotiation on latitude may enable more favourable terms.

Cash talks, and with a SSAS able to move swiftly on commercial property acquisitions you can open the doors to great opportunity. Many of the techniques in this book can be used including collaborating and enabling through a SSAS:

- SSAS acquires
- Loan Back
- Third party unconnected loan
- Joint purchase
- Collaboration
- Limited company purchase

4. OTHER AREAS A SSAS CAN INVEST

In an earlier chapter we have focused on how the power of property assets is one of the more popular asset classes.

Whilst the focus of this book is specifically on how SSAS and Property can work in concert with each other, it is also recognised that diversification plays a large part in considering the right strategy for you across your overall wealth position.

For balance, and to ensure that the reader recognises the importance of considering this, I have included some of the other asset classes that can be considered for investment purposes. Each has a different level of specific due diligence, risk and reward levels hence taking the most appropriate level of advice, experience and counsel will seldom fail to pay a great return.

For completeness here are a list of non-property related investment opportunities that a SSAS can consider:

- Regulated Collective Investments such as Unit Trusts, OEICS and ICVC's
- Gilts
- Bonds
- Fixed Interest stocks
- Investment Trusts
- Direct Quoted Equities

- Trustee Investment Plans
- Loan back to the sponsoring employer
- Equities
- Futures and options traded on recognised futures exchange
- Authorised UK unit trusts and OEICs and other UCITS funds
- Unauthorised unit trusts that don't invest in residential property
- Investment trusts subject to FCA regulation
- Unitised insurance funds from EU insurers and IPAs
- Intangible assets such as intellectual property (IP)
- Deposits and deposit interests
- Traded endowment policies
- Derivative products such as a Contract for difference (CFD)
- Gold bullion
- Peer-to-peer (P2P) Lending/Crowd Funding
- Off-shore funds
- Cash deposits
- Image rights
- Copyrights
- Trademarks

Some of these investment areas may have caveats to them on how they may be allowable - some are only applicable to the UK for instance. It is always appropriate to seek sound advice from your financial advisor or tax advisor when reviewing new investments, ensuring that you stay clear of any potential for tax penalties or loss of tax efficiency.

5. WHAT A SSAS CANNOT INVEST IN

There are certain areas that would attract a significant penalty tax charge if held by, or invested in, through the SSAS.

Rather than say what a SSAS cannot do, it is technically more accurate to identify what investments and activities will become taxable events and thus losing the tax efficiencies of a SSAS. Failure to observe the rules will result in painful tax penalty charges.

In the UK, HMRC lay the tax rules down very clearly and we, the taxpayer, have the requirement to seek great counsel and advice to pay the correct amount of tax for the given circumstances and environment. A SSAS, or a limited company, are two great examples of us creating the circumstances and environment to enable us to have a tax optimised position.

I have never 'nickel and dimed' on great advice, rather seeking instead to build up a great array of counsel, knowledge and wisdom that can be brought to bear to ensure that each decision, investment or deployment is undertaken with compliance, risk management and tax efficiency in mind.

There is a huge diversity of what a SSAS Trustee can consider for their investment strategy and equally there are key guidelines that must be followed to ensure economic viability, tax efficiency and overall compliance. A SSAS can do many things, however stepping over the guidelines and rules will trigger investigations and potentially result in serious tax penalties.

For example - investments currently permitted by primary legislation but subsequently made subject to heavy tax penalties, therefore rendering them un-investable, include:

- Any item of tangible moveable property
- Exotic assets like:
    - vintage cars
    - yachts
    - wine
    - stamps
    - antique furniture
    - works of art
    - rare books
    - oriental rugs
- Residential property
- Plant and machinery:
    - wind turbines
    - solar panels
- Commodities
- Personal loans directly, or indirectly, to Trustees or persons connected with a Trustee
- Investments considered to be personal chattels
- Unsecured loans to the sponsoring employer
- Overseas unquoted equities
- Off-plan hotel rooms
- Carbon credits
- Cloud lending

- Land banking
- Storage pods
- Any taxable moveable property (with a market value that does not exceed £6,000)
- Gold Krugerrands
- Loans to member Trustees or their families
- Jewellery and gemstones
- Residential property is not permitted under any circumstances
- Commercial freeholds where a reversionary interest in residential leasehold exists within the property
- Time shares
- Beach huts

5.1 TANGIBLE MOVEABLE PROPERTY

Tangible moveable property are things that can be physically touched and that are moveable rather than immovable property. Examples might include assets such as:

- Art
- Antiques
- Classic cars
- Plant and machinery owned by a registered pension scheme
- Horses
- Vans
- Yachts
- Watches

- Rugs
- Fine wines & spirits

Certain tangible moveable property, that is specified in Regulations, will not be taxable property so will not be subject to tax charges when held as a scheme investment by an investment-regulated pension scheme. Any specified items will be of a type that is normally held as investments and does not provide any possibility of personal use.

Investment grade gold bullion is an example that has been specified. The definition of investment grade gold is gold of a purity not less than 995 thousandths that is in the form of a bar or a wafer, of a weight accepted by the bullion markets. The gold must be stored by a bullion dealer and cannot be moved or taken home.

I have heard of examples where a SSAS has invested in whiskey as another example. Upon examination, it is based on wholesale barrels of whiskey held in bonded storage facilities would be highly dependent on the mandate of your corporate trustee as to whether it would be approved.

Tangible moveable assets are as complex an area as you want to make it. The rules are very clear and contained in https://www.gov.uk/hmrc-internal-manuals/pensions-tax-manual/ptm125100.

The complexity comes when you start to examine around the boundaries of acceptability. Consider the huge opportunity that a SSAS has to invest and then decide whether the risk of marginal returns against a risk profile, that could incur tax charges, is worth it.

Whatever your desired investment strategy, gaining great advice and support from your SSAS corporate trustee is essential.

6. ENERGY AND THE ENVIRONMENT

As property investors and SSAS trustees we have a very keen interest in energy consumption, energy efficiency and the mindset shift of strategic energy management which is essential to safeguard and optimise our investments.

6.1 ENERGY PERFORMANCE CERTIFICATE (EPC)

An Energy Performance Certificate (EPC) rates how energy efficient your building is using grades from A to G, with 'A' being the most efficient grade.

The Energy Efficiency Regulations 2015 established a minimum level of energy efficiency for privately rented property in England and Wales. From April 2018, landlords of privately rented domestic and non-domestic property in England or Wales must ensure that their properties reach a minimum Energy Performance Certificate (EPC) rating of E before granting a new tenancy to new or existing tenants.

From 1 April 2020, these requirements changed and all domestic private rented properties in England and Wales must reach an EPC E rating, even where there has been no change in tenancy arrangements. It is also expected that the EPC minimum D rating will apply from 1 April 2022.

The regulation changes across the country will mean that landlords and managing agents will need to ensure that EPC standards are met for their properties at a change of tenancy, and whilst there is a cost cap of £5,000 for any required works needed for a property to meet the required EPC banding, there will be fines for non-compliance.

You must have an EPC if you rent out, or sell, the premises or if a building under construction is finished. Commercial EPCs are valid for ten years and can be reused as required within that period. A new Commercial EPC is not required each time there is a change of tenancy, or the property is sold, provided it is no more than ten years old.

You can be fined between £500 and £5,000 based on the rateable value of the building if you don't make an EPC available to any prospective buyer or tenant.

You must display an EPC by fixing it to your commercial building if all these apply:

- Total useful floor area is greater than 500 square metres
- Building is frequently visited by the public
- EPC has already been produced for the building's sale, rental or construction

You can only get an Energy Performance Certificate (EPC) from a commercial energy assessor and the type of assessor you will need will depend on the complexity and features of the building. If you need advice on choosing one, speak to a commercial (non-domestic) energy assessor or contact the approved accreditation scheme they belong to.

The seller or landlord is responsible for ensuring there is a Commercial EPC for the building, or part of the building, being sold or let, even if an agent or another service organisation is acting on their behalf or providing an EPC.

For newly constructed buildings, it is the responsibility of the builder to provide an EPC to the person who commissioned the construction of the building, within five days of completion. An EPC must be obtained before a building is marketed for sale or rent.

6.2 RENEWABLE ENERGY PERFORMANCE ASSETS

Energy efficiency, renewable energy and energy performance assets have long been a part of my corporate life as well as forming a core part of my sustainability ethos personally.

I care deeply about the future of our planet and its unsustainable consumptions levels. The very essence of our Creating Shared Value ethos at our Equa group of companies is focused on CREATING not CONSUMING and this permeates down through each aspect of what we do in our operating businesses.

Examples of energy performance assets are included below and can include any aspects of energy savings, efficiency, and generating investment:

- Solar photovoltaic (PV)
- Solar thermal
- Wind
- Tidal
- Combined Heat and power (CHP)
- Biomass boilers

For us it is important to understand this as a deep societal issue, but also, in order to be a constructive part of the solution, it has to be economically sustainable and hence there is a huge opportunity awaiting those that are prepared to contribute to the solution.

Turning the problem into an investment opportunity with an attractive Return on Investment is smart thinking.

An area to be aware of, which we cover in a chapter of the same name, is Tangible Moveable Assets. Be aware that as a SSAS, you will not be able to own assets that fall with this category so if it can be lifted and moved, then it probably will not be allowed. Check with your corporate trustee on any plans for any retro fitted assets, such as solar panels, to make sure they are fully compliant before installing on SSAS owned property.

Here are some areas in which a SSAS could potentially become involved in Renewable Energy Performance Assets:

- SSAS installs these assets on its property to enhance the energy performance of the building, thus lowering the operating costs

- Invests capital to install energy generating assets, thus creating an additional income stream

- Lease land owned by the SSAS to a company who would install and operate energy generating assets such as wind and solar

- Lease roof space of buildings, owned by the SSAS, to a company who would install and operate energy generating assets such as solar PV

Renewable energy, particularly solar, and to a certain degree wind, has long been trying to embrace the challenge of intermittency. The wind doesn't always blow, or the sun doesn't always shine when the demand is required for electricity. Recent advances in battery technology have now enabled energy storage to become a mainstream proposition which many are taking lucrative advantage of.

Electricity costs more when demand is high throughout the day. The unit rate is the price you pay per unit (KWH) of energy. If you could create a model which harnesses and generates electricity at off peak times, stores it and then sells (exports) the electricity to the grid at peak times, there are very significant advantages that will provide a substantial return on your investment on the capital required.

6.3 ENVIRONMENT SUSTAINABILITY

The following chapter is a BONUS chapter from my book published in 2018, 'Commercial to Residential Conversions: the essential manual for property developers'.

As developers we have chosen a path of responsibility in being catalytic to the creation of shared value.

The mine and burn fossil fuel economy is simply not sustainable over the long term and this planet only has a finite amount of natural capital. If we are designing and creating buildings that have a design life and leaseholds of in excess of 125 years, we would be remiss not to fully consider environmentally sustainable options thoroughly, particularly as in most cases they make sound economic sense also.

Many of you reading this book will have, or may be considering, a family in the future. Therefore, long term horizons come into perspective when considering our future generations and the type of world and array of assets that we leave behind for our children as part of our legacy.

The quicker we see this as a business opportunity, rather than an imposed burden, and not just 'saving the planet', the more integrated our business and personal choices will be over the long term. It is this mindset that is required to truly optimise and transform our vision for the assets we create.

This book focuses on the overall sustainability of your development business - however, true sustainability must involve environmental as well as economic sustainability.

Currently the built environment accounts for approximately:

- 45% of total UK carbon emissions (27% from domestic buildings and 18% from non-domestic)
- 72% of domestic emissions arise from space heating and the provision of hot water
- 32% of landfill waste comes from the construction and demolition of buildings
- 13% of products delivered to construction sites are sent directly to landfill without being used

We must make a decision on whether we want our development business to contribute to the problem or be part of the solution. Without considering the entire life cycle of the building, at the start of the design process, we could be missing huge potential for optimising the developments environmental performance.

Our main areas of focus will be the eight stages of the ENTIRE life cycle of a building, namely:

1. Design
2. Transportation
3. Installation
4. Operation
5. Maintenance
6. Refurbishment
7. Demolition
8. Recovery/Recycle

Our aim should be to minimise the effect on the environment by the following:

- CO2 emission reduction
- Overall reduction in greenhouse gas emissions
- Increase energy efficiency and performance
- Increased renewable energy adoption
- Water reduction
- Waste reduction
- Materials from sustainable sources
- Minimise the use of precious Natural Capital

6.2.1 What is Natural Capital?

Natural Capital can be defined as the world's stocks of natural assets which include geology, soil, air, water and all living things.

6.2.2 Why is Natural Capital an issue?

With financial capital, when we spend too much, we run up debt, which if left unchecked, can eventually result in bankruptcy. With natural capital, when we draw down too much stock from our natural environment, we also run up a debt which needs to be paid back - for example by replanting clear-cut forests or allowing aquifers to replenish themselves after we have abstracted water. If we keep drawing down stocks of natural capital without allowing or encouraging nature to recover, we run the risk of local, regional or even global ecosystem collapse.

Poorly managed Natural Capital therefore becomes not only an ecological liability, but a social and economic liability too. Working against nature by overexploiting Natural Capital can be catastrophic, not just in terms of biodiversity loss, but also catastrophic for humans as ecosystem productivity and resilience decline over time and some regions become more prone to extreme events such as floods and droughts. Ultimately, this makes it more difficult for human communities to sustain themselves, particularly in already stressed ecosystems, potentially leading to starvation, conflict over resource scarcity and displacement of populations.

Source: World Forum on Natural Capital https://naturalcapitalforum.com.

This is another area where modular construction, undertaken correctly, has the opportunity to create massive sustainability advantages and we will look at this in more detail in a future chapter.

Other emerging areas of technological advancement which will aide environmental performance will include:

- The Internet of Things (IoT) & Integrated Automated Building Systems
- Greywater Plumbing Systems
- Electrochromic Glass
- Solar Thermal Cladding
- 3D printing
- Self-healing concrete
- High quality maintenance

Energy remains one of the largest and most impactful industries we have and one which is undergoing a transformation to address years of neglect in environmental terms. Energy also represents one of our largest cost bases from a building owners perspective.

To turn this conundrum on its head, we can challenge tradition, making it possible for a building to become a net EXPORTER of power in the future.

By focusing on two key areas, we can get closer to this point whilst still achieving economic sustainability in parallel and that is the point here – you can have your cake and eat it. These two areas are:

- Driving energy consumption down
- Increasing energy production

Decentralised energy represents an economic solution to an ageing and creaking centralised energy system which has inherent inefficiencies and losses in its distribution system, all of which come at a cost to the environment and the economic equation. Additionally, given that heat is a by-product of energy production, efficient generation of energy close to its point of use enables us to utilise the heat generated and commoditise it as a valuable product in its own right, rather than a waste product.

We have been involved in:

- Enabling many decentralised energy developments including district heating systems
- Enabling incredible levels of community shared value through logical thinking

Many solutions exist that will enable minimum, if any, trade-off for challenging tradition and taking your development down a route of high performance environmentally sustainable credentials. Indeed, this could be the differentiator for you in tomorrow's market that makes your property unique, stands out and a more intelligent investment with dramatically lower operational costs, more secure and possibly with additional income streams.

Types of renewable energy which are being adopted and form part of your designer's checklist include:

- Ground source heat pumps
- Air source heat pumps
- Solar thermal
- Solar photovoltaic
- Biomass
- Wind
- Energy storage
- Intelligent control systems

Each of these technologies should be carefully selected and adopted on solid investment principles, such as funding ROI and IRR calculations.

There are of course many more variant themes of renewable energy and energy reduction methods which your designer will review and discuss with you.

Let me pose a question from a Freeholders perspective - 'walk a mile in another person's shoes'.

Would you pay more for the freehold interests of the property if the building not only had a very low energy consumption, was operationally intelligent and had an effective and minimal maintenance cost base, but also had an additional income stream of energy exporting back to the grid?

This may provide the freeholder a great marketing opportunity to command high rental premiums whilst also providing additional energy security on site. Most publicly traded organisations have a mandate, committed to their shareholders, to operate environmentally effectively and every area of business activity is, and will become, scrutinised including that of leases and the type of properties that are occupied. This is an opportunity to provide socially conscious businesses with products that align with their environmental policies, bottom line positioning and long-term shareholder returns.

This would be much more appealing especially given the challenges that the leasehold/freehold market structuring is facing at present.

The forward-thinking funders are beginning to take an increased interest in this area and, in the future, I expect environmental sustainability to sit within the evaluation and due diligence criteria of funders and investors.

There are many interesting initiatives and processes that are emerging that are lead indicators as to where the world or business may be going, including:

- Carbon cost accounting
- Natural Capital accounting
- Green bonds
- Social impact bonds – remember our section earlier on how society is moving from an input based to an output-based economy?

7. ENVIRONMENTAL, SOCIAL AND GOVERNANCE (ESG)

As SSAS Trustees we have an incredible opportunity to define our investment culture.

Personally, I feel this is hugely important and should sit as a core ethos within every trustees Statement of Investment Principles (SOIP's).

We have the power and the currency to decide what is acceptable and what is not, who we invest in, and how.

Central bodies such as the United Nations are driving this agenda and over the last decade there is a tide of momentum towards taking socially responsible investment decision making – one of which SSAS trustee are increasingly becoming aware of.

But how do we begin to approach this?

Well, leading by example is key as well as adopting a framework that enables your strategy. Increasingly there is a system that is starting to become mainstream.

Environmental, Social and Governance (ESG) is a set of standards and criteria that increasingly socially conscious investors use for due diligence and screening of their investments.

It considers how a company and investment opportunity stands scrutiny in each of the three areas:

- Environmental criteria considers the stewardship of the natural environment
- Social criteria scrutinise how it manages relationships with customers, employees, suppliers and the communities where it operates
- Governance observes how the company operates from shareholder structure and rights, leadership, internal controls and audit

When organisation's like the European Investment Bank (EIB) and United Nations (UN) adopt this approach there will inevitably be much attention from the funding markets and sovereign wealth funds, which will filter down to partial adoption and beyond, in the years to come.

The UN Principles of responsible investing are:

- We will incorporate environmental, social and corporate governance (ESG) issues into investment analysis and decision-making processes
- We will be active owners and incorporate ESG issues into our ownership policies and practices
- We will seek appropriate disclosure on ESG issues by the entities in which we invest
- We will promote acceptance and implementation of the principles within the investment industry
- We will work together to enhance our effectiveness in implementing the principles

- We will each report on our activities and progress towards implementing the principles

Examples of ESG criteria, used by investors, include determining a company's impact on climate change or carbon emissions, water use or conservation efforts, anti-corruption policies, board diversity, human rights efforts and community development.

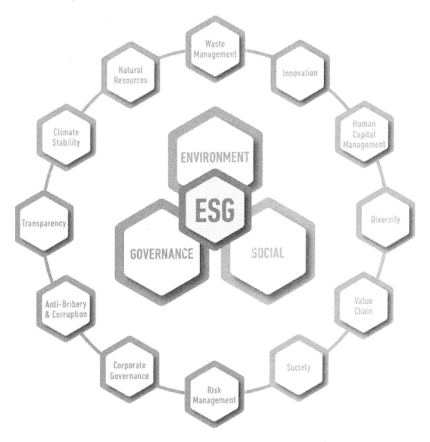

Much work remains to be done in this area. However, I hope this has given you food for thought and the context, opportunity, accountability and responsibility that we, as developers, automatically assume when we take on our deeply meaningful societal role. Whether, and to what extent, we choose to adopt environmental sustainability could well have a fundamental effect on our economic sustainability in the future and the valuation on our business.

At EquaGroup, our development company, we have based our strategy on the principles of ESG which represent an important part of the backbone of our organisation.

8. INVEST IN A BUSINESS

With a SSAS you can become a business investor and given that businesses are a defined asset class, with the potential to create lucrative returns on an annual basis through dividends as well as through sale of shares, it is no wonder that this is an increasingly popular area of interest for trustees.

There are many things a SSAS can do and a relatively small list of things it cannot own, such as residential property. However, the answer to most questions as we have discussed before is - "it depends!"

Even with residential property a SSAS can be involved in investment such as it can invest in a company that owns residential assets. So always start with the end in mind and discuss structures and investments with your professional team to ensure a SSAS (yours or others) can play the role you would like to create positive impact on your strategy.

There is no objection by HMRC to a SSAS making loans to third parties i.e. persons not connected to members or sponsoring employers. Such loans are normally on an 'at arm's length' basis and at a commercial market interest rate.

No more than 50% of the pension scheme's assets can be invested in shares and/or unsecured loans to unquoted UK companies.

The trustees can invest up to 5% of the net asset value of the SSAS in shares of a sponsoring company and are further subject to an overall limit of 20% of the net asset value in any such transactions. For example, the SSAS could invest in five sponsoring companies provided they invest no more than 5% in any one company and no more than 20% in total.

It is important to make sure that the SSAS does not inadvertently take an indirect holding of taxable property through an investment into a company which would create a taxable event.

8.1 ENTERPRISE INVESTMENT SCHEMES (EIS)

The UK government has created a highly attractive array of tax efficient incentive schemes for companies to raise money to help grow their business. It does this by offering tax relief to individual investors who buy new shares in your company.

A SSAS is unlikely to be able to participate and take advantage of an EIS related scheme – however, who said a SSAS was your only option to invest? It would be possible to raise funds through a Loan Back to then onward invest it such an investment scheme, such as EIS, in theory.

The principle of including this chapter in the book is to get you thinking hard - really hard! This is looking at the overall structure of your investments which MUST start with the ORIGINATION OF THE FUNDS in the first place to know what the most efficient method of deployment is.

If you invest via a SSAS it will be with tax free funds. If you invest through EIS or SEIS it would have to be done in your own name so that would be funds probably in a post-tax state where you may have already had anywhere from 7.5% - 45% deducted through tax.

This opens up a really interesting dilemma and analysis on where to best invest from, what was the source of capital, what will the returns be (dividends or capital gains tax) and what the most tax efficient route would be to receive that. Enter into the calculation the tax relief available, it becomes a fantastic array of tax efficient possibilities!

These government investment schemes come in various forms and whilst we won't be going into the detail of each, here are four of them:

- Enterprise Investment Scheme (EIS)
- Seed Enterprise Investment Scheme (SEIS)
- Social Investment Tax Relief (SITR)
- Venture Capital Trust (VCT)

When deciding whether to invest in a company, one of the key decisions will be how to invest. The same investment made through a SSAS or a limited company or a personal investment can create very different risk profiling, as well as tax implications, on losses as well as returns.

Work with your accountant and tax advisor to establish what is the best method of investing for you.

8.2 FRANCHISE INVESTMENT

It is possible to invest your own SSAS funds into a franchise which you would like to become the franchisee. This can be done through a Loan Back to your sponsoring company, taking the security on the company.

We have seen several SSAS trustees undertake this within our SSAS community and they have secured an attractive return for their

SSAS as well as enabled substantial returns in the form of income, dividends and potential business valuations on the franchise over a period of time.

This single investment will then have created multiple income streams, not just for the SSAS but enabled an important array of returns outside of the SSAS in the franchise company.

9. INTELLECTUAL PROPERTY

Intellectual property (IP) can be a key business asset and covers the following:

- Patents
- Trademarks
- Goodwill within a business
- Design types
- Copyright

Valuing intellectual property can be difficult and is generally considered as the 'strength of the IP in the marketplace and financial performance of the IP'.

The choice of valuation methodology will vary on a case-by-case basis depending on the type of IP asset that is being valued. Once the IP has been assigned to the pension, it must be revalued on a regular basis to maintain the integrity of the IP assets.

The type of due diligence that may be required by a SSAS to properly consider an investment in IP might include:

- What is the brand strength of the business
- What IP the business currently has and its perceived or valued strength
- Is the IP registered or unregistered
- How long has the business been trading

- A copy of the last three years' certified accounts and financial review
- Detailed overview of the business and its day-to-day operations and future plans. This would also include an appraisal of the prevailing market
- Ownership and operating structure of the business
- Geographical business coverage
- Key competitor analysis

Ideally a brand or IP related business valuation would be undertaken by an ISO 10668 Brand valuation specialist. These organisations focus on the requirements for monetary brand valuation as specified by the International Organisation for Standardisation (ISO) for the procedures and methods of measuring the value of a brand.

As with an asset class it would be prudent to ensure that consideration is only given on a certain loan to value basis. Hence if the IP valuation is £150,000 then you may make an assessment of applying a loan of say 60% which would be £90,000. Think like a bank - do your bank grade due diligence and preserve your capital with a passion!

10. OP CO AND PROP CO MODEL

The subject of Op Co v Prop Co models comes up very regularly with our mentees and is another example of 'start with the end in mind'. As entrepreneurs it is very easy to become intoxicated with the idea of being involved in everything to 'make a few quid' when, in reality, it is usually sage wisdom that says you should 'stick to you knitting!'

So, what does this have to do with property and SSAS. Well, let me illustrate this with an example.

Imagine securing the purchase of an office block with the intention of converting it to 'residential' accommodation for which you then intend to operate it as Serviced Accommodation.

Now, you may have experience of running a Serviced Accommodation business, but most do not, and it is certainly a very different type of business. It is fundamentally a service-based business rather than a property asset ownership model and therefore there are differing income streams, cost bases and taxation implications, not least of all being VAT. This is a frequent scenario where an Op Co v Prop Co model could be considered.

The Prop Co is the property holding company which is holding the asset. It engages with a Serviced Accommodation business - the Op Co or Operating company - which runs the business of service guest accommodation.

The lease may well be a full repairing (FRI) or internal repairing (IRL) lease which creates a distinct separation between the two parties and their obligations.

Furthermore, the Prop Co will be able to raise commercial finance on the strength of the terms of the leave with the Op Co. This would depend on the specific terms including duration, financials, covenant strength of counter party, breaks in leases and other clauses.

In this model both companies trade within the confines of their core competence, tax is efficient, and risk is separated. One advantage that can be gained over time is that as the Op Co improves in its business model and its covenant strength will grow. Imagine forecasting the next three years audited accounts. Once a lease is then renegotiated in 3+ years' time, the improved covenant plus possibly other favourable movement in terms could well create a significant funding advantage called Compression Yield. This is where the valuation on the lease has improved, when all other areas have remained constant, and is a holy grail moment if you can create that advantage.

So, consider long and hard which type of business model you are running. Is it a property ownership company or a Serviced Accommodation business – the risk and reward profile can be very different, and the resourcing levels can also vary significantly.

Finally, remember that a SSAS has no resources apart from a hunting license and cash! Owning a commercial premise, which is then leased to a company who operate a Serviced Accommodation business, is perfectly possible - subject to usual verifications.

I have used Serviced Accommodation in this example, but you can substitute numerous other business models in this equation.

So, the moral of the story here is - decide what game you are in!

11. FINDING PROPERTY INVESTMENTS

From all the areas we have examined, it is evident that there are a huge and wide-ranging array of options for a SSAS to invest in property. Personal discipline must remain high as shiny penny syndrome and distraction can reign supreme if you let it!! With the options available some may become overwhelmed and suffer from procrastination or worst still, engage in the wrong strategy for them.

If your investment strategy is investing directly into property through your own SSAS or business, there are many ways to identify and secure commercial property opportunities including:

- Commercial Agents
- Private contacts
- Vendors
- Auction
- Estate agents
- Estates Gazette
- Rightmove
- Zoopla
- For Let
- Sourcing agents
- Websites
- Fleurets

- Daltons
- Drive your area
- Land registry
- Local Authorities
- Software – Land Insight etc.
- Airspace
- Other developers
- 'Planning Gain' parties

My business partner of over 20 years, Nigel Greene, runs our land and acquisition team and has invested in, and developed a team and set of skills which deliver to our businesses the pipeline of asset classes we strategically require.

When mentoring our client particularly in the property area, inevitable focus is placed on several key areas for most, including clarity of strategy, finding deals and funding deals.

The chicken and the egg - what comes first? Is it finding the deal or the funding of the deal?

I am very clear that the two must co-exist in parallel and if you have aspirations of scale, both must start NOW. For SSAS trustees there is a unique position here that they have the money anyway, or most of it, and need the deal so they must find a middle ground to keep funds invested, whilst finding property deals to secure.

Place the sourcing of your property opportunities high on your priority list, once you have your investment strategy clear, and start building those all-important skills and relationships NOW.

12. BANK GRADE DUE DILIGENCE

I was contacted recently by someone who asked me a great question - "Why do you refer to bank grade due diligence – after the 2009/10 global financial crisis, surely the banks are not the best example?"

You may agree or disagree with the sentiments of the question so let me explain FOUR reasons why I refer to *Bank Grade* due diligence:

1. As property developers we recognise that we must place seed capital at risk at the commencement of the development/property acquisition phase. Whilst we tend to mitigate as much as we can, deposits, legal search fees, investigations, planning fees and consultants are all required. It is therefore essential that we get the due diligence as close to precisions as we can make it. One of our worst-case scenarios is that the bank and their valuation and credit approval process find a fault, or disagree, with our methodology or assumptions. A subsequent devaluation or decline to fund a deal could well see the end of the acquisition and therefore potential loss of the seed capital

2. The second reason why I use it is that it also gets people talking about risk, due diligence, analysis and critiquing the deal. This can be no bad thing and only serves to provide people with more knowledge and tools, such as

our *Equa*DA tools to establish the power of anticipation. In analysing our deal flow, using the *Equa*DA, we are endeavouring to simulate and anticipate the RICS Red book valuation process and the monitoring surveyors' analysis. If your analysis does not stand scrutiny to either of these tests, then you run the risk of a significant down valuation, enhanced requirement for more private capital, and therefore deteriorating economics of the deal, and quite possibly a failed deal with loss of seed capital. I will leave you to consider the implications of this versus the relatively small cost of becoming well advised, supported and articulate in *Bank Grade* due diligence!

3. You are the bank! As a SSAS you need to get used to the fact that you can operate like a bank. You have that functionality and ability to fund your own deals, and those of others, so it pays to think like a bank might and gain the maximum risk mitigation and transfer as possible, with optimum return profile

4. 'Walk a mile in another person's shoes' - why wouldn't you want to observe and replicate the best parts of what the best parties in the industry do, to create your optimum model. After all, a solid dose of humility will lead you to learn a huge amount from others!

The due diligence phase is, without doubt, the most crucial phase of our investment system and indeed is integral to each and every part. Time is of the essence when securing deals. As time progresses so will your exposure, your costs and the amount of time you invest will increase, therefore it is important to ensure you get the fundamental decision-making criteria correct. That can only be achieved by ensuring that the level of your due diligence is thorough, robust and you are mindful of all risks, right from the offset, in evaluating your potential deal that has arisen. Create a systemised process that becomes your 'checklist' of areas to consistently evaluate and consider when doing your due diligence on a new commercial conversion or development opportunity.

Like all good systems they grow over time, becoming more comprehensive. Your due diligence system will be the same. View it as the backbone of your business, evolving it through tweaks and revisions each time new learning, situations and approaches are experienced. This way you will minimise the chances of repeating the same mistakes and will fine tune and optimise your assessing capability. At the time of writing this book, our *Equa*DA development analysis tool is in the 59th revision, showing how it is an integral part of recording our evolution.

If you would like to access our *Equa*DA in its latest version, it is available at www.equaacademy.co.uk for our mentees.

A number of common errors can occur for the unwary when encountering development analysers:

1. Non-systemised approach to due diligence. This can lead to certain layers of analysis being missed out completely

2. Deal analysers using basic Excel spreadsheets that are incomplete, inaccurate and non-audit checked

3. Core data not taken from reliable sources

4. No sensitivity analysis

5. Costs not fully identified

6. No integrated cash flow modelling

7. No equity waterfall modelling

When you do your due diligence, anything you fail to identify at this stage, which later emerges and impacts your decision-making process, could be extremely expensive. In terms of return on investment, proper structured investment at the start of your process will ensure that your evaluation criteria are formed on solid bedrock, not on shifting sand.

Bank grade due diligence is crucial to understanding how each one of our stakeholders will evaluate, whether that be our commercial funding partners, private investors, valuers and many of the other areas we will look at later on in the process. Once you have systemised your due diligence it will become a relatively swift process to get the core data and initial assessment undertaken. You may eventually be able to get your initial due diligence concluded within a matter of hours – however, as you start your journey in evaluating developments, this may well take several days and with a systemised approach, you will be able to improve on this substantially.

13. AUDIT FILE

A quarter of a century in corporate life, running companies and hundreds of millions of US dollars of global infrastructure, has taught me the powerful lessons of diligence and also record keeping. I have also been a corporate trouble shooter for 20 of those years and have frequently seen how contracts and files are rarely reviewed in the good times, but are always the 'go to' point of information when things come off the rails for various reasons.

Life as a SSAS trustee, being in full control of your personal economy, reminds me of these experiences. Many of you will have heard me talk extensively about due diligence and compliance and one of the core systems you MUST have, in my opinion, is a robust audit file for what you do and the information to establish why and how you do it.

In a SSAS and property context this can be applied in so many essential areas that it is profoundly important to adopt this approach. Areas include:

- HMRC and tax records
- Health & safety on site operations
- SSAS valuations on acquisition of assets
- Legal agreements and reliance data supporting the agreements
- Bank grade due diligence reports

- Capital allowance reports

- Lease documentation

- Condition reports on property at the commencement and completion of all lease periods, as well as interim milestones as required

- External verification and diligence reports with associated professional indemnity cover

- Valuation basis for sale of SSAS assets

- Construction and/or refurbishment process for test and compliance certification

- Structural warranties

- Income and expenditure records

- Bank funding compliance

- Investor compliance

- Planning permission and conditions satisfied

- Investor self-certification of high net worth and sophisticated investor status

- Energy Performance Certificate (EPC)

- Legionella test records

and many more areas.

Maintain and hold your records for the duration of the asset ownership plus at least six years+ in your archives. This will ensure you have all relevant information in your audit file to satisfy tax and HMRC compliance if ever required.

14. LEVERAGE WITH A SSAS

Leverage is the primary route to creating wealth. Without leverage there will be a cap placed on capacity, scale and potential. A SSAS only has three things essentially:

1. An operating license
2. Cash resources
3. Trustee intellect

Leverage that can be deployed can be wide and varied in each of the following areas:

- Time
- Specialist resource
- Intellectual property
- Funds
- People

The primary area of focus for us in this chapter is financial leverage.

It is possible for SSAS pensions to borrow money to provide extra liquidity for any type of investment, including for a property purchase. The borrowing does not have to be secured, although a high street bank is unlikely to offer an unsecured loan to a pension scheme.

A SSAS is limited to borrowing only up to 50% of the net value of the scheme assets at the point a mortgage is taken out. Leverage usually comes in the form of debt and can be from the following sources:

- High street banks
- Development finance
- Other SSAS
- Private capital
- Your own resources

The 50% of net assets limitation is measured at the point of taking out the loan or mortgage. A fall in the value of the pension fund over time may mean that at certain points during the lifetime of the loan, this 50% limit is technically exceeded. However, provided no additional borrowing is taken out, the limit will not be judged to have been breached the rules.

If the 50% limit is exceeded for example, where a SSAS takes out additional borrowing, the excess is treated as a scheme chargeable payment, subject to a penalty tax charge.

For example:

A SSAS is acquiring a commercial property with an offer accepted of £375,000 and could therefore secure a 50% loan to value (on the SSAS fund value) from a bank.

The SSAS currently has no debt and has a value of £750,000.

In securing a SSAS mortgage, the bank would take a first legal charge, at land registry, on the property.

Technically the SSAS can borrow up to 50% of the fund value: £750,000 x 50% = £375,000 so has sufficient funds to acquire the asset with 100% leverage. I say 'technically' as with many things, the simplicity belies the actual reality for a number of reasons:

- The SSAS will have costs including professional fees etc so the cost of purchase will be higher than the agreed purchase price
- It is very doubtful that a bank would loan 100% loan to cost

The way this transaction may happen, in simple terms and excluding fees etc, would be that the bank would loan say 70% loan to value on the agreed purchase price of £375,000 which would be a mortgage of £262,500 and the SSAS would use £112,500 of its cash.

The £262,500 leverage within the SSAS would still be well within the 50% limit of its £750,000 valuation and therefore would be allowable.

This example is for illustration purposes only to demonstrate how the moving parts operate and what is in the art of the possible - you should be acutely aware that whilst leverage is extremely powerful, it can also harbour risks for the unwary.

Where could you gain financial leverage for your SSAS? There are a number of places, as long as they are from unconnected sources, which simply put means that they are not connected to the trustees by way of business or blood. Examples include:

- Another SSAS
- Private investor
- Main high street bank
- Commercial development finance
- Bridge finance
- Family office

Traditional leverage route, via banks and development funders, is certainly possible with many funders able to lend to a SSAS. It would be fair to say that as the popularity and understanding of SSAS comes to the mainstream, demand for SSAS funding will increase and more lenders will begin to serve this market.

Solid preparation with a great broker is always time well spent. Your details, structure and evidence should be well laid out, and professionally presented, and a great broker will spend the time with you to enable this to be presented, in the correct manner, for maximum attractiveness and appeal to funders.

Funders evaluating your proposal will undertake the requisite diligence expected on any commercial acquisition. Sitting right at the heart of this will be the security being provided which will usually be the property you are acquiring, hence the valuation process will be crucial. See the chapter of RICS Red book Valuation.

There will be certain nuances that SSAS funding may highlight which may not be immediately apparent, although they all apply irrespective who the funder is lending to. These include:

- Debt service cover ratio (DSCR)
- Occupation levels
- Sound legal title for the property
- Risk of contamination/environmental damage/Japanese Knotweed/petrol stations etc
- Difficult to insure
- Acquisition of onerous leasehold interest
- High ground rent
- High service charge

- A property is adjacent to other property owned by a connected party
- Possible breaches of pensions legislation requirements or the SSAS trust deed and rules

From a process perspective, below are a list of some of the additional elements of diligence and scrutiny that may be required:

- **Details of Acquisition:** property type, address, description, lease, development proposals, how the purchase is to be funded and contact details of the vendor, tenants, solicitor, insurance details and a VAT indemnity form
- **Borrowing Schedule:** detailing the lender, documentation and the borrowing and repayment terms
- **Surveyor's Report:** RICS Red Book, Structural Survey, Monitoring Surveyors report
- **Borrowing Agreement:** Offer/Facility Letter/ Mortgage Agreement or Legal Charge
- **Transfer/Conveyance Documentation:** via conveyancing solicitor
- **Professional Adviser Appointment Letters**
- **Lease Agreement(s):** comprehensive schedule
- **Insurance:** cover note from exchange
- **Desktop Environmental Report**
- **Energy Performance of Buildings Regulations Compliance**
- **Control of Asbestos at Work Regulations 2012 Compliance**
- **VAT:** registration details and indemnity requirements

- **Specialist Reports:** as required to address any identified risks encountered

One concern I want readers to understand is the potential of stranded assets in their SSAS. By this I mean commercial property assets which have been secured for the purpose of creating a yield with capital growth, possibly over the long term. One of the advantages of a SSAS is that often Trustees have the ability to acquire a property in cash without leverage, quickly and then can refinance a little later down the line.

If leverage via bank finance is expected to materialise later, we must start with the end in mind and ensure that as far as we can, that finance will be available.

I want you to be aware that leverage is available for a SSAS, however it is much more difficult than in a traditional, limited company environment, as there are fewer funders available as it is fairly nascent on any scale and therefore remains niche.

Concern would be particularly for smaller commercial units held in the SSAS where funders may impose a minimum funding level, due to the additional administration required, and differing security levels.

This security would always include asset backed first charge at land registry, but probably not a debenture on a trust, which would not be available, and no personal guarantees on trustees either. Hence funders are few and far between.

Some lenders have placed minimum lending levels in recent times (at the time of writing) of £300k - 500k which would leave asset lending lower than these levels hard to find. The consequence could be stranded assets in the SSAS, fully funded in cash with no leverage from banks.

Is this a bad thing? Well, it depends on your perspective. With no cost of funds, the SSAS would have a greater net yield, which is positive. If the SSAS strategy is to expand rapidly by leveraging and redeploying cash again and again, then this would place severe restrictions on this roll out of further assets.

Retail and high street assets are going through a huge amount of change in recent years, given the exponential increase in on-line shopping as well as the Covid-19 effects. Some funders are restricting lending in the retail space, so proceed with caution and ensure that funding lines are available to you with your strategy. Knowing this early in your strategy may mean the acquisition is still viable but may need to be structured in a different way, such as in a limited company.

Future growth in SSAS awareness and popularity will inevitably draw a greater demand for bank finance and therefore new lenders and products to this market. Create a great relationship with your broker and monitor this position vigilantly.

So, in summary, leveraged bank funding is available but as ever comes with an ever-moving array of products. The relatively low demand for borrowing on SSAS held assets means a current low supply of funding products at present, but this will change over time. Careful consideration of your strategy and structuring is essential to ensure your strategy and its returns are not stalled by stranded cash, unnecessarily.

15. RICS RED BOOK VALUATION

As we discussed earlier in the book, when you are using your SSAS or engaging with someone else's SSAS, a valuation will be required to support the property valuation to the trustees and corporate trustee.

What is a valuation report? The valuation report is governed by strict standards from the Royal Institute of Chartered Surveyors (RICS). They have particular standards referred to as a Red Book Valuation and the purpose of these standards are to ensure that valuations produced by RICS members achieve high standards of integrity, clarity and objectivity and are reported in accordance with a recognised basis, appropriate for the purpose.

The standards define:

1. Criteria used to establish whether members are appropriately qualified

2. Steps necessary to deal with any actual perceived threat to their independence and objectivity

3. Matters to be addressed when agreeing conditions of engagement

4. Basis of valuation, assumptions and material considerations must be taken into account when preparing a valuation

5. Minimum reporting standards

6. Matters that shall be disclosed when valuations may be relied upon by third parties

The RICS Red Book Valuation is a highly governed document undertaken by professionals.

Who relies on the Red Book Valuation? You will rely to a certain extent on the Red Book Valuation and your private investors may have a significant interest. It is primarily your commercial funder who will be interested in the Red Book Valuation. This will be a critical gateway and component of their bank grade due diligence, which they will be required to take to their internal credit committee, to get sign off for your final credit approved offer.

The common challenges that are experienced by many developers are surprises with down valuations. What exactly is a down valuation? Well simply put, it is when the valuer says that the development economics are less than you had envisaged. This may be due to:

- Reduced GDV
- Increased construction costs expected
- Additional professional fees anticipated
- Additional time required
- Additional contingency required
- Property value less than expected

Whilst these are difficult situations, certain measures can be taken to improve your due diligence early in the process and to walk a mile in the valuer's shoes to enable a closer correlation later, during your development's timeline, so that you are more aligned with what the funder is likely to lend, based on the valuation results.

Any significant down valuation will be potentially highly disruptive to your development. At a worst case, the valuation may spell doom for the project and you will lose any costs or seed capital if you cannot find somebody else who may be interested in that development.

Therefore, it makes business sense to invest a significant amount of time to equip yourself with the knowledge and skills to incorporate the systematic process and techniques of a Red Book Valuation, in your development's due diligence. The power of anticipation at work!

If there is a down valuation, and therefore less funds will be loaned by the commercial funder, then it will be your capital, or your private investor's capital, which makes up the rest. Hence a down valuation will mean an increased requirement in private capital and therefore, assuming profitability remains the same, this will correlate to a reduction in return on capital employed on the private investor's returns.

What would a RICS Red Book Valuation have within its contents?

1. Executive summary. This will give an outline of the findings at a high level and enable you to quickly capture the essence of the document

2. Instructions and terms of reference. This will outline the specific instructions that an RICS surveyor is working under, the background of the appointment and the purpose

3. Property statutory and legal aspects. This will cover all areas such as location, situation, any description on the property, the condition of the property, town planning and its current situation, taxation, environmental impact and consideration, any statutory matters, tenure and condition of commercial leases and the occupational lease arrangements

4. Development proposals. This would give a detailed description of the intentions of the developer and their proposed development plans with regards to this site. The proposed construction and accommodation that is being provided, whether that be new homes, new-build apartments or refurbished apartments etc. The construction proposal will include the type of construction, the method, the duration, how the construction is going to be procured, the proposed specification of the final units, its intended purpose and any levies - which would be Section 106, CIL agreements, Affordable Homes etc

5. Market commentary. This would include a market overview of the national markets, of the local market, any information from the RICS housing market surveys and any recent comparable sales transactions of similar properties in a similar area, probably within a 0.5 – 1 km radius

6. The valuation. This will be at a number of levels. This will look at the valuation considerations that are being taken into account, the approach to how the valuation is being undertaken, any residual appraisals, the valuation itself and also, for insurance purposes, the reinstatement costs of the property

7. Security for the loan. This will give an overview as to how appropriate the property will be as loan security for your commercial lender

8. Any general assumptions and conditions for the valuations.

9. Detailed set of appendices which will include the letter of instruction, any detail of layouts, floor plans, elevations, any background residential information that was being relied upon, the developer valuation, development valuation and then a detailed

assessment of the basis of the valuation and its assumptions

As you can see, this is a detailed report and may be anywhere from 50 to 100 pages long, even longer on larger developments.

Anybody can instruct an RICS valuation report as long as they can provide the access to the property. Predominantly the three parties that would instruct would be yourself as a developer, your funder and possibly your private investor. However, your private investor may be happy to rely on your developer's valuation or a transparent sight of the funder's Red Book valuation.

As a developer, whether you have instructed an RICS valuation or not, the lender will always want to instruct one themselves. The RICS valuation must be produced under the instruction of the funder and addressed to the funder. In certain cases, the funder may allow an existing RICS valuation report to be re-directed in the name of the funder. However, this is rare, and most credit committees would insist on a brand-new instruction.

As a developer, that leaves a decision to be made very early on, on whether to invest in a valuation, knowing full well that a further valuation will be required by your chosen funder and possibly a further valuation from your mezzanine funder if you choose that route also. One would hope your commercial broker can make arrangements whereby your mezzanine funder would be content to stand by your senior debt funder's RICS valuation. However, again a revised fee may be required for a rewrite/re-instruction of that valuation in the name of the mezzanine funder.

The strong inference here is to move swiftly in deciding the senior debt funder you wish to proceed with as early as your due diligence allows.

The valuation report is undertaken by an RICS surveyor which can be a local regional practice or can be one of the larger national practices. Each party will have a different level of professional indemnity cover, which is an important criteria of the evaluation of the lender in selecting their surveyors. The commercial funders will typically have a panel of RICS surveyors to choose from - typically, between three and five. You will have the choice in discussions with your funder and broker, to select which surveyor from the commercial funder's surveying panel you wish to instruct.

The instruction will always come from the lender and in doing so the report will be addressed back to the lender. You should expect that the developer will be responsible for paying for the valuation report and this would usually happen at the time of instruction, rather than at the time that the lending facility is approved and drawn down. This will have an impact on your cash flow and should be factored in on day one of your due diligence. Typical RICS Red Book valuation reports can vary from £1,500 up to £10,000 and can go much higher on larger developments - all figures excluding VAT. The range will be dependent on where in the country this is instructed, the type of practice, the amount of professional indemnity insurance requested, the scale, size and complexity of the scheme involved.

In the appraisal summary, often in the appendices, the scheme will have the computations recorded. These elements which will be assessed include:

- Sales valuation units
- Cost per square foot
- Unit price gross sales
- Ground rents

- Ancillary - parking and storage areas as examples
- Net expected realisation

There will then be a detailed assessment of the outlay costs, which will include:

- Acquisition costs
- Stamp duty
- Agent fees
- Legal fees
- Construction costs
- Contingency assessment, frequently between 7.5-15%
- Other construction costs, which may well include items such as utilities

There will be professional fees. These can include:

- Structural engineer
- Quantity surveyor
- Architect
- Project manager
- Mechanical and electrical engineer
- Acoustics
- CDM and Health and Safety
- Marketing and letting costs for the marketing of the units to be sold
- Disposal fees
- Sales agent fees
- Legal fees
- New home warranties

- Show home costs
- EPC costs

There will then be an assessment of funding costs and interest rates for the land, the construction and ultimately provide total funding costs. This will give you a very clear understanding of how the RICS valuer has assessed the development and the funder will take this into account as they provide a final offer 'term sheet' to go to credit.

If these look familiar, then they should! They are all in the simulation of the Red Book valuation in the *Equa*DA.

Take time to look through all of these elements and then review your development analyser and decide if it is comprehensive enough to simulate the Red Book Valuation process.

15.1 Timing

The dilemma for any investor is when to make the instruction for a valuation report, either direct or via your lender. Timing is crucial. It must happen before exchange of contracts, unless you're buying in cash and choose not to have a survey done - which would not be recommended. At the point of exchange, you would want to have absolute clarity on your funder's position. Do not exchange contracts unless you are clear you have all the key components in place to fund the transaction through to completion.

The dilemma for developers is by investing in the valuation too early, you potentially have duplicate costs because your funder will want a valuation report redone later down the process. If you do it too late, you may have abortive costs if the development becomes un-fundable.

One point to make with the RICS Red Book Valuation process is they work off current and historical information only and not future forecast information. While they might note certain trends and observations on how the market may be moving, their reliance data will always be based on historic demonstrable costs that have been realised in the market and not on a future assessment of where the market may or may not be going.

When you are understanding the due diligence of one of your developments, look at how a lender will instruct the valuation and how the valuer will look at that. The valuer has a professional job to do and will be putting his professional indemnity insurance on the line with his report. They will look at it realistically and it will not be a racy valuation. It's important for you to understand that in your due diligence.

You may choose to look at having a range of values on your GDV. We have a:

- Low end – supported by Red Book Valuation
- Medium – midway between low and high
- High end – based on where local agents predict the market might be at point of marketing

The best advice is always to under promise and over deliver!

Note that when you are designing your building there are certain elements in the valuation process that can impact the valuation level of each one of your units. These might include the floor level that the unit is on, the orientation and the aspect of each apartment as an example. Be aware of this at the design stage and you may be able to optimise your scheme.

16. CREATING AND RETAINING VALUE

There are many property investment strategies and each one is designed to bring a different level of benefit and risk profile to the investor - in this case primarily the SSAS Trust.

Your SSAS may have a strategy that encompasses one or a number of the following:

- Long term income stream
- Adding value to refinance and minimise funds retained in property
- Long term capital appreciation
- Retained income in your circular economy – an example would be for a SSAS to own your business premises and it pays a fair commercial rent to your SSAS pension
- Corporation tax or income tax reduction through capital allowances. Note that capital allowances cannot be claimed by a Trust or property held in your SSAS. However, if structured with this is in mind, a property could be acquired using a SSAS to off-set these taxes in part, for many years to come.
- A low cost of capital and recurring funding line

The fundamental principle of most property investment is to add value where possible. Examples of adding value can include, but not be limited to:

- Gaining a change of use through Full Planning Permission
- Gaining a change of use through Permitted Development rights
- Adding leases to previously vacant properties
- Negotiation, restructuring and rebasing commercial leases
- New leases on expiry of old, with better terms and counter party covenant strength
- Develop, extend, refurbish and improve the property

If you are investing in property with your SSAS, take time to consider your strategy. Quite often the best strategies are the ones that create substantial value on the way into the deal, rather than during, or at the end of ownership.

17. YOUR TIME

Of the thousands of SSAS trustees I have met, I have yet to meet one who wants a full-time role managing their SSAS pension. The reality is that we all wear multiple hats to allow us to manage our business, personal and SSAS investment interests, as well as family life.

Of all the commodities, our time is the most valuable. It is the one that we cannot extend but we can leverage it so that we achieve more with other people's expertise and time, rather than ourselves just piling more and more time in. Those results would not be sustainable, and something would give – often breaking relationships and missed opportunities in life.

Your Return on Time Invested (ROTI) is an important consideration, especially given that your SSAS has no personnel apart from its member trustees. In your previous Defined Contribution or Defined Benefit Schemes your time employed was probably very low – mine tended to be 10 minutes glancing at my pension statement once per year and I suspect I am not alone.

Ensure that you factor your time into the equation when planning your overall investment strategy. Your availability of time may well have a fundamental effect on your strategy or, at the very least, choosing how you leverage the expertise of others to help enable and facilitate your investment management.

18. ATTRACTING FUNDS

Raising investment through relationships with SSAS trustees is a skill which needs to be acquired. There are many compliance and governance checks that need to be made within your business to establish the 'if' and the 'how', yet many have achieved this and it has created powerful relationships that often turn into personal friendships which create shared value time and time again, in many forms.

And that is what any relationship should, in my opinion, be based upon.

Creating Shared Value

As with any investment model, strong considerations on governance and compliance are essential. Do not cut corners - take great advice, create compliant systems and know the legal framework which you must remain compliant to. This professional approach should not be feared, but embraced and care, time and attention, as well as investment, will pay a handsome return for all parties. Failure to comply will put you and your investors in harm's way.

18.1 PROMISED Model©

I have managed investor relations within our businesses for many years and have been responsible for well over £20m of private capital fund raising and, through this, have evolved a professional system and approach which has served our organisations well. We created the PROMISED Model© to help others create an operating framework which enables them to become successful in achieving the fund raising they need to meet their objectives.

Here is the outline summary of the PROMISED Model© to help you:

Process: You must have a clear, compliant and identifiable process to engage potential and actual investors. This will be a roadmap, from start to finish, to ensure compliance and auditability at each stage and will enable a very professional and robust investment model for your business.

Returns: Returns come in many forms. Firstly, decide what structure and returns are viable for your fund raise. Then, walk a mile in your potential investor's shoes and understand what they are looking for as a basket of benefits, one of which will be economic. We will discuss these later in this chapter.

Options: You offer debt and I want equity/profit share – end of conversation! However, if you have multiple investment options then we will be having a more detailed conversation as to the most appropriate option for the investor circumstances.

Model: Always have a model – an economic equation that feeds your overall goal and strategy. This can be multiple models – however, having a clear, documented operating system for each is paramount. It will enable each model to evolve and grow momentum, quality, trust, evidence and relationships over time.

Investable: Becoming investable isn't an act, it is inherent in who you are, what you do and how you do it. It is how others see you over time. Being investable is incredibly important and starts by being investable firstly at a personal level, then at a business level. Without achieving these two levels of trust, your specific property investment memorandum will not see the light of day with most investors.

Security: Security comes in all shapes and forms (see specific chapter in the book on Security) and you will need to decide what security your system can offer to meet compliance, availability and appetite from both you and your investor's perspective.

Engagement: Many developers miss the post investment engagement and communications with investors. To investors, this is important. Many investors wish to be kept informed on a regular basis, to understand the progress, to share the passion, learning and understanding of the journey of an investment. We all like to feel valued and appreciated, rather than kept in the dark. Most investors have one thing in common - once the investment concludes, they have to find the next opportunity; could they remain in your investment eco-system and build extended trust over many years?

Draw: Decide how you are going to attract interest for your investment opportunities. Being mindful of compliance on FCA 13/3 etc, how will you market what you do, your track record and create that attraction and draw of interest to your door. This could be through presentations, podcasts, website, interviews, social media etc. You will need to find an array of these 'mini assets' that are congruent to who you are and create a programme of engagement that will assist in meeting your objects.

And finally, don't forget your STORY. Most potential investors want to understand who you are, what you are trying to achieve, your background and experience and what drives you. Find ways to share your bigger 'Why' with people so that they can appreciate your motivation. Do not fear judgement from others – after all, it is your 'Why', is deeply personal and unique to YOU.

As part of our *Equa*Mentorship programme, Nigel Greene and I support and guide people through the process of property, business and life. This frequently involves enabling them to become eminently investable, whilst building systems where raising private finance becomes second nature.

Imagine the growth in your business and the life changing impact in your life if you could raise all the private finance you needed. Drop me a confidential note if you would like to explore this further at mark.stokes@equassas.co.uk.

19. YOUR FUND VALUATION

For most people their pension is the largest 'bank account' they own. It is perhaps surprising that a very small percentage of the population actually know what the value of their pension is. As SSAS trustees we can monitor and measure our funds' performance at frequent intervals and actively engage in its management and determine outcomes.

As Peter Drucker said, "you can't manage what you can't measure".

At the time of starting your SSAS you have a determination of value through the transfer values of current pension schemes or Cash Equivalent Transfer Value (CETV) as it is known. This is a great start and a defining 'line in the sand' you are crossing, of moving from old habits to new dynamic ones of 'self-management'.

The principle of understanding the valuation of your fund, and the forecasting of it moving forward, should never leave your subconscious thought. It is the fundamental to much of the mechanics that enable you to operate a SSAS to its optimum effect.

As well as growing your wealth, there are a few other reasons why technically you will need to understand the net valuation on your fund i.e. the valuation of your fund less all borrowing.

Once you have a SSAS there are five fundamental reasons why you should understand what your fund value is on a regular basis:

1. **Growth:** The growth rate of your Fund – presumably this is one of the core reasons why you are operating your SSAS in the first place!

2. **Maintain:** To enable you to decide what, within your SSAS fund, is working effectively and what requires attention. You may find that certain assets are underperforming and may require disposal in favour of other assets that are working particularly well and requiring additional concentration and investment.

3. **Leverage:** Your SSAS fund can leverage (borrow) up to 50% of the fund value. You should monitor this level from a compliance perspective as well as from an opportunity angle.

4. **Loan Back:** You can loan up to 50% of the fund value to your sponsoring company(s).

5. **Compliance:** Given that punitive tax penalties exist for failure to comply with SSAS rules set out by HMRC, it is important for you to continually assess the above -particularly in relation to points three and four.

6. **Lifetime Allowance:** Each trustee should monitor their fund value, as part of their regular wealth reviews, to measure valuation against their lifetime allowance.

Your SSAS may be structured with anywhere between one and eleven Trustees. Each Trustee has a proportion of the trust fund valuation at any time. Each Trustee has a specific personal requirement for their proportion of that fund long term, which may include providing a pension in later life. It is important that the fund valuation is reported on a regular basis to ensure that this is understood and audited to the satisfaction of each Trustee.

The Trustees, normally via their trust administrator, should ensure that there are financial statements prepared every year, setting out the fund valuation in total and the allocation of the total fund between the members.

The financial statements can take the form of a simple balance sheet, more formal accounts or even audited accounts, depending on the Trustees' requirements.

In between accounting periods for reasons quite often associated with a larger investment, the scheme administrator can commission an ad hoc or informal update at the direction of the Trustees.

20. LEGACY AND THE NEXT GENERATION

CREATING EXTRAORDINARY LEVELS of compounding wealth - that is the true power of a SSAS, taking centre stage right at the very heart of a hugely compelling multi-generational wealth creation juggernaut!

The key is the power of compounding, the snowball effect that happens when your earnings generate even more earnings. You receive interest not only on your original investments, but also on any interest, dividends and capital gains that accumulate - so your money can grow faster and faster as the years roll on.

Why not jump in the car and show your kids your legacy of property – much more powerful than a pension statement!

What better way to show the powerful effects of compounding than planning your legacy whilst your children are growing up?

The word Legacy is huge to many – I also believe the words custodianship are equally powerful. Most of us enjoy not only growing a substantial legacy, but the real joy is nurturing the next generation to become responsible and knowledgeable benefactors of the legacy, as well as the learnings and experience of growing it.

The SSAS pension is a multi-generational, highly tax efficient structure and is an asset which can be inherited and, therefore, kept within the family across generations.

That is why it is often referred to as a 'family pension'.

A SSAS can be a catalyst to a Multi-Generational Family Plan that will work actively in concert with other investments and income sources you may have, providing a balanced and long-term set of principles that will serve your future generations in a supportive and yet protective environment.

If I were to bring just one subject matter into the schooling curriculum it would be compounding, and that is why the word figures so prominently in the title of this book.

To become a SSAS Trustee one has to be 18 years old. To become a shareholder in a limited company you can be any age. We can see here a powerful combination of creating and preserving wealth which can commence at any age and enable the younger generation to benefit and grow up with the powerful combination of property & SSAS in their lives.

My own children were as young as eight when they became shareholders in one of our companies. At that age they were not incredibly knowledgeable about what a shareholder was, however, the objective was to ensure they became more knowledgeable about being a shareholder by the time they become 18 than ever I did when I was 18!

Image turning 18 and having already been a shareholder for over a decade and fully understanding the potential of a SSAS pension – powerful stuff indeed, if nurtured in a responsible manner.

21. BUSINESS BENEFITS OF A SSAS

Beauty is in the eye of the beholder as every one of us will have differing personal and business circumstances. A SSAS invariable can add a huge array of business benefits to your entire business, and indirectly, your personal interests. A few examples include:

- Utilising the General Unallocated Fund – see chapter in my SSAS Pensions book
- Can reduce Corporation Tax every year as contributions are made
- Lend your sponsoring company at low cost of borrowing rate – you choose where you want the value
- Family engagement
- Enhance your security
- Protect the assets within your company with additional security
- Be the bank by lending to others
- Enable wealth creation outside of your SSAS as well as within it – double compound curve
- Received tax free rental income
- No income tax on allowable investments
- Invest in your own company shares
- If selling your company, you keep the assets and the income stream for years

- Aggregation of funds with others
- Increased ability to raise funds within the SSAS and outside
- Provides an enhanced array of options at Trustees and Board of Directors disposal
- Can receive a large pension contribution up to £500k and receive Corporation Tax relief in the current tax year
- Can receive carried forward pension contribution allowances of up to £120k per Director
- Company and personal contributions are deductible against tax
- Can receive pension contributions, with or without cash, from the business
- Can lend to the sponsoring employer
- Can buy your business premises
- Can create multiple options for expansion
- Can borrow money to purchase commercial property
- Can receive rent, tax free, on commercial property
- Purchasing commercial property to be leased back to your business (or third party)
- No capital gains tax due on disposal of investments
- Can resolve auto enrolment issues for business owners
- Can hold all existing pension funds in one place under personal control
- Can reduce pension administration fees
- Can allow more flexible HMRC approved investments than alternatives

- Can increase a pension fund through tax free and compound growth
- Trustees (business owners) can access 100% of the fund at age 55 (may not be tax efficient above 25% though)
- A tax-free lump sum on death before retirement
- Investing in your company by buying an equity stake
- A tax-free lump sum from age 55 on retirement
- Transferring assets from you, or your family, personally ('in-specie' transfers)
- Provides business owners with control and efficiency
- Creates protection of assets outside of the company structure
- Create your own circular economy

This list can provide you with a checklist of potential options that you can consider ensuring your SSAS fits into your overarching strategy to maximum effect.

22. TAX

This book is not a tax manual and nor am I qualified to provide tax advice. However, the tax efficiency of what we do is fundamental to the growth of our SSAS and overall wealth.

Compliance is everything and great advice and counsel from your professionally appointed team will enable you to drive a highly tax efficient and compliant approach, whilst benefitting from many years of compounding.

22.1 STAMP DUTY LAND TAX

Stamp Duty Land Tax is a tax which a SSAS must pay, as with any other commercial property transaction. Most commercial property acquisitions by a SSAS will usually be substantially under £1million, which makes commercial property generally still a tax efficient investment.

As a SSAS will only be acquiring non-residential property, commercial SDLT rates apply. Non-residential SDLT includes:

- Commercial property, for example shops or offices
- Property that isn't suitable to be lived in
- Forests
- Agricultural land that's part of a working farm, or used for agricultural reasons
- Any other land or property that is not part of dwellings,

gardens or grounds
- Six or more residential properties bought in a single transaction

The current rates and bandings for non-residential SDLT at the time of going to print are:

Purchase Price	Stamp Duty
0 – £150,000	0%
£150,001 – £250,000	2%
£250,001 +	5%

Stamp duty is payable on the proportion of the purchase price that falls into each band.

Example 1

Stamp duty on a £450,000 purchase would be calculated as follow:

0% on the first £150,000 = £0

2% on the next £100,000 = £2,000

5% on the final £200,000 = £10,000

Total SDLT = £12,000

Example 2

If you buy a freehold commercial property for £235,000, the SDLT you owe is calculated as follows:

0% on the first £150,000 = £0

2% on the next £85,000 = £1,700

Total SDLT = £1,700

22.2 VAT

VAT is one of the more complex areas of tax and it is important to understand the areas where VAT knowledge is required.

The following are some of the areas you should be aware of and draw them to the attention of your solicitor, accountant and corporate trustee.

VAT on commercial property purchase – in most cases the property may be elected for VAT and therefore the purchase price will have a 20% VAT levied. In certain cases, the property may not be elected for VAT due to aspects of the vendors circumstances. Always ask whether a property is elected for VAT at the time of enquiry.

VAT on conversion to residential purchases – where the intention is to convert the property to residential, a HMRC1614D form can be used to dis-apply VAT on the property purchase price. The complication here is that the acquiring party, the SSAS, cannot own residential property. Detailed discussions with your professional team should be held as to the best structuring of the transaction.

VAT on purchases of services and products – differing levels of VAT apply, depending in intentions or service/product. These vary from non-applicable; zero rated, 5% and 20% depending on the category. Make sure you catalogue all costs to ensure the correct level of reclaim is processed and also that cashflow is accurately calculated.

Recovery of VAT – If the entity is registered for VAT then VAT can be recovered from HMRC. A SSAS can be registered for VAT and interestingly so can an individual property within a SSAS. The process works in a very similar way to usual VAT recovery process within a Limited company environment with either your SSAS corporate trustee or accountant undertaking the process. Your VAT recovery periods are usually 3 months however can be monthly should you wish to preserve cashflow – something we do on many of our developments.

Cashflow impact of VAT – Is VAT a cost?

Well, the answer lies in whether it can be recovered or not – you can see how structuring is so crucial yet again.

Undoubtedly VAT has a cost, even if it can be recovered, as there will be a time period for the VAT recovery, hence there will be an impact of both funding and cashflow.

22.3 CAPITAL GAINS

A SSAS does not pay capital gains tax. No capital gains tax is due on disposal of investments. This means that a property investment can generate substantial returns on top of all the tax relief already available, by also not paying tax on the capital gain once a property is eventually sold. If this is repeated multiple times, over many years, the compounding effect would be very significant indeed, proving just how powerful a SSAS can be in the right hands!

22.4 TAX ON INCOME

A SSAS does not pay tax on income generated on investments. Herein lies yet another layer of massive tax efficiency which will compound over many years, to create yet further return.

22.5 CAPITAL ALLOWANCES

Many listening or reading to this book may be fellow property developers and may have read another of my books 'Commercial to Residential Conversions: The essential manual for property developers'.

One of the very significant advantages that many developers and commercial property investors value are capital allowances.

At this stage I want to be very clear with you that capital allowances are <u>NOT</u> directly applicable to a SSAS, which is already a tax efficient vehicle.

The clue though is in the word 'directly'. We have discussed earlier my passion for creating multiple compounding benefits through the use of a SSAS. Whilst not directly benefitting to the SSAS, a detailed awareness of capital allowances in all their forms are a great example of where additional, and extremely valuable, tax efficiencies can be deployed, within the overall sphere of your personal economy. Having the knowledge of what capital allowances are, and how they can be used, could possibly be one of the determining factors on whether you structure a deal within your SSAS, outside of your SSAS or part within and part outside of your SSAS.

As an additional bonus, you will find this chapter on the more illuminating detail on capital allowances. I hope this will be of particular interest in demonstrating the compounding benefits you can access outside of the SSAS, from strategic considerations deployed in concert <u>with</u> the SSAS.

Capital allowances are a tax relief in lieu of depreciation and are claimed on the cost of plant and machinery existing within a commercial property.

They can significantly reduce tax liability, can sometimes result in a tax rebate and are therefore an important consideration in any property developers' tax planning. Specialist advice from a tax specialist(s) is again crucial in this area and interpreting the tax rules is essential.

It is possible to get tax relief on plant and machinery which can be defined broadly as:

- Heating
- Lighting
- Power Supplies
- Sanitary Ware and kitchen installations
- Carpeting
- Air conditioning

You cannot get tax relief on the following categories of a building:

- Foundations
- Bricks and Walls
- Roof
- Flooring
- Drainage

The summary components of a capital allowances tax relief claim include:

- Capital allowances can only be claimed once in the lifetime of any property – establish if there has been a historical claim
- Allowances can be off set against any income stream
- Sideways loss relief, depending on the structuring of your group of companies
- Holiday lets, serviced accommodation, commercial

properties and certain residential works

- Residential property generally is not allowable
- From 5% - 150% of your capital investment can qualify
- Can include purchase price of property and certain refurbishment costs
- HMRC say 96% of available allowances have NOT been claimed

It is important for the developer to agree the plant value in the building, with the vendor, within two years of purchase:

- Fail and you get nothing
- Endeavour to agree as part of the sale negotiations
- If the vendor will not agree – potential for a Tax Tribunal
- It is a business cost in your accounts, reduces your 'taxable' profit and hence your tax
- Only the 'owner' of the property can claim
- Parties that may claim include:
  - You
  - Your spouse
  - Partnership
  - Limited company you control
- Non-Dwelling premises only

A word of caution for you in this area. Whilst capital allowances can indeed be an incredibly powerful stimulus for your business, as it is intended to be by HMRC, it is also an area where you will require specialist advice. You will require your accountant, a specialist capital allowances surveyor and possibly your solicitor to work closely together.

It is worth noting that you can outsource for advice, but you cannot outsource decision making and the ultimate accountability that comes with that. I strongly suggest that you use your accountant, solicitor and capital allowances surveyor to test each party's opinions and advice to the point where maximum clarity is achieved, before deploying this strategy. Failure to comply, or inaccurate use of the rules, will result in you and your business feeling the full weight of HMRC and their penalty process.

The legal entity that you are claiming capital allowances within can make a substantial difference in the tax efficiency of your strategy.

Certain legal entities are already highly tax efficient and therefore are unable to claim capital allowances. Three examples of this may include:

- Trusts
- Charities
- Local Authorities/Government

Should your strategy and business be seeking the substantial benefits of capital allowances, you can certainly apply this knowledge when approaching and acquiring land, and commercial property opportunities, by understanding what legal entity the property is currently owned in which potentially could result in the most commercially beneficial advantage for you. A cautionary note would be to consider the lifetime of the ownership of the assets as previous owners could have claimed capital allowances and they can only be claimed ONCE.

Experience has generally shown that if your strategy is 'buy, develop and sell' then the C3 use class apartments that you are creating would be held as 'stock' on the balance sheet in your SPV accounts, for a relatively short period of time, and therefore would not be eligible under HMRC rules for capital allowances.

Should your strategy be 'buy, develop, hold' then the apartments would be held as fixed assets on the balance sheet of your company and therefore capital allowances may well be something you should consider.

Once again, we see that the phrase 'start with the end in mind' will pay enormous dividends by ensuring you establish the correct structure and approach to your business interests. In identifying the type of property you are searching for, and your intended purpose for that property, you will be able to incorporate the most appropriate advice from your professional team and ensure maximum efficiency and compliance over the term of your business interests.

There are numerous tax efficient allowances which you might consider with your specialist tax team, some of these include:

1. **Capital Allowances:** as discussed earlier in the chapter

2. **Enhanced Capital Allowances:** The Enhanced Capital Allowance (ECA) energy scheme aims to encourage businesses to invest in certain energy saving technologies. The ECA energy scheme lets your business claim 100% first year tax relief on investments in qualifying technologies and products. This means you can write off (i.e. deduct) the whole cost, or up to the published claim value of buying the energy-saving product, against your taxable profits in the year of purchase. ECA's bring forward tax relief so that you can set it against profits from a period earlier than would otherwise be the case

3. **Land Remediation Relief:** Land Remediation Relief is a

relief from corporation tax only. It provides a deduction of 100% plus an additional deduction of 50%, for qualifying expenditure incurred by companies in cleaning up land acquired from a third party in a contaminated state. Land Remediation Relief can enable up to 150% tax relief under certain circumstances - it pays to be informed! Land or buildings are in a contaminated state if there is contamination present as a result of industrial activity such that:

- It is causing relevant harm.
- There is a serious possibility that it could cause relevant harm.
- It is causing, or there is a serious possibility that it could cause, significant pollution in the groundwater, streams, rivers or coastal waters

'Relevant harm' includes significant adverse impact on the health of humans, animals or damage to buildings that has a real impact on the way the building is used.

Qualifying expenditure includes the cost of establishing the level of contamination, removing the contamination or containing it so that the possibility of relevant harm is removed. There is, however, no relief if the remediation work is not carried out.

Land Remediation Relief is available for both capital and revenue expenditure. However, the company must elect, within two years of the end of the accounting period in which the expenditure is incurred, to treat qualifying capital expenditure as a deduction in computing taxable profits.

In addition to the deduction for the cost of the land

remediation, the company can claim an additional deduction in computing its taxable profits. This additional deduction is 50% of the qualifying expenditure. A company can claim this additional deduction at any time within the general time limit for claims under Corporation Tax Self-Assessment. HMRC does not specify any particular form for the claim. A computation reflecting the claim and submitted in time is sufficient. The 50% additional relief is given in the same period as the actual expenditure is charged to the profit and loss account.

I hope you enjoyed that exert from my other book and it has helped trigger some thoughts on how this specialist knowledge may be able to assist your wider economic interests in property. For instance, if you are investing in a commercial property in one of your other legal entities, using funds from a loan back as an example, then the knowledge of the power of capital allowances may well save you a very substantial amount of tax in the future.

Lateral thinking is extremely powerful. Your SSAS is NOT an isolated asset, it is one of possibly many parts of your personal wealth economy and there is no reason why you cannot look at how they interact with each other and serve your wider objectives - as long as each legal entity, including your SSAS Trust, acts with the correct governance, compliance and probity within each legal entity.

22.6 LIFETIME ALLOWANCE

The Lifetime Allowance is a limit on the amount of pension benefit that each individual can draw from pension schemes and can be paid without triggering an extra tax charge, including lump sums or retirement income.

In tax year 2020/21, the Lifetime Allowance is £1,073,100 and it is likely to increase in line with Consumer Price Index inflationary levels at the end of each tax year. This is something to keep an eye out for each year in the Chancellor of the Exchequer's Budget speech!

The likelihood of you reaching your Lifetime Allowance will depend on a number of factors including:

- Level of contributions into your pension to-date
- Level of contributions into the pension in the future
- Growth rate of pension fund
- Investment strategy
- Duration of pension

While many people may initially feel they are not affected by the Lifetime Allowance, you should take action if the value of your pension benefits is approaching, or likely to approach, this limit. If you are younger, you never know how successful your strategies may be in the coming decades!

As pensions are normally a long-term commitment, what might appear a relatively small amount today could exceed the Lifetime Allowance by the time you want to take your benefits – particularly if you have taken the decision to have a SSAS and have operated it wisely and successfully!

It may be necessary to take your pension early or stop contributing to the scheme/plan, even though you have not retired, to avoid your benefits exceeding the Lifetime Allowance. The test for the Lifetime Allowance is done each time you access a pension benefit.

The Lifetime Allowance was introduced in 2006 and in subsequent years, when it has been reduced. Following pension reforms, those with benefits valued in excess of the Lifetime Allowance have been able to apply for 'protection' to protect the value of benefits they have built up, and future benefits that may accrue, from tax charges.

These protections include:

- Primary protection
- Enhanced protection
- Fixed protection
- Individual protection

Each have different conditions attached to them.

22.7 SSAS TAX CASE STUDY: SHAZ NAWAZ - How to use a SSAS to extract money and save tax

Many of you operating as a limited company might be in the higher rate tax bracket for your personal income tax. The challenge is always to extract money from your company without incurring a huge tax burden and there are several strategies that will help you with tax-efficiency. Here is one which uses SSAS.

Let us look at the case of Sarah, who is the director and shareholder of X Ltd. She is already a higher rate taxpayer and she wants an additional sum from the company of £40,000, net of income tax.

Well, to start with, let us look at the maths. If she were to pay herself a dividend then once she's taken into account the income tax on dividend income (32.5% for someone who is already a higher rate tax payer) she would have to receive a dividend of £59,259 in order to get £40,000 in her hands. The company should have pre-tax profits of £73,159 (or distributable reserves) on which it will pay Corporation Tax at 19%.

So, what if you could extract £40,000 from the pre-tax profits (reducing the Corporation Tax payable), without incurring a massive burden in personal income tax?

Suppose the company contributes to a SSAS on Sarah's behalf as her employer - the annual maximum is £40,000. The contribution will qualify for Corporation Tax relief (if it satisfies the rule of being wholly and exclusively for the benefit of the business - which for business owners or key employees it should usually be the case). So, the tax relief will be £7,600 and the company pays Corporation Tax on £73,159 - £40,000 - £7,600 = £25,559 instead of on £73,159.

There is no taxable benefit-in kind to Sarah as an employee - as long as the company's contribution is within the annual limit - and no income tax payable on investments within the scheme, nor any Capital Gains Tax on disposals. Sarah will get a tax-free lump sum of 25% at 55 years of age plus a pension. The company can make further contributions each year and she can also make contributions from her own income, subject to the £40,000 limit, plus the lifetime pension allowance.

How does she get the benefit of the extra £40,000 as we said at the beginning? Well, the short answer is that she does not get it as a payment straight away. What she does get is an investment in her future income position, via a pension, which she would otherwise have to fund from her own income.

The SSAS is a form of trust and it is usual for the 'members' to be trustees themselves (plus ideally a professional pension trustee). Sarah will retain a considerable measure of control. It is also possible for a connected company to take a 50% loan back from the SSAS, thus avoiding the need to approach third party lenders.

Any assets passing into the SSAS, whether from the company or from Sarah herself, will be trust assets. Any capital growth that takes place within the trust are not within either the company or Sarah's personal estate, so there are savings for Inheritance Tax as well. Sarah can draw down benefits from age 55 (or earlier if she is in ill-health) and if she dies before taking her full benefits, then, as with most pension trusts, the benefits will be available to her nominated beneficiaries - but still outside Sarah's personal estate for Inheritance Tax (IHT) purposes.

One additional benefit is that these assets are now held outside the company so are not at risk from liability for the company's debts.

So that is a fairly simple example. Now let me show you how else you could use this.

Imran originally purchased offices to use for his business, buying jointly with a partner for £225,000 ten years ago. The market value has grown to £325,000, and the premises are not subject to mortgage, nor opted to tax for VAT.

Imran's key objectives are much the same as Sarah's:

- Minimise personal income tax
- Reduce CGT
- Reduce IHT
- Plan for future retirement
- Grow the assets in the pot
- Safeguard assets by holding them outside a limited company

The first step is to sell the premises to the trading company (the trading business). Of course, Imran and his partner must pay CGT on the chargeable gain and the limited company would pay SDLT, but this is a relatively minor outlay when set against the ultimate tax savings. Had the property been VAT-opted, then the limited company would also have had to pay VAT on the purchase price.

The company now owns a property worth £375,000 and instead of the purchase price being paid out there and then, it remained in the accounts as a director's loan.

The next step is for the company to sell the property to the SSAS, the members of whom are Imran and his partner - this is by way of transfer at market value. You can avoid paying SDLT twice by using the sub-sale relief. I suggest you seek advice on this matter so that the transaction is carried out properly in line with tax guidance. The SSAS then immediately leases the property to the trading company.

We now have the following taxation advantages:

- The company pays rent, so this is a deductible expense for computing the company's taxable profit (so a reduction in Corporation Tax)
- The company maintains the property and pays for insurance, which is also deductible for Corporation Tax, and means that the SSAS does not have to pay for this
- The SSAS does not pay tax on the rent received (which grows the investment quicker within the SSAS)
- The property is secure in the SSAS and cannot be liable for the company's debts
- Future capital appreciation is in SSAS, so no CGT
- The value of the property is removed from the purchasers' personal estates and is no longer a company asset which inflates the value of the shares, so will not be taken into account for IHT

- The SSAS is providing security for the future in a tax-efficient way

To give you an idea of immediate savings, if the rent is £37,500 per annum and for 10 years is paid to the SSAS, this is tax-free income of £375,000. If this had been paid to Imran and his partner, then after deduction of tax, (assuming no change in income tax rates) this would have been £225,000. So that's £150,000 tax saving.

The £375,000 remaining outstanding on the director's loan would attract personal income tax at 32.5% if it were paid out in dividends. That is £121,875 tax saving.

The Corporation Tax saving on the £375,000 contribution to the SSAS is £71,250 (at 19%).

So total tax saved is £150,000 + £121,875 + £71,250 = £343,125.

To achieve this, Imran and his partner had to pay the CGT on the net gain when the property was transferred to the limited company (at 20% = £25,200) plus the SDLT (£8,250). There may be relief available for SDLT on transfer to the SSAS, so this will not have to be paid twice as highlighted earlier.

Net tax savings £309,675!

That's not taking into account the investment power of the SSAS using the £37,500 annual rent, the tax-efficient and flexible ways in which the pension provision can be paid out to you, and the notional potential savings in IHT (plus the personal security of having your retirement provided for). Plus, if you are a property developer and use the 50% loan back option, the return on investment is even greater.

As an accountant, I am all for the proactive approach. My practice,

Entrust Property Tax Experts, based in Peterborough, provides all the usual accountancy services but what my team and I really aim for is to help our clients be the best that they wish to be, in terms of business success, maximising profits and enjoying their chosen work-life balance, whilst minimising the burden of tax. I emphasise that the tax-planning strategies we recommend will all be entirely legal. No tax-planning is entirely without the risk of challenge by HMRC, but part of our service is to explain how this might arise and how the challenge can be successfully met.

You will also see from the above that I can bring my own experience to the table, both as a successful business-owner and as a taxpayer, as well as that of a professional adviser. In recent years I have established a keen interest in tax-planning for property-related issues.

23. BANKING

At first glance, it may not seem that banking has much to do with Property and SSAS but on further analysis it has everything to do with it. Some of the most frequent questions I get asked within SSAS Alliance are related to the protection of cash deposits in the bank. Given that SSAS fund values, in our nationwide annual SSAS Alliance Survey, have consistently shown average valuations of £350,000 plus, it is the right question to ask as part of your investment philosophy on what protection and return your cash will receive, whilst held in the SSAS bank account.

23.1 THE FINANCIAL SERVICES COMPENSATION SCHEME (FSCS)

The Financial Services Compensation Scheme (FSCS) is the UK's statutory deposit insurance and investors compensation scheme for customers of authorised financial services firms. The FSCS is an operationally independent body, set up under the Financial Services and Markets Act 2000 (FSMA), and funded by a levy on authorised financial services firms. The scheme rules of the FSCS are made by the Financial Conduct Authority (FCA)

FSCS is free to consumers and, since 2001, has helped more than 4.5 million people and paid out more than £26 billion.

In 2008/09 the FSCS made payments totalling nearly £20 billion to protect consumers from bank and building society failures, with the cost of Bradford & Bingley's eventual failure resulting in payments of £15.75 billion.

Mark Neale, Chief Executive of FSCS in 2017 said "Public trust in the banking system is essential for the economy to function. FSCS will continue to make improvements to our systems so we are ready to respond if another major failure should occur. Consumers should be reassured that in the event of a future failure, FSCS will protect them and ensure that they automatically receive their money back in seven days or fewer."

FSCS protects your money up to £85,000 for all banks, building societies and credit unions that are authorised by the Prudential Regulation Authority (PRA) and the Financial Conduct Authority (FCA). It is important to understand eligibility criteria that apply, however, generally it protects individuals and most businesses, and this also covers SSAS Trust bank accounts.

If you hold money with a UK-authorised bank, building society or credit union that fails, the FSCS automatically compensate you for your loss up to certain exposure limits. These are:

- up to £85,000 per eligible person, per bank, building society or credit union.
- up to £170,000 for joint accounts.

It protects up to £85,000 of savings per individual, per financial institution (not just per bank), and also covers mortgages, insurance and investments.

The FSCS protects deposits made with high street banks, building societies and credit unions.

If your provider collapses, you will receive compensation for deposits of up to £85,000. If you hold a joint account, you could receive compensation of up to £170,000.

You get protection for up to £85,000 for each institution you make a deposit with.

For example, you might deposit £130,000 at a single bank and it later collapses. You would only receive £85,000 in compensation from the FSCS.

You might eventually get the other £45,000 back through various claims routes, or this may be unrecoverable.

Due to the ceiling to this support, many deem it wise to hold £85,000 with one bank and any additional cash reserves with another provider with FSCS protection.

In this scenario with £145,000 placing £85,000 in one bank account and the additional £45,000 with another provider, you would receive compensation for £145,000 in total should, in the unlikely event, both banks fail.

There may be some products which aren't protected by the FSCS. Providers will be able to tell you if the scheme covers their accounts. If you are at all in doubt that this protection applies to any account you open, ask the provider.

Banks are regulated by the Financial Conduct Authority (FCA) which gives banks, building societies, and other financial firms authorisation to operate.

However, some banks are part of a larger banking group. Each bank might be operating under one group authorisation from the FCA.

This means that you could only get compensation for up to £85,000 across all accounts you hold within the group.

Say that you hold £50,000 with one bank within a group and

£50,000 with another. If both collapsed, you'd only get £85,000 back in compensation in total from the FSCS.

If each bank within a group has its own separate FCA authorisation, you're covered for up to £85,000 with each bank. In the above example, you'd get your entire £100,000 back if both banks had their own authorisation and both failed.

If you have a lot of money stored in bank accounts, it's important that you check this. You need to know that your money will be fully protected by the FSCS in a worst-case scenario.

Some investments are also covered by the FSCS, up to a limit of £50,000.

This protection only applies when a provider fails and cannot return your money to you. This does not apply if you have lost money through your investments of course!

Investing always comes with risks. So, if you've lost money because your investments have lost value, you cannot make a claim. This is the case even if you have invested money in a company that collapses. If any of your shares become worthless, you will not get any compensation from the scheme.

Stocks and Shares ISAs might be eligible for compensation of up to £85,000. However, this depends on your provider and the contract between you and them. The rules get complicated here, so it's best to ask providers what cover you would receive from the FSCS.

The FSCS may protect certain qualifying temporary high balances up to £1 million for up to twelve months from when the amount was first deposited. Below is an exert from the FSCS (www.fscs.org.uk) website on these scenarios.

Temporary high balances

FSCS protects temporary high balances in your bank account of up to £1million for up to twelve months. The protection begins from the date the temporary high balance is credited to an individual depositor's account, or to a client's account on an individual's behalf. This date may be earlier than the date the temporary high balance was credited to your account with the failed firm.

Certain life events could have caused a temporary high balance in your bank account, including:

- Real estate transactions (property purchase, sale proceeds, equity release - relating to your main residence only).
- Benefits payable under an insurance policy
- Personal injury compensation (unlimited amount)
- Disability or incapacity (state benefits)
- Claim for compensation for wrongful conviction
- Claim for compensation for unfair dismissal
- Redundancy (voluntary or compulsory)
- Marriage or civil partnership
- Divorce or dissolution of their civil partnership
- Benefits payable on retirement
- Benefits payable on death
- A claim for compensation in respect of a person's death
- Inheritance
- Proceeds of a deceased's estate held by their personal representative

To prove you've held a temporary high balance the FSCS ask for proof, which could include (but not be limited to) the following:

- A property sale receipt or agreement
- A court judgement
- A will
- A letter from an insurer regarding an insurance pay-out
- A letter from a lawyer, conveyancer, mortgage provider, former employer, pension trustees
- Court orders
- Social security statements
- Probate/letters of administration
- Death/marriage certificate
- Land register and HMRC records

This list is not exhaustive, and the evidence required will depend on the life event of your individual circumstances. If you provide the relevant supporting evidence, the FSCS will provide compensation within three months.

23.2 ALTERNATIVE CASH MANAGEMENT STRATEGIES

Depending on your strategy you may have funds sat in cash in your SSAS bank account for some time. Some trustees find that there is a small part of their funds left in the account not working for them for a lengthy period of time. If this were a few thousand pounds to a few tens of thousands, that money is eroding over time against inflation.

There are alternative cash management strategies that can be used rather than leaving funds to languish in the bank account. Opening multiple bank accounts to benefit from ever changing rates is impractical and far too time consuming.

These maybe in a liquid or semi-liquid state whereby the funds are available at short notice and at least earn more interest than they otherwise would.

Alternative cash management organisations offer a service where they have the relationships with fund managers, banks, savings platforms etc and through your established account they draw upon economies of scale and open access to products in the market that may be otherwise inaccessible.

23.3 OPERATIONAL BANK ACCOUNT

As we have discussed previously, there are many good reasons for having multiple bank accounts for your SSAS and indeed many areas of your business and personal interests.

Have a discussion with your corporate trustee to consider if you should have control of a day-to-day operational bank account to pay sundry expenses such as utility bills and agent fees etc. This can save a lot of time and enable the corporate trustee to focus resources on more value-added activities.

However, having cash sat in any bank account is not necessarily the best use of optimising funds from an investment perspective.

At this stage, I would say that being sat in cash for certain periods of time may be a crucial and enabling part of your strategy. It all depends whether you are approaching this to maximise returns in the short-term, month by month, or playing a long term of waiting for great opportunities at very short notice. A few examples of this might include:

- Auction Property acquisition - there can be some great

opportunities available through the auction process. The speed of the auction process with typically four weeks to review the auction lots and 21-28 days to legally complete, post successful auction, means that those with cash can certainly gain an advantage through speed, less dependency in the buying process and reduction in costs. For larger purchases bridge finance may be used, in conjunction with cash, to also enable swift transaction efficiency. Other advantageous auction scenarios could be to acquire pre auction or post auction on unsuccessful lots

- Buying from banks - properties in receivership are often sold through the banks and they often have a policy where no offers are accepted but it is almost a 'first past the post' system of getting to legal completion
- Waiting for the market to correct in times of volatility and overheating
- Period of absence, illness or time when concentration may not be at its highest

23.4 SPECIAL PURPOSE VEHICLE BANK ACCOUNTS

SPV's are a term often banded about by property developers and, in reality, it is a separate legal entity, almost always a limited company established for the purpose of doing one thing, such as a property development which is being acquired, developed and sold.

There could be a number of reasons why a separate company would need to be established for this including:

- Different shareholding structure
- Separation from other assets
- Lending banks prefer no previous trading issues

- The business can be closed in a controlled manner at the end of its useful life

Whilst not a necessity, it would be good practice to establish a separate bank account for each SPV to maintain control and governance, especially if a different shareholding structure prevailed. An SPV bank account is no different to any other bank account and is set up in the usual way.

24. INSURANCE

Having a SSAS does bring home the responsibility (and opportunity) we have in managing our pension. In many property strategies we are almost always steered by the bank and their requirements for minimum insurance provisions, and indeed this can also be true for a SSAS where leverage is utilised. However, given the availability of cash, more properties are actually being bought in cash without bank debt, or maybe because of third party unconnected loans and loan backs in limited companies being used.

So, given this absence in bank oversight we, as trustees, are required to find our own way to ensure the correct insurance is in place. For this we will need to engage ideally with an appropriate insurance broker as well as our corporate trustee. It is worth repeating again that different corporate trustees will have differing mandates, so make sure you have one that has the right level of enablement to suit your strategy.

Insurance is a specialist area and will certainly be a requirement to one degree or another, based on:

- Business owner
- Developer
- Strategy obligations
- Senior debt provider
- Private investor lenders
- SSAS trustee policy

A detailed understanding of your insurance strategy and structure is where an insurance broker will serve your SSAS and business well as a key part of your professional team.

Some of the levels of insurance that you will need to consider for your business may include:

- Business insurance
- Property insurance - buildings and contents insurance
- Joint names policy
- Contractors all-risk
- Professional indemnity
- Key man insurance
- Public liability
- Employers' liability

There are many variant themes of insurance and your specific strategy must be discussed openly with your insurance broker to ensure you have the correct cover required.

You must always insure the property you are purchasing at the point of exchange. At exchange, you're legally obliged to purchase the building at a period of time in the future (stated in the exchange contract). As mentioned earlier, should that building burn down between the point which you have exchanged and your specific completion date, you will still have to complete on the purchase - therefore it is vital that full insurance is in place at the point of exchange.

Engagement of your professional team, and also your main contractor, will be very important in the assurance process of which insurance covers a critical layer of diligence. Your senior debt funder will also be highly observant and will want to understand your insurance structure and the levels of which public liability, professional indemnity and employers' liability cover are engaged. So do bear this in mind, in your due diligence and prequalification of your professional team and main contractor and make the insurance requirements a condition of contract.

Other areas for consideration for cover may also include:

- Rebuilding Costs – e.g. reinstatement value
- General damage – e.g. by fire, lightning, explosion, storm, flood, burst pipes, riot
- Malicious Damage
- Terrorism
- Public Liability
- Legal Expenses
- Loss of Rental

Should you have a bank providing leverage, their minimum insurance cover requirements will preside.

25. SECURITY & SECURITY TRUSTEE

A Security Trustee holds the form of security on trust for the beneficiary (let us assume a SSAS in this case) and is an important member of the team for many SSAS Trustees.

A SSAS may take security on an asset that it otherwise may not directly own without incurring a tax charge. An example may be a residential property.

What must be ensured is that irrespective of any event or default, the SSAS can never end up owning an asset which losses its tax advantages and incurs as tax charge.

Who can act as a Security Trustee?

There are many professions that can act as security trustee. However, one of the most frequently used for SSAS Trustees is the SSAS Corporate Trustee - this often brings efficiencies of cost and time.

A security trustee is usually, but not always, an independent entity which is regulated by the Financial Conduct Authority. This could include solicitors, SSAS administrators and some accountants.

There are many considerations which may require your structuring of deals to require a security trustee:

- To ensure that the SSAS is never placed in peril by becoming the owner of the asset by which the security is placed on, however still preserving its ability to benefit from the security value and strength

- If there are numerous beneficiaries of the security and too many to appear on the security documentation. An example of this would be the registering a charge at Land Registry on a property

- In the event of a default situation occurring, where the security needs to be enforced, the security trustee would act impartially in taking all necessary parts of the process to enforce the security and distribute the proceeds of the security to the beneficiaries

- The beneficiaries of the security may in some structures change over time. This can be a costly and time-consuming process of transferring the security provisions from one party to another. By the appointment of a security trustee the process become much more flexible, swift and economically viable

Loan Back value: to its sponsoring company with security being on a buy to let residential property.

Loan back value:	£90,000
Security:	First legal charge on residential property independently valued at £170,000
Loan to value:	53%

If the sponsoring company fails to pay back annual capital and interest payments for the loan back, and ultimately this leads the SSAS invoking its security package, meaning the SSAS could end up owning the residential property by default. We must avoid this happening and the best way to do this is at the start of the loan back process, and not at the end!

By placing the security with a security trustee, who is often the SSAS Corporate Trustee, the asset which the loan back is secured on, can be seized and liquidated if necessary, returning the loan back amount, plus interest and costs, back to the SSAS in cash. Any surplus funds would be returned to the sponsoring company.

This way security is held on trust by the security trustee and the SSAS can enjoy the benefit of the security of the asset, whilst not taking unnecessary risks on the loan back investment.

Another scenario where a security trustee is important is where the entity holding the various security interests is created on trust, for multiple creditors. This structure avoids granting security separately to all creditors which would be costly and impractical.

This may occur where a developer is raising funds from numerous investors (SSAS and private investors for instance). The security trustee can hold the security charge for all parties, rather than each investor signing a specific agreement with the developer.

25.1 TYPES OF SECURITY

There are many scenarios in property and business where security charges are utilised and these can be many and varied – however, they are an essential consideration in almost all forms of funding. Here are 11 types of security that may be utilised within investment and funding circles and may be relevant to your SSAS, business and property considerations:

1. First charge – on a property registered at Land Registry

2. Second charge – on a property registered at Land Registry. This form of charge will almost certainly require approval of the first charge lender (who is at no obligation to allow a second charge)

3. Restriction/RX1 – a form of security charge where the beneficiary cannot invoke action, but it provides a restriction on the sale of the property until lifted. This may frequently be held on an unencumbered property as security against a loan

4. Shareholding – security in the form of a shareholding (often in the SPV) which can be presented in the form of differing share classes, and subject to conditions held within the shareholder agreement

5. Deed of Trust – a legally binding agreement registering the financial arrangements between joint owners of a property, as well as other parties, who may have an active financial interest in the property. The agreement is generally made at the time of purchasing the property and is designed to clarify exactly what happens to all interested parties' financial interests in the future, thus minimising disputes

6. Debentures – this is frequently requested by the first charge lender on a development company in addition to its usual first charge security. The debenture gives the funder security on all other assets held by the company

7. Floating charges – generally available only to companies and is usually an equitable charge on all the company's assets, both present and future. This may also include a charge on a specific type of asset such as stock, vehicles or machinery

8. Personal Guarantee – frequently commercial funding is conditional on the directors of the company entering into personal guarantees. In entering into this form of guarantee, the lender may well demand

Independent Legal Advice (ILA) be taken from a separate solicitor to ensure that an audit trail can be achieved, clarifying that the director entered into the guarantee on an 'eyes wide open' basis and was fully aware of the implications of what they were signing

9. Parent Company Guarantee – this form is usually reserved for corporate transactions or where you have multiple SPVs and hold your interests in a formalised holding company with an asset base of value. It is worth considering this more fully when presented with this demand as this does extend the security package requested from the lender to well beyond the boundaries of a first charge, debenture and personal guarantees

10. Stocks and Shares – security could take the form of stocks, shares and bond certificates which are deemed an asset class which security could be assigned to

11. Legal recourse – it may be often overlooked, however, the most basic security would be the legal agreement you sign. This will give you certain rights to take legal recourse and sue through the legal system in the event of a default

It is worthy of note that one party has an even greater level of security than any of the other security charges mentioned above – and that is HMRC. Hence you may well find your first charge funder being very specific about the professional compliance, governance, fiduciary duties and probity levels that you, as a company director, operate your company to. Your failure to comply with HMRC obligations could be one of very few events that could trump their security package of first charge and debenture and leave them picking the bones out of the business after a tax failure and following HMRC recovery proceedings.

26. YOUR PROFESSIONAL TEAM

One of the phrases that has served me well over 30+ years in industry is 'well advised'. I have been involved in some phenomenally complex transactions, as well as many which are straight forward, and I can testify to the increased assurance that ensues by having the humility to engage qualified professionals.

Some of the benefits include:

- Expertise: leveraging and expanding your team exponentially and tapping into a huge amount of experience
- Accountable: Enabling you to transition from trying really hard to having clear accountable and professional indemnity backed input
- Scalable: You engage them on a case-by-case basis

One myth that often circulates is that a SSAS is an unregulated environment which is not correct. A SSAS is not regulated by the Financial Conduct Authority (FCA), however it is regulated by The Pension Regulator (TPR) and as most trustees have little passion or interest for understanding the intricacy of the pension manuals, most choose to engage the corporate trustee services to manage compliance.

The extent of your advisor network will depend on your investment strategy. Here is a selection of some of the parties you may use in your strategy, in no particular order:

Tax advisor

This function could well be through your accountant – however, I have kept it separate to illustrate that certain more complex transactions may require specific advice which may be out-with of the expertise of your accountant for SSAS corporate administrator role.

As Trustees we should not leave anything to chance. A SSAS is a highly tax efficient vehicle at one end of the spectrum and a vehicle that, if operated ineffectively, can induce significant penalties and liabilities for the uneducated and naive.

A great tax advisor is always recommended, and this may be an appointment you make in conjunction with your accountant's role or separately. You may also choose to combine this role (albeit through a separate engagement contract) with other tax advise that you seek for your other wealth interests.

26.1 Security Trustee

We discuss this important function and services at length in the Security chapter. The security trustee is an appointment often held by the SSAS corporate trustee whereby the security for a transaction is held on trust by the security trustee and in the event of default, has the ability to liquidate the security and return cash to the SSAS without fear of the SSAS owning an asset where a tax charge may ensue.

26.2 Independent Financial Advisor

Independent Financial Advisers (IFA) are professionals who offer independent advice on financial matters to their clients and recommend suitable financial products from the market.

Typically, an Independent Financial Adviser will conduct a detailed survey of a client's financial position, preferences and objectives;

this is sometimes known as a 'fact find'. The adviser will then recommend appropriate action to meet the client's objectives and, if necessary, recommend a suitable financial product to match the client's needs.

Individuals and businesses consult IFAs on many matters including investment, retirement planning, insurance, protection and mortgages (or other loans). IFA's also advise on some tax and legal matters. Some IFA's may not be aware of SSAS pensions in any detail - hence do your research and ensure you secure the advice of an IFA who truly does understand all the viable options available to you.

To offer financial advice, an individual must represent or be an appointed representative of a firm registered with the Financial Conduct Authority (FCA).

26.3 SSAS Administrator

The SSAS administrator is the entity who runs the pension scheme. As well as this general duty, the SSAS administrator has particular obligations to provide information to HMRC, the pension scheme member and The Pensions Regulator.

The SSAS administrator is the party responsible for notifying, within the deadline, any reportable events including the annual HMRC pension scheme return and accounting for any tax due. They are the party who will provide the overwatch and administration of the day-to-day operations of the Trust, on behalf of the Trustees. This is the responsibility of the Trustees, who in most cases will decide to outsource this function to a specialist SSAS administration organisation.

Throughout this book we refer to the generic term 'SSAS administrator'.

However, there are four types of roles which you may consider in driving your SSAS Trust, as follows:

- **Member Trustees:** These have the ultimate responsibility to The Pension Regulator and HMRC for the overall SSAS compliance with pension law

- **Scheme Administrator:** This role oversees the scheme and its assets in a formal engagement by the Trustees to assist them in complying with pensions law. The Scheme Administrator is also responsible for completing and submitting returns to HMRC. Often the scheme administrator will be a sole signatory bank account from which all financial transactions are made - this enables the Member Trustees to delegate the administration of transactions and can help ensure that valuable pension assets remain protected from breaching HMRC rules

- **Professional Trustee:** or 'Independent Trustee' is appointed by the Trustees to support them in complying with pensions law. A Professional Trustee will be a co-signatory on scheme assets and can act to prevent certain investments and actions if they will cause harm or high levels of risk to the SSAS or give rise to HMRC charges

- **Scheme Practitioner:** Whilst a scheme *must* appoint a Scheme Administrator, a Scheme Practitioner is not a formal role but supports the Scheme Administrator and the member Trustees in complying with pension law

Should you engage with an external scheme administrator you will be asked to sign an Administration Service Agreement (ASA) which will be your contract between all parties.

The scheme administrator's role is to advise the Trustees on the ever-changing administration and tax rules set out by HM Revenue & Customs. As HMRC does not offer any ongoing guidance or support to your SSAS directly, it is strongly advisable to have an experienced scheme administrator in place. The penalties levied by HMRC for any unauthorised payments by your scheme can be severe.

The scheme administrator may be a member of a recognised industry body such as AMPS (Association of Member-Directed Pension Schemes) or possibly SSAS Alliance. AMPS has more than 150 member firms representing many parts of the member-directed pensions industry, including SSAS administrators.

Your scheme administrator will provide you with all administration and technical advice relating to your SSAS, as well as give you all of the required scheme documentation. They will also maintain scheme records in accordance with the Information Commissioner Office data protection requirements, including GDPR.

Your scheme administrator will also complete all required HMRC reports, assist Trustees regarding the purchase and sale of scheme assets, and provide any calculations for members' benefit payments.

A scheme practitioner is also invaluable in the event of a dispute between members and would be able to mediate without having to involve regulatory bodies or solicitors.

Running a SSAS is not an easy task; HMRC rules are very stringent and it is not usually advisable for Trustees to act as administrators, or not until they have become very experienced, although there are exceptions.

Some SSAS administrators have very specific investment

opportunities, or associated funds, that they may overtly open up to you for investment. You will need to decide how comfortable you see this service. Do you see it as a benefit? Is it an opportunity? Does it sit with the objectives of your statement of investment principles? Is it being sold to us? Does it make economic sense, compared to the other opportunities you are considering? Will it restrict our investment strategy?

Most SSAS administrators play an entirely independent role and only have a financial interest in terms of fees, for a schedule of services provided.

Some of the functions that are undertaken by the scheme administrator include:

- Registering the pension scheme with HM Revenue & Customs (HMRC)
- Setting up a bank account
- Operating tax relief on contributions under the relief at source system
- Reporting events relating to the scheme and the scheme administrator to HMRC
- Making annual returns of information to HMRC and The Pension Regulator
- Register the pension scheme with The Pensions Regulator
- Reporting events relating to the scheme and the scheme administrator to The Pensions Regulator
- Providing information to scheme members regarding the Lifetime Allowance, benefits and transfers
- Pension scheme documentation to address changes in

legislation

- A scheme takeover service where required
- Pre-investment review service to assess proposed investments
- Annual member statements
- Calculation and periodic review of pension benefits
- Trustee meetings as required
- Pension Payroll Services

For many, the path most trodden is to engage with a SSAS administrator who will be a company. As any company can have challenges along the way, let us touch on your protection should your SSAS Administrator go out of business, for whatever reason. If this happens, your pension assets will be safe, and the following process would happen:

- All funds are held in your Trust and do not form part of any other legal entities balance sheet so cannot be accessed by creditors
- You have FSCS protection for regulated investments such as the pooled Trustee bank account which protects you where the bank fails
- A receiver would be appointed to handle transfer of any administrator's business activities to other providers
- The receiver is likely to maintain staff to ensure this process operates smoothly

Whilst the likelihood of this happening is probably very low of course, any organisation can encounter issues, hence it is sensible and pragmatic to ensure you engage with a well-known and well-structured company, with a substantial track record, that can offer the services you require. Whilst there would be some inconvenience for sure, the process outlined above would broadly ensure there is no disadvantage to you other than some possible administrative delays while your pension scheme is moved.

26.4 Builders

Builders and main contractors are a fundamental part of your supply chain if you are developing property. For some reason I frequently see them referred to separately from your professional team, however I would argue that whilst they are structured differently, they are most certainly just as important as other professions in your ability to deliver assured outcomes.

I cover some of the frequently asked questions and process in my chapter 'Managing the development phase' and I would recommend that you read my other book 'COMMERCIAL TO RESIDENTIAL CONVERSIONS: THE ESSENTIAL MANUAL FOR PROPERTY DEVELOPERS' where you will gain a very detailed insight into the processes required. Some of these areas include, but not limited to:

- The Pre-Contract Phase
- Contract selection
- Procurement route selection
- Pre-tender contractor selection
- Tendering
- Funder requirements
- Selecting your professional team
- Cost Management
- Contract Management tracking
- Construction management

- Cash flow management
- Programming and planning
- Progress reporting
- Change control
- Disputes resolution
- Handover process
- Structural Warranties
- Home User Guide
- Alternative construction techniques, e.g. Modular Construction

26.5 Solicitor

A solicitor may be required for numerous elements of SSAS activity. You may choose to take advice in areas such as independent legal advice as a Trustee, to review any contracts, to oversee investor loan, and the SSAS may appoint a solicitor to undertake transaction work such as property transactions.

Should a lender be appointed to provide financial leverage, they may specifically require personal guarantees from the individual Trustees. Should this be the case, you will need to ask a suitably qualified solicitor to take advice and they will have to certify that you signed the personal guarantees in the certified knowledge and understanding of what you were signing - and not under duress.

26.6 Accountant

Depending on the complexity of your SSAS operations, you may choose to appoint an accountant to manage the process of your records and filings.

Many SSAS administrators undertake this process as a matter of course, as part of the engagement process, and you should check thoroughly if the services you are contracting covers these areas.

If engaging a separate accountant due to the diversity, quantum and specialism of your SSAS investments, then interview and research the potential accountant's expertise, specifically in the area of SSAS pension schemes, as there are crucial requirements which will need to be adhered to.

As the old saying goes, "you wouldn't want an eye surgeon operating on your heart!".

Many Trustees may choose to provide additional responsibility to their existing accountant who is familiar with their overall personal economy, including personal tax returns and any company account management. This can simplify the process significantly.

26.7 Bank

A bank account is an important part of establishing your SSAS and enabling your pension funds to be transferred into.

Your governance process will need to structure how you finalise your bank mandate in terms of the protocol of who can operate the bank account, how payments are made and maintain audit and control at all stages.

The Government are increasingly tightening the checks that banks need to make in order to approve the opening of a bank account. These checks fall under the Anti Money Laundering (AML) checks, covering areas such as 'Know Your Client' (KYC) due diligence.

If you have decided to engage a SSAS administrator, then this is something that they frequently deal with.

26.8 Insurance

Insurance is a specialist area and may be a requirement to one degree or another, based on the agreed operations of your SSAS. You may have to consider other parties' requirements as well. For example, if you are bringing in leverage in the form of senior debt funding from a bank, possibly for a commercial property acquisition, they will make insurance a condition precedent in the funding documents which must be satisfied prior to the loan/mortgage being drawn down.

A detailed understanding of your insurance strategy and structure is where an insurance broker will serve your business well as a key part of your professional team.

Some of the levels of insurance that you will need to consider for your business may include:

- Business insurance
- Buildings and contents insurance
- Joint names policy
- Contractors all-risk
- Professional Indemnity
- Key man insurance
- Public liability
- Employers' liability

There are many variant themes of insurance and your specific strategy must be discussed openly with your insurance broker to ensure you have the correct cover required.

One of the more complex areas for insurance is property and if this is part of your SSAS investment strategy, you will need to be clear on what type of investment you are considering.

As an example, if you are acquiring a retail premises with a single, full repair and insure (FRI) lease in place with a commercial tenant, that would require one set of insurance policies. The insurance considerations would be very different if purchasing a commercial property and then developing through partial demolition, rebuilding or extension.

You must always insure the property you are purchasing at the point of exchange of contracts. At exchange, you're legally obliged to purchase the building at a period of time in the future (stated in the exchange contract).

Should that building burn down between the point which you have exchanged and your specific completion date, you will still have to complete on the purchase. Therefore, it is vital that full insurance is in place at the point of exchange.

Engagement of your professional team and also your main contractor will be very important in the assurance process of which insurance covers a critical layer of diligence. Your senior debt funder, if you have one, will also be highly observant and will want to understand your insurance structure and the levels of which public liability, professional indemnity and employers' liability cover are engaged.

Do bear this in mind in your due diligence and pre-qualification of your professional team and main contractor and make the insurance requirements a condition of contract.

26.9 Commercial property agent

Agents will be a useful source of deal origination for you. They can bring you opportunities to lease or acquire commercial property of almost every shape and size and they will also assist you in the disposal of assets overtime. As many SSAS trustees and associated business will have the aspirations to hold commercial units, the commercial agents will assist you in managing the premises and lease on a monthly basis. They will assist you in finding leases and negotiating terms, guiding and supporting you at every stage of the process.

26.10 Commercial funding broker

Leverage represents one of the huge opportunities for a SSAS to utilise when acquiring property and a great commercial funding broker will help you navigate the intricacies of this market.

26.11 Health & Safety/CDM

We cover the responsibilities that you will have under health, safety and CDM in a separate chapter and this will be one area where you should not try and 'nickel and dime' the process. People's lives and well-being are at stake in any construction or refurbishment phase – it is as simple as that. This will be the one area that you could go to prison if you get this wrong, so making sure you have your obligations well understood and covered by a professional in this area is vital.

26.12 Commercial property solicitor

Your solicitor is required to manage the commercial acquisition, including all leases. They will conduct all searches and the transaction process of the purchase of a property and its filing at Land Registry. They will also support each lease and its varying stages from initial offer through to signing, renegotiations, extensions, exit and breaks.

26.13 Energy Performance Assessor

It is a legal requirement that commercial property holds a valid Energy Performance Certificate. An energy performance assessor is the professional party who will produce this report for you.

26.14 Project Manager

Project Managers come in all areas and disciplines. You may choose to employ a specialist required to oversee property development, as an example.

26.15 Private Investors

Depending on your strategy and funding stack, there may be a requirement to engage with private investors who could be fellow SSAS trustees, individuals, companies etc. There are many rules, requirements, skills and observations in this area which I support people on a frequent basis. Drop me a line if you require support in this area.

26.16 Contractors

We have covered builders in an earlier part, however you will require varying trades throughout the property ownership period. This could include repairs and scheduled maintenance, asset refresh and modifications and upgrades.

26.17 Monitoring Surveyor

A useful relationship to have and primary the monitoring surveyor will be engaged by the bank, providing you leverage – however, I have placed it in this section as understanding this role, their process and requirements can provide us with another area of expertise to tap into.

Oh, and another thing - we are paying for their services anyway so why not use it!!

Commercial Manager: usually employed to manage property development contracts and cost control. This can often be combined with the duties of the project manager.

Surveyors: these can be many and varied and are typically involved in property purchases. They may include party wall surveyors, structural surveyors, environmental engineers, contamination specialists, building surveyors, refurbishment and demolition surveyors etc.

Planning Consultant: required should you look to enhance, or change, the property through development or for planning gain purposes.

Design team: required for property development including architect, building services, structural and environmental etc.

RICS Valuer: this is the surveyor that will undertake the RICS Red Book Valuation required by the SSAS, bank lenders and possibly investors.

26.18 Interior Designer

Creating wonderful interiors will enhance the value and attractiveness of your property. The point I would add here is be very aware of your market with commercial property. If you are establishing long term FRI leases, often a shell and core, or basic fit out provision is sensible as each lease will have a very different set of requirements. You may think you have designed a great interior but the requirements of a mobile phone shop or a coffee shop would be very different.

26.19 Structural Warranty provider

When creating new residential units, structural warranties will be required by mortgage providers and new owners so this needs to be built into the process right from the start. This is an insurance backed product and hence the warranty provider should be engaged early as they will want to understand the builders track record, quality control, inspections, documentation etc to ensure that they can sign off the warranties at the end of the construction phase.

This area is a classic case of 'start with the end in mind'. One may have every intention of holding residential units long term and with no leverage, and think you don't need warranties. However, what if something changes along the way – you decide to sell or re-mortgage for example? The mortgage provider will almost certainly request these warranties. Always best to cover your options and then you have a wide array of choices in the future.

26.20 VAT specialist

VAT is one of the more complex areas of property and taxation and each acquisition can potentially bring about different requirements. Your accountant and solicitor may be able to handle most scenarios – however, we frequently find that additional specialist advice is required also. Bear in mind that VAT can have significant cashflow impact, hence getting it correctly planned from the outset is vital to the prosperity and health of your investment interests.

26.21 Stockbroker & Fund Manager

You may have a diversified strategy including stocks, shares, tracker funds, CFD's etc. A specialist array of expertise will be required to keep you well advised.

27. HEALTH, SAFETY & CDM

"Do not complain about getting old, it is a privilege denied to many" - Mark Twain

I have witnessed suffering to mankind that I would not wish others to experience. We all expect each other to come home safely to loved ones, at the end of each day and a few points of common sense, self-awareness and consideration of our actions to others, goes a long way to ensure this happens.

As SSAS trustees we may well be acquiring properties within, or outside, of our SSAS and if we are making improvements through construction and refurbishment, or letting the property of a commercial basis, we are taking on legal obligations to provide a safe environment.

It is imperative that we understand our legal obligations and put in place the correct systems and process to manage and fulfil these duties. We will usually be doing this through a strong, professional team who have the skills, resources, competence and insurance to fulfil these duties.

It is important whilst finding property, to consider health and safety from the earliest point when you will almost certainly be conducting site visits. Be aware that site visits can be hazardous, even if these are not in a construction area. Please take suitable care and attention and form your own risk assessment prior to any visit.

Be prepared and always have available your personal protective equipment including safety boots, hard hat, high visibility vest, gloves, eye protection and use your risk assessment to understand what the risks are, and what the most appropriate plan is.

Always remember that your first line of defence in health and safety will be your own common sense and reading the situation that you're about to step into. Always make sure that you are responsible for yourself and also assume responsibility for others, ensuring their access and actions on site are safe. Particularly be careful when accessing roof spaces, loft access, ladders and any areas at height. Many of the properties you will visit will be in a distressed condition - be aware these could possibly have been used by uninvited guests and may include unhygienic situations and potentially, drug paraphernalia. Always report unsafe acts or conditions to the agent or property vendor.

Occasionally you may be visiting construction sites and certainly you will be if your development moves to the next stage. During your assessment of principal contractors, you may well be visiting their current sites as part of your due diligence.

Irrespective of whether you are visiting your own construction site or another development, you will be expected to attend the site induction. This is a great opportunity for due diligence when you can check your principal contractor's case study sites during your due diligence phase of contractor selection. Make sure they abide by the rules on other developers' sites - be mindful whether the safety practices and culture on the site is something you would welcome on your development.

Ensure you know and follow all the regulations; the Health and

Safety Executive (HSE) has a lot of very good quality guidance on their website. I recommend that you go to this website for guidance.

From a business perspective you must ensure you have these things in place in considering health and safety:

- Health and safety policy
- Health and safety statement
- Correct equipment
- Sufficient expertise and resource
- Training
- First Aid book
- Method statements
- Risk assessments
- Responsible person
- CDM F10 notification to the HSE
- Appointment of professionals where required to do so

The Health & Safety Executive is a great place to understand your duties and how to fulfil them - visit www.hse.gov.uk.

As with every other element of due diligence in your business, evaluate the expertise and knowledge available and consider engaging a professional to support you formally in this area to ensure compliance.

Health and safety should be at the top of everyone's agenda. We all have a right to enter and leave the workplace in a safe manner.

At the age of 19 I was at Hillsborough on that fateful day on 15th April 1989 for the FA Cup semi-final between Liverpool and Nottingham Forest which, as events were to unfold, turned out to be the largest single loss of life in any UK sporting event where 96 people lost their lives, 38 of them under the age of 18.

This event left a life lasting impression on me, leading me to change my BSc Construction dissertation to Managing Health & Safety in the Construction Industry.

Why is this relevant to a book on property and SSAS pensions? Well, it has everything to do with the duty of care one assumes when acquiring property, particularly commercial property or rental property. If you are, or intend to be, a SSAS trustee and are considering property investment in one form or another it is essential to recognise that this comes with responsibility for compliance in health and safety.

This responsibility may well be discharged under contracts and if it does not, then the burden of responsibility lies with you - the SSAS trustee.

Areas where health and safety may apply include, but not limited to:

- CDM
- Electrical tests
- Gas Safe certification
- Safe access and egress
- Legionella
- PAT testing
- Fire management
- Evacuation
- Covid19 measures
- Smoke and Carbon Monoxide Alarms

- Furniture and Furnishings Regulation
- Building and renovation works

Construction Design and Management Regulations

The Construction (Design and Management) Regulations 2015 (CDM 2015) cover the management of health, safety and welfare when carrying out construction projects.

A construction project is notifiable if the construction work is expected to last longer than 30 working days and have more than 20 workers working at the same time, at any point on the project, or exceed 500 person days.

Some of the scenarios where this would be relevant to SSAS trustees include:

- New build commercial property
- Commercial to residential conversions
- Refurbishment of commercial property
- Commercial conversions to other non-residential use
- Dilapidations and strip out
- Demolition

Whatever your role in construction, CDM 2015 aims to improve health and safety in the industry by helping you to:

- Sensibly plan the work so the risks involved are managed from start to finish
- Have the right people for the right job at the right time
- Cooperate and coordinate your work with others
- Have the right information about the risks and how they are being managed

- Communicate this information effectively to those who need to know
- Consult and engage with workers about the risks and how they are being managed

CDM 2015 is divided into five parts:

- Part 1 deals with the application of CDM 2015 and definitions
- Part 2 covers the duties of clients for all construction projects. These duties apply in full for commercial clients. However, the duties for domestic clients normally pass to other duty holders
- Part 3 covers the health and safety duties and roles of other duty holders, including:
  - Designers
  - Principal designers
  - Principal contractors
  - Contractors
- Part 4 contains general requirements for all construction sites
- Part 5 contains transitional arrangements and revocations

Usually, the duties under CDM are passed to professional parties to deploy. However, the owner/client still has some responsibilities primarily to appoint these professionals.

The three main parties in the UK under the CDM regulations will be:

- Client - which may well be you as the SSAS trustee/ developer

- Principal designer
- Principal contractor

The principal designer will take full responsibility of all of the design process. This would usually be part of your consideration, when selecting your professional team, to appoint your principal designer and all obligations sit within that designer, such as health and safety or any of the other project requirements. This can aid the communication throughout the entire project.

The main contractor's responsibilities for health and safety, particularly under the CDM regulations, will be very clear. This is a similar process for your principal contractor where you are appointing one party and allowing them to use their expertise to deploy, through sub-contractors and suppliers, their obligations.

To summarise your five main responsibilities as the developer or client are to:

- Appoint the principal designer
- Appoint the principal contractor
- Ensure a CDM co-ordinator is appointed
- Submit the F10 notification to the Health & Safety Executive
- Ensure the F10 is displayed on the site

28. MANAGING THE DEVELOPMENT PHASE

If your intentions are to develop your commercial property or undertake commercial to residential conversion, refurbish or rebuild, the managing of the development phase for an assured outcome will be defining for your investment.

I recognise the need for managing this phase exquisitely with a great professional team – after all, this is what we do in our own development business on a day-to-day basis on schemes ranging from £1m - £20m gross development value (GDV).

It is not my intention to turn this book into a development operational manual as that already exists!

We have already prepared two comprehensive sources of this information for you to follow:

1. Commercial to Residential Conversions: The essential manual for property developers

2. *Equa*Academy, where you will find a catalogued and array of hundreds of videos, templates and systems for you to gain a detailed understanding of these systems. This is FREE and can be accessed at www.equaacademy.co.uk

29. PROPERTY & ASSET MANAGEMENT

Whether you own the property in your SSAS or a company, you are now in the asset management business. The duties, obligations and liabilities, as well as enhancement opportunities, will vary depending on what specific asset class it is.

The usual Property Management activities will need to be attended to, however, with commercial property likely to be held in a SSAS, often for many years, we must bring our attention to the more value-driven Asset Management.

Most commercial property owners, whether a SSAS or within a limited company, will normally engage the services of a commercial agent to manage those duties.

As well as the standard responsibilities of making sure that landlord and tenant obligations under the terms of the lease are complied with by both parties, the asset management element is important as this will look at taking a medium to long term view of how revenue can be increased, and capital value be enhanced for the asset.

This could include areas such as:

- Rebasing leases
- Extending outwards or downwards with basements for additional floor space

- Utilising air space rights to increase area - see chapter on Air Space
- Using future changes in the planning system to consider additional value that can be added through redevelopment
- Create a change of use to alternative use classes
- Replace existing leases with high covenanted counterparty
- Refinance property with additional gearing to withdraw equity to reinvest elsewhere in the portfolio
- Invest in energy generating assets to create additional income streams. Examples include wind, solar PV or solar thermal.
- Create or engage in community district heating schemes
- Invest in energy efficiency assets to increase the attractiveness for tenants with lower cost of operations
- Negotiation extension of short leases to create increased valuation.

Many of these will be reviewed on a 'project by project' basis where capital may be required to be invested to create a clear return on investment. The asset management function is all about business planning and driving additional value into the asset.

30. STRUCTURING

"Those who think they can and those who think they can't are both usually right." – Confucius

The word Structure should now be resonating with you as it is repeated numerous times throughout this book – it is crucial. Structure encompasses:

- A clear plan
- Knowing what you are trying to get to
- Compliance
- Inter-connection between moving parts
- Something that can evolve and be fine tuned
- Something that is understood by others

The Confucius quote is great as those with a SSAS have an extra piece of kit in their toolbox. When you have a SSAS, usually whatever the question is, the answer can usually be **Yes** – the details lie in the **How**.

When you have a mindset and are equipped with the knowledge to achieve that, then you have something extremely powerful indeed.

So, what do I mean by a structure? The word structure comes from the Latin word *structura* which means 'a fitting together, building'. That is what we are creating with our property deals. We know where we need to get to, and it is planning an organised set of resources and events to ensure that we achieve the most efficient outcome.

With a SSAS in your toolbox you have a wide range of structures to apply to any number of scenarios when acquiring property. Here are a few:

- Ownership with no debt
- Ownership with bank debt
- Ownership with bank debt and private capital
- Ownership with private capital
- Co-ownership – share of ownership
- Ownership of shares in company that owns property
- Company purchases with Loan Back
- Company purchases with bank debt and Loan Back funds
- Company purchases with loans from un-connected SSAS/ private capital
- Company purchases with bank debt and loans from unconnected SSAS/private capital

30.1 DUE DILIGENCE

Literally everything gets considered when structuring your deal from the due diligence of the property through to its funding and building. The list is far too exhaustive to list comprehensively, however, those that have our legendary EquaDA will know many of the areas anyway and other aspects can be found in my *Commercial to Residential Conversions'* book. So here goes with a checklist of some of aspects of due diligence to consider:

1. Gross Development Value

The GDV is where we calculate the likely end valuation of our finished product which generally will include leasehold sale of apartments, freehold sale, sale of gardens, car parking and storage areas.

2. Local comparable statistics

This is the base data from sold comparables of similar products in the area. For instance, if our product is a one-bedroom apartment on a ground floor location of 40sqm then we would be searching for similar criteria within 0.5 km (ideally within the same postcode!) to determine past evidence of sold comparables.

3. Freehold Sale and Ancillary items

There is uncertainty in the market in this area with government intervention endeavouring to control the often historically found issues of unfair practices of indexation on ground rents well above that of inflation and retail price index levels. The other areas of valuation interest are car parking, storage units, any garaging, gardens and other ancillary areas of benefit.

4. Build/Refurbishment costs

This would be the anticipated refurbishment of the property based on existing and proposed floor areas, with additional certainty being provided through our professional team.

5. Professional fees and other costs

a. Pre-exchange costs

This includes all costs that would be expended using seed capital prior to your development private capital being deployed. If the development failed to exchange contracts, then this would be the ultimate value of any abortive costs.

b. Costs from exchange to completion

These are the costs that enable the development to progress to legal completion, after exchange of contracts. Given that you are now committed to purchasing this property after exchange of contracts, decisions can be made on the risks of taking planning/permitted development to the next stage, subject to conditionality, as well as seeking final utility quotes and progressing the detailed design etc.

c. Allowable/non-allowable costs

Your senior debt funder will fund certain 'allowable' costs and others costs they will not entertain. It is important for the developer to understand the correct terminology and which costs sit in which category, as this will affect cash flow and private investor funding levels required.

d. Transaction management

These are the costs and management time required to drive through the legal conveyancing, funding and private investor on-boarding as well as establishing the company secretarial aspects of formalising a new company.

e. Selling costs

The selling costs will include, but not limited to, brochures, computer generated images (CGI), sales and marketing, estate agent's costs, legal fees for conveyancing (leasehold and freehold), title splitting and furnishing show apartments etc.

6. Contingency

Always apply a contingency within your numbers, typically somewhere between 5% and 20%, depending on your experience, the complexity of the scheme, the condition of the building and how many knowns and unknowns you have at this stage. Your contingency will be allocated in several areas including build costs, duration of development, funding, professional fees, cash flow and GDV. See the separate chapter on contingency.

7. Property area data

This will be the original base data of the property and your assessment of what can be undertaken through your particular planning strategy to create new homes. The base data must be accurate so conduct checks on the area/dimensions. Through an initial assessment of circa say 45 – 50 sqm (500spft) m per apartment, you will be able to make a very high-level assessment on how many apartments might be designed into a property. If you find this difficult to assess initially, always utilise a designer to support you.

8. Development returns and summary

With all the data you are processing, you will need to assess how to pull the information together, to make sense of it and to make informed decisions. This will include your gross and net profit positions. You may include tax implications on your development model also although, due to complexity, this is often kept separate and all numbers discussed are net of tax.

9. Finance costs – senior debt, bridge mezzanine etc

Cost of funds usually ranks third in magnitude after purchase price and refurbishment costs, hence this needs careful thought on your chosen strategy. This analysis would be supported by a draft term sheet from your broker typically, who would be able to turn this around within 24-48 hours.

10. Private capital

Private investors will be your source of capital through a variety of channels. What the development analyser should show you very clearly is what amount of private capital you require for this development.

11. Development Statistics

Establishing trends in your systems is important - the more analysis you undertake, the more valuable trends you will see and the more confident your language will be when discussing developments with funders, private investors and commercial agents. Key performance indicators (KPIs) and data for internal analysis, hurdle rate assessment and risk evaluation will often come from this source and will help you to assess your forecast performance versus actual and aide continuous improvement.

12. Cash flow

Cash flow is frequently missed from many development analysers I have seen, however it remains a fundamental element. Your cash flow will affect the amount you are asking your private investors for and hence getting an accurate range of private investor capital early is essential to avoid any corrections later.

13. Sensitivity Analysis

An important part of risk management is sensitivity analysis in understanding what happens if two or more variables move in different directions. If GDV reduces, we have a problem; if build costs increase, we have a bigger problem; if build duration increases, then we have extended funding costs as well so we would be experiencing exponential economic downward pressures. Likewise, if GDV increases, the build came in under budget and most of the contingency remains unspent, the profit will increase.

14. Land Purchase

Finally, once all the other elements have been analysed, we use our equation: GDV – All Development Costs – Developers' Profit = Maximum Purchase Price to ascertain the maximum price we are prepared to offer on the property purchase.

Our comparables will be taken from historic prices only and we must understand how the sale price relates to the actual unit that has been sold in the past. We achieve that by using the national EPC Register (www.epcregister.com) to identify the sales unit rate (sq. m & sq. ft) of the house or apartment that has been sold. We then apply that as an average of those examples in the local area, within as tight as possible proximity – ideally a 0.25-0.5 km radius maximum.

Ensure that you look at the sensitivity of whether we are in a rising market or a falling market. How far in the past was each comparable sold? The presumption is that property price increase over time, however the time scale of our due diligence is over a short period of time and we must understand where we are in the property cycle.

We will also evaluate potential sales with the local agents and their aspiring view as to what those units, once created in 9-24 months, might realise in sales.

30.2 GENUINELY DIVERSE COMMERCIAL VEHICLES

If a SSAS holds an indirect interest in taxable property by investing in a vehicle that has any interest in taxable property, and the vehicle is not a Genuinely Diverse Commercial Vehicle, the investment will give rise to tax charges.

This could happen if the SSAS purchases shares or makes a loan to the vehicle which has interests in what would be taxable property, if it were held in the SSAS.

The important consideration here is that the entity must be a Genuinely Diverse Commercial Vehicle.

These vehicles can include:

- Trading companies/concerns
- Investment companies/special purpose vehicles
- Other collective investment schemes including unit trusts, open ended investment companies and UK REITS
- Individuals

A vehicle is a Genuinely Diverse Commercial Vehicle if it, and the investment in it, satisfies the following criteria, not only when the SSAS makes the investment but all the time that it holds that investment.

Where the vehicle is trading:

- The vehicle's main activity is the carrying on of a trade, profession or vocation
- The SSAS Trustee, either alone or together with associated persons, do not have control of the vehicle
- Neither the SSAS Trustee nor a person connected with the Trustee is a controlling director of the vehicle or any other vehicle which holds an interest in the vehicle directly or indirectly
- The SSAS does not hold an interest in the vehicle to allow a Trustee or a person connected with a Trustee to occupy or use taxable property

A controlling director is a person who is a director or manager and is either on their own or with others, a beneficial owner of, or able, directly or indirectly, to control 20% or more of the ordinary share capital of the company. A bit of a mouth full but important to understand!

31. CONTINGENCY

When most hear the word contingency, they might immediately relate to a 5%-15% contingency on build costs for their property.

Risk is about the probability of something happening versus the impact of if it happens. The probability of something happening may be small but the impact if it does happen could be immense.

Imagine a fatality on site. The probability is very low, however, the impact if it happens is enormous in terms of loss of life, family impact, emotional, financial, time, investigations and cost etc. This is clearly a sensitive subject and one that I have been close to in my career and the personal impact on family members is not lost on me.

At the other end of the scale, it is likely that during a strip out of a building there will be things that emerge such as rotten wall plates or small structural cracks that require attention.

A top tip that we use on our larger developments that could serve you well. We phase our strip out to happen whilst the design and main contractor selection and tendering is underway. That way designers and tenderers all have the opportunity to see the strip out complete, assure themselves that all unknowns are now known, incorporated into the design and tender documentations and duly priced for. This phasing, certainly on larger projects, is simple in concept and highly effective in minimising variations of cost and time throughout the build phase.

There are many layers of contingency which are there to address or mitigate risk in various ways – however, the ones we are going to focus on, are ones that you may include financial allowances against.

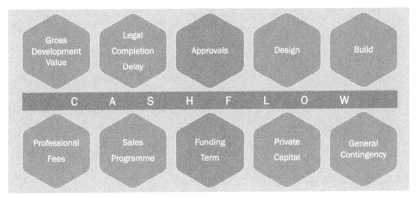

Suggested standard contingency areas for your checklist include, but should not be limited to:

- **Gross development value:** This will be important when raising long term funding, when holding property, due to the valuation and lending phase. This is a subject in its own right, however, suffice to say that considered analysis and careful preparation is required to assure a route to an optimised outcome. From an internal planning perspective being conservative in your base case assessments on valuation levels is the prudent approach

- **Legal completion timing:** Achieving legal completion on your purchase can seem like the end of a lengthy process but the reality is that it is one of the first major milestones ahead of you, each with a series of dependencies such as strip out, design, procurement and various appointments to move your project forward

- **Approvals:** Gaining necessary consent and approvals along the way may not always be straight forward and in your control. Examples might include gaining planning permissions and/or permitted development, discharging planning conditions, bank pre-commencement conditions, building control sign off, CIL and S106 legal agreements etc. Any delay in any of these could incur time and cost issues

- **Design:** It is easy to run away in your mind with a great design and loose control of the costs. Be passionate about what you are creating but don't get too emotionally attached as this can obscure the clarity of your financial plan. Scope creep can eat away at cost budgets due to unforeseen within the building so contingency will be required

- **Build:** Depending on the complexity of the build and the type, this could vary from 5%-25%

- **Professional Fees:** Any change in time and cost may well require someone to manage it or any knock-on effect, so a contingency allowance should also include professional team costs to manage the other contingency events

- **Sales programme:** If your property, or part of it, is being sold then additional contingency should be allowed for delays in the process, including funding costs

- **Funding term:** If using institutional funding, the bank and their monitoring surveyor will be very keen to ensure you have sufficient term on the loan to satisfy their assessment and diligence. This will include many of the aspects already considered

- **Private capital:** Depending on your structure, you may or may not require private capital from external sources. From personal experiences, I can testify that there is a distinct sense of freedom when one can undertake a project with one's own funding resources. However, whilst this may be possible, scale of ambition can create a desire to extend to additional funding lines, other than the bank. Ensure these funding lines are carefully considered and planned well in advance, as usually private capital is required at the purchase/legal completion stage early on and any delay would potentially mean breaching your completion date, which can be painful

- **Cashflow:** Generally, one of the most common contingencies that is forgotten. Unless your development analysis tool has integrated cashflow modelling, such as the EquaDA, then it is difficult to assess the volume of private capital required accurately. Cashflow is the core reason why most business businesses fail. Do not let your SSAS or development run short of cash

- **General contingency:** Recent global political and health challenges are a timely and vivid reminder that uncertainty can happen, even when you think you have everything covered. An assessment should be made in context with all other contingencies to ensure you have sufficient headroom for most eventualities

If you allow for a contingency against each item highlighted above, you may be well covered – however, you may not get the deal as well!!!

Application of contingency should be taken against certain specific items you are concerned about, and then holistically considering all other areas. Never make the deal fit by ignoring these areas, or your gut instinct, until fully investigated.

Who owns the contingency?

A strange question to add, however, the answer depends on who is asking the question. If a bank is funding the development, then development finance will view the contingency as part of their security package considerations in assessing lending risk. The bank, through their monitoring surveyor, will monitor committed costs against contingencies to ensure that the contingency pot remains healthy.

If the contingency pot remaining reduces to a low level, it is possible that the bank loan agreement allows the bank to ask the borrower to inject additional funds (think cash) to 'top up' the contingency pot.

Now, as a SSAS, if we had this situation, think of the impact. Let us say we were leveraged to the full 50% permissible and had to inject additional cash. If the SSAS has no liquidity left, as all other funds are out on long term loans for instance, and because we are 50% bank leveraged, there could be no other means to inject funds. This scenario, whilst theoretic, could happen and if it did it would create a serious issue.

The point of raising this is not to instil fear, but real awareness and careful thought of the detail that is required when engaging with bank finance.

32. RESILIENCE

Resilience is one of the driving factors behind many successful people - having the ability to weather most storms and having the freedom of choice in all areas of life.

For many, Covid-19 has had terrible personal impacts, as well as seeing others lose their jobs or being put on furlough. This experience has been of the most significant change in the economy in living memory where the pace of change has increased dramatically - where jobs for life no longer exists and where employers see diversity and frequently changing roles as a positive, and not a negative.

Massive shifts in employments patterns, decentralisation of whole industries, such as hotels and travel and restrictions on movements, are changing the way we work and play. The words 'furlough', 'staycation', 'masks' and 'testing' have now become part of daily lives and will probably remain with us for many years to come.

So how does this relate to SSAS and property?

Well, a SSAS, for those with the knowledge and education, provides an opportunity for many to create and operate their own highly accountable investment fund. A pension may have been that fund previously but the distinct accountability of a SSAS and trustee provisions, allow an entirely different feel, structure and opportunity along with, for many, a sizeable fund value to make informed investment choices which can be truly life changing.

So a SSAS, combined with diversified property, enables multiple opportunities to take control of your personal economy and invest in assets classes which can create equity appreciation in an asset, cashflow and capital growth. These can often be within a SSAS, as well as outside of a SSAS, if one has the business acumen to create the right structuring.

So, throughout this book we have highlighted a wide array of property and SSAS interactions that can create enormous layers of compounding wealth and heighten your levels of resilience for you and your loved ones.

Covid-19, climate change, exponential technological advancements and global political trends are just some examples of threats for some - and opportunities for others. We all need to make decisions on whether we wish to be subservient to change, or to embrace it.

The only certainty is change – our mindset and actions around this will define our future level of resilience.

33. PROPERTY EXIT

Start with the end in mind. Sound advice that should be heeded by all. It is important to know where you are going, what your strategy is and why. Only then can you track a purposeful course to getting incrementally closer to your goals.

Whether you are a developer of commercial conversions, hold long term commercial units, have a buy-to-let or a HMO portfolio - this is true.

Many will immerse themselves straight into the property deal analysis and, it is true that without the deal, there will be no return – however, the impact of the investment will usually also depend on the structuring of the deal (see chapter on Structuring). Careful thought and consideration of how you are going to structure, position, fund and possibly collaborate on your deal, will be a defining and precious time which could have huge implications on the end outcome.

The starting point, as we look at any potential deal or assess our area, should be to understand what our exit strategy or strategies are. Always prepare at least two exit strategies, but ensure you are comfortable with your core strategy.

There are a number of dependencies in your business operations and how you select your exit strategy might be based in part on:

- Business structure

- Tax strategy
- Type and volume of your target market
- Expertise
- Time availability
- How you fund the deal
- Legal entity
- Shareholding and ownership structure
- Aspirations of your JV partners and their exit strategy

What could your exit options look like?

Typically, they fall into a number of categories. You could:

- Buy, develop, title split and sell
- Buy, develop and sell a non-title split block
- Buy, develop and hold
- Buy, develop and partially hold and sell some units
- Buy, add value and sell before developing
- Buy, add value and sell, retaining some equity
- Contract and develop and this would typically be working with alternative funding, typically 100% loan to cost structures
- Control the property through purchase lease options
- And many, many more permutations!

Time spent at the start of an investment, deciding on the plan, is seldom wasted and will represent a significant ROI for you.

34. WHEN A SSAS SELLS PROPERTY

There could be many reasons why a SSAS may sell a property. All property portfolios should continually reassess yields, risks and changing demands in the market.

As we have also discussed throughout this book, there could also be very specific reasons for a sale, such as gaining planning permission for residential conversion and deciding to sell the property for a planning gain, prior to the conversion process.

Many sales transactions will be simple and straightforward, based on a commercial sale to an unconnected third party. However, we must ensure we have compliance at the forefront of our mind.

There are a number of considerations to take into account when deciding to sell a property from your SSAS.

Reason for selling:
There will be a clear reason or reasons for the sale. It is important to document this and to make sure that the correct protocol is understood. This may affect the price and speed of transaction for instance.

Avoid Trading:
A SSAS cannot trade and care should be taken to avoid repetitive behaviour and intent that could be construed to mean trading has happened. That is not to say that a SSAS cannot buy a property

and then sell at some future date however reasoning, strategy, frequency and performance would all need to be supported by evidence to avoid any investigation.

Method of sale:

What is the selected route for sale of the property asset? This could be an open market sale, auction, private sale etc.

Who the SSAS is selling to:

We must be careful to consider connected party transactions. There is nothing at all wrong with making a sale to a connected party and this is undertaken quite frequently in a commercial to residential conversion type transaction process. The concern that we must be wary of is to ensure a robust asset valuation is made to evidence that the asset is being sold at fair market value.

Valuation:

Usually, the valuation process will be instructed by the SSAS through a RICS Red Book valuation (as discussed in the chapter in this book). This will be a key document in your audit file that will be shared with your corporate trustee to demonstrate fair market value of the asset being sold and independently verified by a qualified valuer. Costs should be allowed for within your budget for this.

Conveyancing:

Usual conveyancing should be followed including CPSE (Commercial Property Standard Enquiries) and a commercial conveyancing solicitor will be able to undertake this for you. Allow sufficient time and budget for the sales process to also allow consultation and sign off by your corporate trustee.

Timing:

Timing is crucial in delivering your chosen outcome. If you are looking to sell a property, with or without planning, will alter its valuation. A vacant commercial building held in your SSAS would have a different valuation if it had full planning permission for eight x one-bedroom apartments as an example. At what point are you considering the sale - is it before planning is submitted, during or after?

Where do you want the value uplift - in the SSAS or if selling to your SPV development company, in that entity? You may choose a timing to better suit the outcome you are looking for.

Another timing consideration would be if you are considering when to undertake the construction phase of a conversion, if selling to your own SPV development company. Technically it is possible to part-construct the asset within the SSAS, using your SSAS funds. However, as we know from previous chapters, if the conversion is to create residential units, the SSAS must have sold it substantially prior to the 'Certificate of Habitation' audit file being completed. This is all fine in theory, however, imagine trying to raise funds on a partially constructed building site!

Funding:

As mentioned above, funding is important to consider for the buying entity as well as redeeming any leverage and security on the SSAS asset prior to sale, which must be lifted to enable the sale to proceed. Your solicitor will manage this process.

If you are selling to your SPV development company, consideration needs to be given to the necessary certification, leases and warranties in place. Let us take a scenario of a partly converted commercial to residential conversion which is being sold prior to the units being completed as residential. This would be a very high-risk strategy for a number for reasons including:

- Construction contracts and obligations would need to be transferred
- All design, building control, structural warranties, permissions etc would require novating or re-engaging also. This would need to be done in a manner that maintains the responsibilities of all parties, including their Professional Indemnity insurance
- Funding costs would be very high and loan to value/loan to cost lending levels would be low, due to the inherent risk of funding a partially completed asset. This would often be through a specialist bridge product
- The requirement for the buying party to have extensive capital available, given low levels of bank funding, may require substantial amounts of private capital to be raised

Funding is usually the critical path item on any programme when considering a property transaction. This area of fundability, costs, time will be the area to place most attention on, in ensuring the smoothest transition of the sale.

Audit file:

Always create a detailed audit file of evidence you have used in creating your decision making, assessment, valuation and overall process. HMRC could investigate at any time, checking that compliance was maintained. This should ensure that a SSAS has not sold assets at a value lower than the market value, thus possibly leading to concerns on pension liberation.

35. WANT TO LEARN MORE?

"The greatest discovery of all time, is that a person can change their future by merely changing their attitude"

OPRAH WINFREY

Why not visit www.equaacademy.co.uk and join our FREE community where you can gain access to hundreds of videos, templates, guidance notes and case studies to help you progress your journey to taking control of your personal economy.

Learn from trusted experts and property professionals who care

We know that whether you are transitioning from the 9-5 career or trying to build a portfolio of buy-to-lets, HMO's through to larger, more ambitious commercial to residential developments – it can feel like a big leap. And it can be. The risks are higher, the deals more complex and there are a lot of moving parts to keep on top of.

Having made many business leaps ourselves over the last three decades, we know the value of a continuous, first-class education, access to a bank of shared knowledge and a network of trusted professionals who have walked the walk.

Add to this the responsibility and accountability of combining these property strategies with your SSAS pension and the stakes are high and yet the returns can be simply life changing. Your next steps are crucial in ensuring you are following a clear and proven strategy with step-by-step guidance from those who have experience in these areas.

Our property mentoring programme, EquaMentorship, provides all the support, training and resources you need to build a successful property development business.

EquaAcademy help hundreds of people each year to create their strategy and focus on creating a powerful property asset base and enabling a multi-generational legacy.

If you are interested in exploring EquaMentorship or EquaEarn & Learn, then book a no obligation call with me personally at **https://calendly.com/markstokes/introductory-call-non-equaacadamy-members**

These options include:

SSAS Alliance

SSAS Earn & Learn

EquaMentorship

*Equa*Mentorship

For Property Investors & Developers

Success in property is achieved by adopting a robust **strategy** that provides a clear roadmap, accountability and impact.

*Equa*Mentorship is a highly accountable mentoring programme designed to enable YOU to achieve your goals with bespoke personal sessions and strategic counsel. Learn from experts in property development and investment through 1-2-1 calls and guided strategic development. Join now!

The *Equa*Mentorship Programme

A 12-month mentorship with Mark Stokes and Nigel Greene, experts in property development, business and SSAS:

- 1-2-1 strategy meeting/s
- Quarterly review meeting/s
- Monthly accountability meetings
- Fortnightly *Equa*Mentorship group sessions
- Monthly webinars - guest speakers, Q&A's and property updates
- Full access to *Equa*Portal resource centre
- *Equa*DA, our unique deal analysis tool
- SSAS Commercial Property Investment Masterclass
- Free Membership to SSAS Alliance

Scan the QR code or visit
www.bit.ly/_bookacall
to book your call with Mark Stokes now.

*Equa*Academy

✉ info@equaacademy.co.uk   🖰 www.equaacademy.co.uk

OTHER BOOKS BY THE AUTHOR

COMMERCIAL TO RESIDENTIAL CONVERSIONS

The essential manual for property developers

SSAS PENSIONS

Creating extraordinary levels of compounding growth

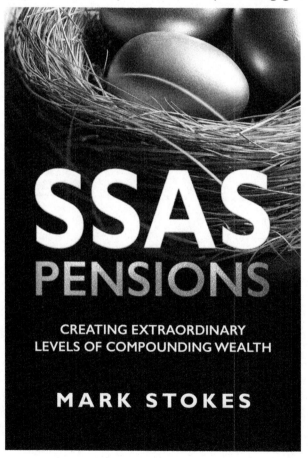

ADVICE TO YOUR YOUNGER SELF

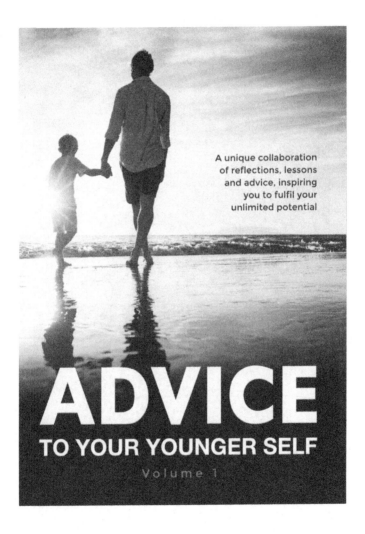

SSAS SUPERSTARS:

How 10 entrepreneurs unlocked their pensions – without waiting to retire

SSAS*

SUPERSTARS!

HOW 10 ENTREPRENEURS UNLOCKED THEIR
PENSIONS – WITHOUT WAITING TO RETIRE

*Small Self-Administered Scheme

LOUISE RIGHTON
MARK STOKES

ACKNOWLEDGEMENTS

There are many people who have had a profound effect and impact on my life; some remain great friends, others I have met briefly on my journey of life and others, sadly, are no longer with us today. Each of you have helped shape me to be the man I am today.

This book has taken a lot of effort and support from several key people who I owe a particular debt of gratitude.

To Avnie Shah at Art by Avnie for your wonderful support and counsel in designing once again another great book cover in my series of books. Your patience and insightful questions continue to be a revelation to me and have been immense in creating truly professional artwork. Thank you.

To Steve Baker at EBooks by Design for turning the final manuscript into the final book you hold today. Much appreciated again Steve.

To Nigel Greene, my business partner of 20+ years and co-founder of EquaAcademy - your ever-present companionship, drive, counsel and wisdom has been a constant source of inspiration to me.

To my wife Sharon for her proofreading of the book and her patience with me through the process of writing yet another book! Love you Sharon xx

And a huge thank you to those who put their passion to paper and have provided such wonderfully inspirational case studies for the book:

- Gareth Alexander
- David Ball
- Sam Cooper
- Jon Dale
- Voon Fui Lai
- Nigel Greene
- Chris Henry
- Alex Impey
- Ian Kavanagh
- Richard Kennedy
- Shaz Nawaz
- Chris Paton
- Tatiana Preobrazhenskaya
- Louise Righton
- Toby Spanier
- Kevin Whelan

Many others have provided the inspiration, requests and questions to enable this book to be written. I thank you all.

Mark

ABOUT THE AUTHOR

As an experienced Business Executive, Entrepreneur and Investor, Mark has a passion for creating and developing enduring businesses that enable the creation of shared value. With 26 years of board level business and property expertise in data centres, energy, construction and telecommunication industries, Mark has founded and operated many businesses (home and abroad), deploying complex global infrastructure projects from £1million - £1billion. Mark is a highly sought-after business mentor and speaker with vast experience internationally in risk management, leadership, trouble shooting and business - from founding, acquiring and growing through to selling a business.

Having sold his equity in a leading management business and then leaving corporate life in 2015, Mark established a number of pioneering investment and development companies.

Having career long company pensions, Mark set out to explore different opportunities to take control of his personal economy and quickly settled on a SSAS, which is now an active part of his long-term investment and wealth creation strategy.

Mark and Sharon are proud parents to four wonderful children - Ben, Jack, Katy and Emily.

Mark has a passion and ethos for creating shared and sustainable value through property, investments and building a powerful and enduring legacy for future generations.

Mark has mentored people for over 20 years and has been a non-executive director for over a decade and specialises in Business, Commercial Property Investment and Development and SSAS pensions.

If you are interested in knowing more about mentorship, visit www. equaacademy.co.uk.

Mark, Nigel Greene and Kevin Whelan run the UK's largest independent members group of SSAS trustees - SSAS Alliance. Find out more at www.SSASAlliance.org.

GLOSSARY

AA	-	Annual Allowance
AH	-	Affordable Homes
ASA	-	Administration Service Agreement
AVC	-	Additional Voluntary Contribution
BAFO	-	Best and final offer
BCE	-	Benefit Crystallisation Event
CA	-	Capital Allowances
CDM	-	Construction Design Management
CETV	-	Cash Equivalent Transfer Value
CIBSE	-	Chartered Institution of Building Services Engineers
CIL	-	Community Infrastructure Levy
CIOB	-	Chartered Institute of Building
COSHH	-	Control of Substances Hazardous to Health
CPD	-	Continuous Professional Development
CPSE	-	Commercial Property Standard Enquiries
CSV	-	Creating Shared Value
D&B	-	Design & Build
DB	-	Defined Benefit scheme
DC	-	Defined Contribution scheme
DCC	-	Double Compound Curve
EPC	-	Energy Performance Certificate

ESG	-	Environmental, social and governance
FCA	-	Financial Conduct Authority
FRI	-	Full Repair and Insure Lease
FSCS	-	Financial Services Compensation Scheme
GDCV	-	Genuinely Diverse Commercial Vehicle
GDV	-	Gross Development Value
GEA	-	Gross External Area
GIA	-	Gross Interior Area
GUF	-	General Unallocated Fund
HCA	-	Homes and Communities Agency
HMRC	-	Her Majesty's Revenue and Customs
HoT's	-	Heads of Terms
HSE	-	Health & Safety Executive
HTB	-	Help to Buy
ICO	-	Information Commissioners Office
ICVC	-	Investment Company with Variable Capital
IHT	-	Inheritance Tax
ILA	-	Independent Legal Advice
IPMS	-	International Property Management Standards
ISE	-	The Institution of Structural Engineers
ITT	-	Invitation to tender
JCT	-	Joint Contracts Tribunal
JV	-	Joint Venture
KBI	-	Key Business Indicator
KPI	-	Key Performance Indicator

LDC	-	Lawful Development Certificate
LLP	-	Limited Liability Partnership
LOI	-	Letter of Intent
LTA	-	Lifetime Allowance
LTC	-	Loan to Cost
LTV	-	Loan to Value
MEES	-	Minimum Energy Efficiency Standards
MPAA	-	Money Purchase Annual Allowance
NEC	-	New Engineering Contract: Standard form of Contract
NIA	-	Net Internal Area
OEIC	-	Open-Ended Investment Company
P2P	-	Peer to Peer
PAT	-	Portable Appliance Testing
PDR	-	Permitted Development Rights
PEA	-	Predicted Energy Assessment
PPF	-	Pension Protection Fund
PTM	-	Pensions Tax Manual
PV	-	Photovoltaic (solar) panel
REIT	-	Real Estate Investment Trust
RIBA	-	Royal Institute of British Architects
RICS	-	Royal Institute of Chartered Surveyors
RIDDOR	-	Reporting of Injuries, Diseases and Dangerous Occurrences Regulations
ROCE	-	Return on Capital Employed
ROI	-	Return on Investment

ROTE	-	Return on Time Employed
S106	-	Section 106
SAP	-	Standard Assessment Procedure
SDLT	-	Stamp Duty Land Tax
SIPP	-	Self Invested Personal Pension
SME	-	Small to Medium Enterprise
SoIP	-	Statement of Investment Principles
SPV	-	Special Purpose Vehicle
SSAS	-	Small Self-Administered Scheme
TOGC	-	Transfer of Going Concern
TPAS	-	The Pensions Advisory Service
TPR	-	The Pension Regulator
VAT	-	Value Added Tax
VBC	-	Vacant Building Credit
VC	-	Venture Capital
VOA	-	Valuation Office Agency

HELPFUL LINKS

EquaAcademy	www.equaacademy.co.uk
SSAS Alliance	www.SSASalliance.org
My personal website	www.markstokesuk.com
The Pension Regulator	www.thepensionsregulator.gov.uk
Financial Services Compensation Scheme	www.fscs.org.uk
Pension Tax Manual	https://www.gov.uk/hmrc-internal-manuals/pensions-tax-manual/ptm121000
Investments in Shares and Equities	https://www.gov.uk/hmrc-internal-manuals/pensions-tax-manual/ptm122000
Loans and general principles	https://www.gov.uk/hmrc-internal-manuals/pensions-tax-manual/ptm123100
Pension Ombudsman Service - Pensions Ombudsman Helpline 020 7630 2200	https://www.pensionwise.gov.uk/en/guaranteed-income
The Pension Ombudsman	www.pensions-ombudsman.org.uk
The Financial Conduct Authority	https://register.fca.org.uk
The Money Advice Service	https://www.moneyadviceservice.org.uk/en

The Governments Actuary's Department	https://www.gov.uk/government/organisations/government-actuarys-department
The Pension Tax Manual	https://www.gov.uk/hmrc-internal-manuals/pensions-tax-manual
Construction Design & Management Regulations	https://www.hse.gov.uk/construction/cdm/2015/index.htm

YOUR NOTES:

YOUR NOTES:

YOUR NOTES:

YOUR NOTES:

Printed in Great Britain
by Amazon